Commonsense Methods for Children with Special Educational Needs – 4th Edition

D0202670

The worldwide trend towards inclusive education has made it even more necessary for mainstream teachers to develop an understanding of the learning characteristics of children with special educational needs. Not only must all teachers understand and accept students with disabilities and learning difficulties or behavioural problems, but they must also possess a wide range of teaching and management strategies to meet the needs of these students in the classroom. This book offers sound practical advice on suitable intervention methods.

This fully revised and updated fourth edition includes expanded chapters on learning difficulties, effective instruction, behaviour management, self-regulation, the teaching of literacy and numeracy skills, and differentiation across the curriculum. In addition, the book includes new chapters on the learning characteristics and specific needs of students with intellectual, physical or sensory disabilities. In all cases the practical advice the author gives is embedded within a clear theoretical context supported by current research and classroom practice.

This book is essential reading for practising teachers and student teachers worldwide.

Peter Westwood is Associate Professor in Special Education at the University of Hong Kong.

Commonsense Methods for Children with Special Educational Needs – 4th Edition

Strategies for the Regular Classroom

Peter Westwood

RoutledgeFalmer
Taylor & Francis Group

LONDON AND NEW YORK

First published 2003 by RoutledgeFalmer
11 New Fetter Lane, London EC4P 4EE

Simultaneously published in the USA and Canada
by RoutledgeFalmer
29 West 35th Street, New York, NY 10001

RoutledgeFalmer is an imprint of the Taylor & Francis Group

Typeset in Times by RefineCatch Limited, Bungay, Suffolk
Printed and bound in Great Britain by
TJ International Ltd, Padstow, Cornwall

British Library Cataloguing in Publication Data
A catalogue record for this book is available from the British Library

Library of Congress Cataloging in Publication Data
Westwood, Peter S.
    Commonsense methods for children with special needs :
strategies for the regular classroom / Peter Westwood. – 4th ed.
        p.   cm.
    Includes bibliographical references and index.
    ISBN 0–415–29848–2 – ISBN 0–415–29849–0 (pbk.)
    1. Children with disabilities – Education.   2. Mainstreaming in
    education.   I. Title.
LC4015.W44 2003
371.91—dc21   2002068295

ISBN 0–415–29849–0 (pbk)
ISBN 0–415–29848–2 (hbk)

To my dear friend Lau Yu Yee (Wendy)

Contents

5   The management of behaviour   **65**

6   Improving social skills and peer group acceptance   **84**

7   Developing early literacy skills: principles and practices   **98**

Introduction

This book is primarily about learning and teaching. The material comes from my own experience as a teacher and educational psychologist, but I have also drawn extensively on international literature covering classroom research and practice.

In this fourth edition of *Commonsense Methods for Children with Special Educational Needs* I have attempted to provide generic information and practical advice that can be applied in any country and under any education system. I have avoided, as far as possible, relating the content of the chapters closely to the special education administrative procedures, legal mandates, regulations, codes and terminology used in any one country. Where reference to a particular system has been necessary I have usually compared the situation under discussion to similar situations in other countries. Children with special needs, no matter where they are in the world, display remarkably similar learning characteristics and require almost identical forms of effective intervention. Similarly, it is my experience that high-quality teaching can be identified by a set of generic competencies applicable anywhere in the world. It is of great interest to me to know that earlier editions of my book have been translated into Japanese and Chinese languages, thus supporting my view that practical ideas have international relevance and appeal.

This edition has introduced for the first time two new chapters covering the learning characteristics and educational needs of students with intellectual, physical or sensory disabilities. I felt this to be necessary because over the past decade the movement towards 'non-categorical' discussion of special needs has gone too far, giving an impression that all students with disabilities are the same and have no unique features. While it is true that students with and without disabilities are more alike than they are different one from another, it is also true that specific disabilities or impairments often have implications for the effective teaching and management of the children concerned. I have tried to provide teachers with a basic understanding of these implications.

Chapters covering self-regulation in learning, social skills development and behaviour management have been expanded and updated. The main focus on teaching basic academic skills to children with special needs has been retained, but this edition also provides a comprehensive and critical coverage of the topic of adapting other areas of the curriculum. Differentiation of teaching method, curriculum content and resources is considered to be a key component of inclusive classroom practice; but as I have indicated later, teachers do not find differentiation in the classroom easy to implement or to sustain over time. These problems are discussed in the final chapter.

I hope this book will enable teachers to increase their repertoire of management and instructional strategies – but in particular I hope that reading this book will help all teachers understand better their students' special educational needs.

Peter Westwood
University of Hong Kong
2002

Chapter 1

Special educational needs, learning difficulties, and effective instruction

A child has special educational needs if he or she has a learning difficulty that calls for special educational provision to be made for him or her. A child has a learning difficulty if he or she has a significantly greater difficulty in learning than the majority of children of the same age, or has a disability which prevents or hinders the child from making use of educational facilities of a kind generally provided for children of the same age in schools within the area of the local education authority.

(adapted from *Education Act 1996*, Section 312, cited in Frederickson and Cline 2002: 35)

The extract above presents a definition of 'special educational needs' accepted in England and Wales at the present time. Most developed countries have fairly similar views on what constitutes a 'special need'. In Australia, for example, Lang and Berberich (1995) explain that the term 'children with special needs' refers primarily to children whose physical or intellectual capacities have been affected to some degree so that their participation in teaching and learning situations requires assistance. These writers add later that 'Special needs children are those whose needs are usually beyond the training and prior working experience of many classroom teachers and administrators' (Lang and Berberich 1995: 16). In the US, under a Federal Law definition, students with special needs are those who are eligible for special services because their disability or impairment affects their educational performance. Included within this broad category are children with learning disability, speech or language disorders, mental retardation (intellectual disability), emotional disturbance, autism, hearing impairment, vision impairment, deaf-blindness, orthopaedic impairments, traumatic brain injury, chronic health conditions, and severe and multiple disabilities. To this long list one can also add children who have been described in the past as 'slow learners', children with attention-deficit hyperactivity disorder (ADHD), and children who are at risk of developing learning problems due to second language difficulties (Friend and Bursuck 2002). Many writers point out that gifted and talented students also have special educational needs – but not all countries include the category of gifted in their policies for special education services. With or without the inclusion of gifted and talented children, the population of students with special educational needs is extremely diverse, and the education of these children presents a major and ongoing challenge to teachers everywhere.

In an attempt to clarify definitions and descriptions of students with special needs the OECD (2000) suggested three broad categories:

- students with identifiable disabilities and impairments;
- students with learning difficulties not attributable to any disability or impairment;
- students with difficulties due to socio-economic, cultural, or linguistic disadvantage.

For many children in all three categories (other than those with severe and complex disabilities) the worldwide trend now is towards placement in mainstream classes. Although not yet fully implemented in most countries, this policy of inclusive schooling has created a situation where all teachers must gain information about students with special needs and how best to meet these needs in regular classroom settings.

Inclusive schooling and special educational needs

Over the past twenty years students with milder degrees of disability or difficulty have been retained in mainstream classes whenever possible, rather than being segregated or withdrawn into special groups (Rea, McLaughlin and Walther-Thomas 2002). This move towards inclusion began tentatively in the 1970s under the banner of 'integration' or 'mainstreaming'. It gained momentum in the late 1980s and 1990s under the influence of policies of social justice and equity. Inclusion was given additional impetus by *The Salamanca Statement and Framework for Action on Special Needs Education* (UNESCO 1994), a document that advocates strongly for providing education for students with special needs within the regular education system.

Policies of inclusion have changed very significantly the nature of special education provision – from serving students mainly in special settings and remedial programmes to supporting teachers and students in mainstream classrooms. Inclusive schooling has had a major impact also on the role of regular class teachers who are now required to cater for the needs of an increasingly diverse group of students, and on the role of special education teachers who must now work more closely and collaboratively with regular class teachers (Wearmouth 2001).

Underpinning inclusive education is the principle that each and every child, regardless of gender, ethnicity, social class, ability or disability, has the basic right to be educated in the regular classroom. This principle has been accepted to varying degrees in most developed countries and has influenced educational policy-making in the United States, Canada, Britain, Australia, New Zealand, Scandinavia, and much of Europe and Asia. However, in many of these countries the implementation of inclusive classroom practice is still lagging well behind the stated policies – and often the rhetoric of 'education for all' is far ahead of the reality in schools (Kavale and Forness 2000). Some countries have been slow to promote integration and inclusion, in part because many teachers and principals were not strongly in favour of teaching all children in the mainstream (Soodak and Podell 1998). Sometimes there has been opposition from parents of both disabled and non-disabled children, concerned that classrooms containing a very wide range of ability may end up failing to meet the needs of any of the children (Farrell 2001). Other obstacles have been a lack of funds for providing an adequate system of support to integrated children and their teachers, and difficulties in providing sufficient additional training for teachers to enable them to teach students with special needs (Rose 2001).

Although there is fairly general acceptance of the idea that students with mild disabilities should be included in the regular classroom, policies that advocate the inclusion of *all* students with disabilities in regular classes are not without their critics – with some educators arguing that regular class placement is not the least restrictive learning environment for some children (e.g. Dymond and Orelove 2001; Hockenbury, Kauffman and Hallahan 2000). Many tensions still remain between those who advocate inclusion for all and those who believe strongly that some children with special needs can have those needs met most effectively in separate settings with alternative curricula and readily-available support services. For this reason it is often argued that the full range of placement options, including special schools and special classes, should be retained, thus allowing for responsible choices to be made concerning the most appropriate educational setting for each individual with a disability. In Britain, for example, the Department for Education and Employment (1997: 43) has stated clearly:

> There are therefore strong educational, as well as social and moral, grounds for educating children with special educational needs with their peers. We aim to increase the level and quality of inclusion within mainstream schools, *while protecting and enhancing specialist provision for those who need it*. We will *redefine the role of special schools* to bring out their contribution in working with mainstream schools to support greater inclusion [emphasis added].

The practical problems surrounding inclusion are most obvious in the case of individuals with severe and multiple disabilities, since many of these students require a high degree of physical care and management over and above their educational needs. However, there is some evidence to suggest that where schools (particularly preschools) are prepared to accept the challenge of full inclusion, it is indeed possible to provide appropriate programmes for these students with significant disabilities (Hammill and Everington 2002; Llewellyn 2001).

By comparison, the inclusion of students with milder forms of disability and with general learning difficulties presents fewer problems. It is believed that regular class teachers can adopt teaching approaches that are more adaptive to the specific needs of such students (Bauer and Shea 1999; Grenot-Scheyer, Fisher and Staub 2001). On the other hand, some doubt has been expressed that children with specific learning disability (LD) can benefit from full-time placement in the mainstream (Klinger *et al.* 1998) and there is evidence to suggest that for these students intensive teaching in special groups on a part-time but regular basis is more effective than in-class support. Children with LD, who have major problems in acquiring basic academic skills, usually need at least one period per day when they are withdrawn from class and taught individually or in small groups. Within the regular classroom it is virtually impossible to provide remedial instruction of the intensity, frequency and duration required by these students. The same may well be true of other students with very special instructional or therapeutic needs.

Factors associated with successful inclusion

Research is really only beginning to determine which school and classroom practices – and what balance between in-class and out-of-class support – result in the most effective inclusion and ensure optimum progress for all students (e.g. Hunt and Goetz 1997; Marston 1996; Nelson, Ferrante and Martella 1999; Rea *et al.* 2002). It seems that as a very minimum the following ingredients are required if students with significant learning or adjustment problems are to be successfully included in the regular classroom with appropriate access to the general curriculum:

- strong leadership on the part of the school principal;
- development of a whole-school policy supportive of inclusion;
- positive attitudes in staff, parents, and children towards students with disabilities;
- commitment on the part of all staff to work collaboratively and to share expertise;
- development of mutual support networks among staff;
- regular assistance from paraprofessionals (classroom aides);
- effective links with outside agencies and services;
- adequate resourcing in terms of materials and personnel;
- regular training and professional development for staff;

- close liaison with parents;
- where possible, parental involvement in a child's educational programme;
- adaptation of curriculum and teaching methods (differentiation).

In recent years many books and articles have been written on the theme of inclusive education, mainly from philosophical, political or managerial perspectives. Some titles have been included in the Further Reading list at the end of this chapter, but readers will have no difficulty in locating recent titles in any education library. Inclusive education will continue to be a topic of debate for many years to come.

How many students have special educational needs?

When mainstream teachers are asked to identify the number of students with special needs in their own classes they tend always to identify significantly more children than the official prevalence figures would predict (McKinnon and Gordon 1999; Westwood and Graham 2000). This may be because teachers have a vested interest in reporting high prevalence rates in order to gain additional resources or support for the school; on the other hand, official figures may be underestimating the true number of children with disabilities, learning difficulties or behaviour problems. An OECD report on inclusive education states that it has been widely accepted in many countries that on average between 15 per cent and 20 per cent of students will have special needs at some time in their school careers (OECD 1999). Some studies have suggested a much higher figure – even as high as 32 per cent if all students with general learning difficulties, low achievement, and behaviour problems are included (Westwood and Graham 2000). Very significant emotional and behavioural difficulties are reported in approximately 9 per cent of the school population (Croll and Moses 2000). The percentage of children with significant intellectual, physical or sensory disabilities is relatively small, possibly about 3 per cent of the school population (Colbert and van Kraayenoord 2000).

The largest single group of students with special needs comprises those with general and specific learning difficulties that are not related to any disability or impairment. Estimates suggest that this may be close to 20 per cent of the school population (Louden 2000). These learning difficulties most frequently manifest themselves as problems in acquiring basic literacy and numeracy skills. Difficulties with reading, writing and calculation then impact adversely on a child's ability to learn in most subjects across the curriculum.

The remaining sections of this chapter will address the special needs of students with general and specific learning difficulties. In later chapters the characteristics and instructional needs of children with various types of disability will be discussed; but the very important point must be made here that the instructional needs of all these children *are much more alike than they are different*. While there are some special approaches needed by students with severe and complex learning problems, or with physical and sensory impairments, in general *all* children with special needs require what has been described as teaching that is '. . . efficient, intensive, relentless, carefully sequenced, and carefully monitored for effects' – in other words, high-quality effective instruction (Hockenbury *et al.* 2000: 9).

Students with general and specific learning difficulties

The term learning difficulties is a very general one, used widely and without much precision to refer to the general problems in learning experienced by some 20 per cent of the school population. Usually the term is applied to students whose difficulties are not directly related to a specific intellectual, physical or sensory disability, although some students with disabilities often do experience problems in learning and in social adjustment. Students who have been referred to as 'slow learners', 'low achievers', or simply 'the hard to teach', certainly fall within the category 'learning difficulties'. So too do the children described as learning disabled (LD) – those of at least average intelligence who for no obvious reason experience great difficulty in learning the basic academic skills (American Psychiatric Association 1994).

Possible causes of general learning difficulty

Hilty (1998) has remarked that the cause of a learning difficulty usually cannot be attributed to a single factor. Most learning problems arise from a complex interaction among variables such as curriculum content, learners' prior knowledge and experience, learners' cognitive ability and task-approach strategies, teacher's instructional method, complexity of teachers' language, suitability of resource materials, learners' confidence and expectation of success, and the perceived relevance or value of the learning task. Many additional factors may also contribute to a failure to learn, such as distractions in the learning environment, the health or emotional state of the learner, and the interpersonal relationship between teacher and learner.

Despite the many and varied possible causal factors associated with learning difficulty it seems that most teachers, psychologists and researchers have tended to focus almost exclusively on so-called 'deficits' or weaknesses within the learner to account for children's problems in coping successfully with the school curriculum (Sternberg and Grigorenko 2001). Rarely have curricula, teaching methods, or materials been diagnosed as possible causes of a learning difficulty: the tendency has been always to 'blame the victim' for his or her own difficulties (Bearne 1996; Croll and Moses 2000). Even parents tend to assume that there is something wrong with their children if school progress is unsatisfactory; and it is common to find such children being referred to educational psychologists and general practitioners for evaluation or diagnosis.

Many writers have attempted to summarise characteristics of students with learning difficulties, resulting in lists similar to the one below – often referred to as the 'deficit model of learning difficulties'. The deficit model suggests that learning problems are due to:

- below average intelligence;
- poor concentration span;
- problems with visual and auditory perception;
- difficulties in understanding complex language;
- limited vocabulary;
- low motivation;
- poor recall of previous learning;
- inability to generalise learning to new contexts;
- lack of effective learning strategies;
- deficient self-management skills;
- poor self-esteem;
- learned helplessness;
- behavioural and emotional reactions to failure.

While these weaknesses do exist for many students with learning difficulties they should not be viewed as obstacles too difficult for teachers to overcome, but rather as clear indications of the students' need for high-quality teaching. The deficit model does at least highlight specific difficulties the students may have that need to be taken into account when planning and implementing classroom programmes.

Perhaps perspectives on causality are beginning to change. Robertson, Hamill and Hewitt (1994: 1) have observed that:

> Low attainment is no longer seen as solely rooted in an individual's intellectual characteristics. Many other factors are now accepted as having an important role in influencing attainment. The curriculum itself can contribute, perhaps being pitched at an inappropriate level or paced too quickly. Also, teaching strategies might not be suited to the ways that pupils learn most effectively.

Rather than blaming the victim it is usually much more productive to examine factors outside the child, such as quality and type of instruction, teacher expectations, relevance of the curriculum, classroom environment, interpersonal dynamics within the class social group, and rapport with the teacher. These factors are much more amenable to modification than are factors within the child or within the child's family background or culture. Trying to identify how best to help a student with general learning difficulties involves finding the most significant and alterable factors that need to be addressed, and providing students with high-quality instruction.

There is, however, one much smaller sub-group of students with learning difficulties – those with a learning *disability* – whose problems may stem mainly from internal factors related to weaknesses in language processing, perception, or cognition.

Students with learning disabilities (LD)

Learning disability is the term applied to students whose difficulties cannot be traced to any lack of intelligence, sensory impairment, cultural or linguistic disadvantage or inadequate teaching (Bauer, Keefe and Shea 2001). This disability manifests itself as a marked discrepancy between ability and academic achievement (Kirk, Gallagher and Anastasiow 2000). This small group, less than 3 per cent of the school population, exhibits chronic problems in mastering the basic academic skills of reading, writing, spelling and mathematics. Some students with LD may also have problems with social skills, and a few have minor difficulties with physical skills.

The most widely recognised learning disability is, of course, *dyslexia*. This form of reading problem is thought to be present in approximately 1 to 2 per cent of the school population – although some reports place the prevalence rate very much higher. Dyslexia is often defined as a 'disorder' causing difficulty in learning to read despite conventional instruction, adequate intelligence and sociocultural opportunity. The dyslexic student typically has great difficulty in:

- understanding and applying phonic decoding principles;
- building a vocabulary of words recognised by sight;
- making adequate use of contextual cues to assist word recognition;
- developing speed and fluency in reading;
- understanding what has been read.

The oral reading performance of dyslexic students tends to be very slow and laboured, with maximum effort having to be devoted to identifying each individual word, leaving minimum cognitive capacity available for focusing on meaning. The student tires easily and avoids the task of reading if possible.

Other forms of learning disability described in the literature include *dysgraphia* (problems with writing), *dysorthographia* (problems with spelling), and *dyscalculia* (problems with arithmetic). It is doubtful, of course, that these pseudo-medical terms have any value, particularly in determining an intervention programme for an individual child. The *Diagnostic and Statistical Manual of Mental Disorders* (APA 1994) describes the same problems under the categories of 'reading disorder', 'mathematics disorder', and 'disorders of written language'. These disorders are recognised mainly by a marked discrepancy between a child's high scores on an intelligence test and low scores on tests of attainment in reading, spelling or mathematics.

It is often argued that the difficulties of many students with learning disability are not recognised early enough in school, and many LD students are considered simply lazy or unmotivated. Some of these students go on to develop social and emotional problems and some present with major behaviour difficulties (Hallahan and Kauffman 2000; Smith 1998). Studies have shown that a significant number of students with LD leave school at the earliest possible date and do not pursue studies later as adults (Sabornie and deBettencourt 1997).

Characteristics of students with learning disability

Over the years, children with learning disabilities have been described as having some of the following characteristics:

- a history of late speech development (and continuing immaturities in articulation and syntax);
- visual perception problems resulting in frequent reversal of letters and numerals (some individuals reporting distortion or blurring of print when reading);
- auditory perception problems (including difficulties in developing phonemic awareness);
- poor integration of sensory information (for example, the student can't easily learn to associate and remember phonic letter-to-sound relationships);
- difficulty in recalling words, or quickly naming familiar objects (*dysnomia*);
- weak lateralisation (no strong preference for left or righthandness; directional sense confusion);
- minor signs of possible neurological dysfunction;
- hyperactivity and/or attention deficits;
- poor motor co-ordination;
- low level of motivation;
- inefficient learning strategies;
- poor self-management;
- secondary emotional and behavioural problems due to persistent failure;
- learned helplessness;
- anxiety;
- depression.

It must be noted that almost all of the problems listed above may also be found to varying degrees in students who have *general* learning difficulties rather than LD, so the list does not help to differentiate between those who have a genuine learning disability and those who are often referred to as having 'garden variety' learning difficulties (Badian 1996). To add to the problem of identification it is also the case that any one child with LD may not exhibit more than a few of the characteristics in the list.

The traditional method for identifying LD is to assess the student's level of intelligence using a standardised intelligence test, then to obtain standardised measures of attainment in academic skills such as reading, spelling, and mathematics. Any marked discrepancy between level of intelligence and level of attainment (an indication of so-called 'under achievement') might indicate the presence of a learning disability. There have been many objections raised to the rigid use of this discrepancy approach to identification, since it might exclude from receiving additional remedial support some students who have obvious learning difficulties, simply on the basis of IQ (Sternberg and Grigorenko 2001).

Possible causes of learning disability

Some authorities in the learning disability field tend to attribute the learning problem to neurological deficiencies within the student. Bender (2001), on the other hand, points out that the neurological perspective, although capturing researchers' keen attention for nearly 70 years, has failed to produce any useful treatment strategies or teaching interventions.

Although much emphasis has been placed upon the possible organic and biological causes of learning disability, and interest has also been shown in possible genetic factors in some cases, recent studies have suggested other possible causes. In particular, attention has been directed towards inefficient learning style (Bradshaw 1995; Gregory and Chapman 2002). In many cases of learning disability the children do not appear to have an effective system when approaching a task such as word recognition, phonic decoding, writing a story, or completing an arithmetic problem. Their lack of effective strategies produces high error-rate and rapid frustration. It has become popular in recent years to say that these students need to 'learn how to learn' so that they can tackle classroom activities with a greater chance of success. The important thing to note is that current evidence suggests that children can be taught to use more efficient learning strategies and can then function at significantly higher levels (Paris and Paris 2001; Sullivan, Mastropieri and Scruggs 1995).

One particular factor considered to cause the learning problems typical of students with a specific reading disability is a lack of awareness of the phonological (speech–sound) aspects of oral language. This difficulty in identifying component sounds within words impairs their ability to master phonic principles and apply the decoding strategy for reading and spelling (Torgesen 1999). It is now believed that in the most severe cases of reading disability this poor phonological awareness is often accompanied by a 'naming-speed' deficiency in which the student cannot quickly retrieve a word or a syllable or a letter-sound association from long-term memory. These combined weaknesses create what is termed the 'double deficit' and make it extremely difficult for the child to develop effective word recognition skills or become a fluent reader (Miller and Felton 2001; Wolf and Bowers 1999).

Is the concept of 'learning disability' useful?

Learning disability remains a very controversial topic. Stanovich (1999: vii) remarks: 'The field of learning disabilities is littered with dead ends, false starts, pseudo-science, and fads.' While some experts argue strongly that, for example, a severe reading disability is qualitatively and etiologically different from any of the more general forms of reading failure, others regard it as merely a different point on the same reading-difficulty continuum. It is fairly clear that the study of LD has not resulted in any major breakthrough in tailored teaching methods or instructional resources. In terms of pedagogy, it is difficult to visualise that any teaching method found useful for children with general problems in learning to read or calculate would not also be highly relevant for other children identified as dyslexic or dyscalculic – and vice versa. If one examines the literature on teaching methodology for children with LD (e.g. Bender 2001; Chinn and Ashcroft 1993; Ott 1997; Silver and Hagin 2002; Thompson and Watkins 1990) one usually finds not a unique methodology applicable only to LD students but a range of valuable teaching strategies that would be helpful to all children. As Thomas (1999) has observed, it has taken us a great deal of time to learn the lesson that the search for unique methods for LD is hollow and illusory.

Any child with a learning problem requires assistance, and there seems little to be gained from seeking to differentiate between LD and 'non-LD' students; the need for high-quality, effective instruction is equally strong in both groups (Tunmer *et al.* 2002). Allington and Baker (1999) suggest that all children who find learning to read and write difficult are best served by designing and delivering sufficient and appropriate instruction, rather than by identifying them with a label.

Correlates of learning difficulty: reduced motivation and learned helplessness

Teachers often blame a student's learning problems on his or her lack of motivation. According to Driscoll (2000) teachers believe that this lack of motivation is the underlying reason that students avoid class work, refuse to become fully engaged in a learning task, fail to complete work they could easily do, or are willing to complete a task only for some extrinsic reward it may bring. It is almost as if teachers believe motivation to be an innate trait of learners, rather than a variable that is significantly influenced by outside factors. On this issue Galloway *et al.* (1998: 17) have remarked:

> Too often, motivation is seen as a characteristic of pupils, perhaps not quite as unchanging as age or eye colour, but nevertheless firmly embedded in their make-up. We have argued that it can be seen as the product of an interaction between pupils and the varying situations in which they find themselves at school.

For many students with learning difficulties the problem is certainly not an innate lack of motivation but rather a marked reluctance to take risks or make any new commitment in a learning situation (Covington and Teel 1996). This reluctance is due to prior experiences of lack of success.

Students' past causal inferences about their own successes and failures are major determinants of future motivation and achievement (Ho *et al.* 1999). There is abundant evidence that obtaining poor outcomes from personal effort to learn can have lasting negative effects on the students' self-esteem, and feelings of self-efficacy (Alderman 1999). If students come to believe that they lack the ability ever to succeed they may try to avoid participating in achievement-oriented activities simply to protect their feeling of self-worth – believing that if they don't attempt the task they will not be seen by others to have failed (Ormrod 2000). As Cross and Vidyarthi (2000:13) remark, some students with difficulties are unable to separate 'failing in class' from 'failing completely as a person'.

Students who encounter continual failure and disapproval may regress over time to a state of learned helplessness, with a very significant decline in motivation and effort (Rholes, Palmer and Thompson 2000). Learned helplessness is the situation in which an individual never expects to succeed with any task he or she is given, and feels totally powerless to change this outcome (Carver and Scheier 1999; Valas 2001).

Observation of young children suggests that, even at an early age, they can begin to regard themselves as failures in certain learning situations. If, for some reason, a child finds that he or she cannot do something that other children are doing easily, there is a loss of confidence. This loss of confidence leads to deliberate avoidance of the type of activity associated with the failure, and sometimes even avoidance of any new or challenging situation. Avoidance leads to lack of practice. Lack of practice ensures that the individual does not gain in proficiency or confidence, while other children forge ahead. The effects of early failure are thus cumulative, and may contribute later to many instances of learning difficulty in school.

While there are different individual thresholds of tolerance for failure among students, it must be acknowledged that failure is not a pleasing experience, and given sufficient exposure to it almost any student will develop avoidance strategies and learned helplessness. One of the ways of remedying this situation is through attribution retraining (Winebrenner 1996), an approach to be discussed later. The main challenge for teachers is to try to use teaching methods and learning activities in the classroom that will lead all students to feel successful. Prevention of a learning difficulty in this way is so much more effective than remedial support provided after failure has become well established.

Impact of students' learning difficulties on teachers' motivation

Unfortunately, children's learning problems can have a negative impact on teachers' attitude and motivation. The poor learning habits, low achievement, and reduced motivation seen fairly frequently in students with learning difficulties can influence the attitude teachers develop towards such students. According to studies reviewed by Eggen and Kauchak (2001) teaching students with learning problems, particularly if the students are in bottom-stream classes, can have a very negative effect on teachers' own enthusiasm and motivation. Researchers have suggested that teachers' expectations for students' progress and improvement are lowered in the case of bottom-stream classes (Chang and Westwood 2001; Harlen and Malcolm 1997). Teachers can become demoralised by students' poor attitudes towards learning and their often-uncooperative behaviour in the classroom. As a result the teachers are less likely to spend time preparing interesting and innovative lessons, or in devising new ways of motivating their students. In general, most teachers would prefer to teach higher-ability students rather than those of lower ability.

Teachers' negative beliefs and attitudes are extremely significant because they are communicated all too easily to students. Feeling valued as a human being is known to be a powerful motivator (McCarty and Siccone 2001) and students' interpretations of how peers and teachers perceive them exert a critical influence on their level of motivation and feelings of self-worth. When the teachers' attitudes towards the students are perceived as negative they often exert detrimental influences on students' self-esteem and willingness to work (Weinstein 1998). Students' self-esteem and self-efficacy are built out of the ways in which teachers behave towards them; and as Biggs (1995: 98) remarks, 'Any messages that suggest incompetence are damaging.' The everyday actions and reactions of teachers when teaching low-ability classes may add to students' own perceptions of being incompetent in school. Even unintentional cues from teachers – such as providing simplified materials, easier tasks, too much praise, too much help – may cause students to believe they are lacking in ability or that teachers believe them to be so.

Alderman (1999) lists 'communicating low expectations' as one of the key factors contributing to negative motivation; and Brophy (1998) has summarised 18 different ways in which teachers, albeit unwittingly, communicate reduced expectations to students they perceive as having low ability. The end result is a lowering of the students' feelings of self-efficacy. When students believe their teachers regard them as 'dull' or 'no-hopers', the development of learned helplessness becomes more likely. In situations where students do not feel successful and fail to reach personal goals, and where they feel undervalued by others, motivation and self-esteem are likely to suffer.

In terms of students' progress and teachers' motivation it is important to consider which teaching approaches tend to produce the most successful learning. In this final section of the chapter attention will be given to methods and strategies that reduce learning failure by enhancing opportunities to learn.

Teaching approaches

Several educators have suggested that student-centred approaches to learning have most to offer children with special educational needs (e.g. Goddard 1995; MacInnis and Hemming 1995). These 'process-oriented approaches' – which often seem to emphasise social development rather than mastery of curriculum content – are thought to be more accommodating of student differences. However, research evidence suggests that students with disabilities and learning problems most frequently do best in structured programmes where direct teaching methods are employed (Kavale and Forness 1999; Swanson 2000a; Vaughn, Gersten and Chard 2000). A carefully structured and direct teaching approach has also been found to facilitate the inclusion of children with disabilities into the mainstream curriculum (Ward and Center 1999).

There is some evidence to suggest that these student-centred process approaches do not necessarily meet the needs of all students, and in particular are not the most effective way of developing basic academic skills for students with learning problems (Harris and Graham 1996; Mastropieri, Scruggs and Butcher 1997; Swanson 2000a). Care must be taken to ensure that a process approach to learning as an example of inclusive practice is not simply a soft option that allows students with disabilities and learning difficulties in the mainstream classroom to fade into the background without being intellectually challenged and without really making progress through the curriculum. To be effective, inclusion should result in more than minor gains in social development.

The viewpoint underpinning this book is that student-centred process methods should be used frequently with all children – but their use should be reserved for the types of learning and stages of learning where they have most to contribute. For example, the development of higher-order cognitive skills and problem-solving strategies necessitates, in part, a process approach. So too does the application of strategies and skills to new situations in order to facilitate generalisation and transfer of learning. However, a process approach if used alone is usually inadequate for the beginning stages of learning important basic literacy and numeracy skills. Direct and explicit forms of instruction appear to achieve most in the early stages of learning basic academic skills (Westwood 1998, 2000). Over many decades, despite the popularity of student-centred, activity-based learning approaches, clear evidence supports the value of direct and explicit teaching, often delivered through the medium of interactive whole-class teaching (Galton *et al.* 1999; OFSTED 1993). Effective teaching not only raises the attainment level of all students but also reduces significantly the prevalence of learning failure.

Based on a meta-analysis of outcomes from many different types of teaching approach Swanson (1999) draws the conclusion that the most effective method for teaching basic academic skills to students with learning difficulties combines the following features:

- carefully controlling and sequencing the curriculum content to be studied;
- providing abundant opportunities for practice and application of newly acquired knowledge and skills;
- ensuring high levels of participation and responding by the children (for example, answering the teacher's questions; staying on task);
- using interactive group teaching;
- modelling by the teacher of effective ways of completing school tasks;
- teaching children how best to attempt new learning tasks (direct strategy training);
- making appropriate use of technology (e.g. computer-assisted instruction);
- providing supplementary assistance (e.g. homework; parental tutoring, etc.).

Many of the same features are identified by Sideridis and Greenwood (1998) who add the following ingredients to create the most effective approach for students with learning difficulties and developmental disabilities:

- Abundant guided practice; the teacher provides frequent feedback and correction during the lesson.
- Reinforcement; students are rewarded through descriptive praise and encouragement.
- High levels of student participation and engagement.
- Fast pacing of lessons.
- Positive student-to-student interactions; peer assistance and discussions.
- Student-to-teacher interactions; frequent asking and answering of questions.

Effective teaching practices are those that provide students with the maximum opportunity to learn. These practices increase student achievement levels through maintaining on-task behaviour. The term 'academic engaged time' is often used to describe such on-task behaviour. Academic engaged time refers to the proportion of instructional time in which students are actively involved in their work. This active involvement includes attending to instruction from the teacher, working independently or with a group on assigned academic tasks, and applying previously acquired knowledge and skills. Studies have shown that students who are receiving instruction directly from the teacher spend more time attending to the content of the lesson than students who are expected to find out for themselves. Effective lessons, particularly those covering basic academic skills, tend to have a clear structure.

The research on effective teaching in general (e.g. Jacobsen, Eggen and Kauchak 2002; Killen 1998; Rosenshine 1995; Wilen *et al.* 2000) suggests that very effective teachers exhibit the following important characteristics.

Effective teachers tend to:

- have well-managed classrooms;
- provide students with the maximum opportunity to learn;
- maintain an academic focus;
- have high expectations of what students can achieve;
- adopt a style that is business-like and work-oriented;
- show enthusiasm;
- use strategies to keep students on task, motivated and productive;
- impose structure on the content to be covered;
- present new material in a step-by-step manner;
- employ direct and explicit instructional procedures;
- use clear instructions and explanations;
- demonstrate appropriate task-approach strategies;
- monitor closely what students are doing;
- apply high rates of questioning to involve students and to check for understanding;
- adjust instruction to individual needs, and re-teach when necessary;
- provide frequent feedback to students;
- use a variety of resources;
- spend significant amounts of time in interactive, whole-class teaching.

Wilen *et al.* (2000: 283) have remarked, 'As to which types of learners benefit most from this systematic approach, research tells us that it is helpful for young children, slower learners, and students of all ages and abilities during the first stages of learning informational material or material that is difficult to learn.' Where explicit teaching is used, students with learning difficulties appear to make much better progress and become more confident and effective learners.

The use of explicit teaching methods in the early stages of learning something new in no way precludes the student from ultimately developing independence in learning; indeed, direct teaching in the early stages facilitates greater confidence and independence in later stages (Pressley and McCormick 1995).

Further reading

Ashman, A. and Elkins, J. (eds) (2002) *Educating Children with Diverse Abilities*, Sydney: Prentice Hall-Pearson Educational.

Barton, L. and Corbett, J. (2002) *Inclusive Education: Difficulties and Possibilities*, London: University of London.

Carpenter, B., Ashdown, R. and Bovair, K. (2001) *Enabling Access: Effective Teaching and Learning for Pupils with Learning Difficulties* (2nd edn), London: Fulton.

Corbett, J. (2001) *Supporting Inclusive Education: A Connective Pedagogy*, London: RoutledgeFalmer.

Franklin, B.M. (ed.) (1998) *When Children Don't Learn*, New York: Teachers College Press.

Frederickson, N. and Cline, T. (2002) *Special Educational Needs, Inclusion and Diversity*, Buckingham: Open University Press.

Henley, M., Ramsey, R. and Algozzine, R.F. (2002) *Characteristics of and Strategies for Teaching Students with Mild Disabilities* (4th edn), Boston, MA: Allyn and Bacon.

Minke, K. and Bear, G.C. (eds) (2000) *Preventing School Problems, Promoting School Success*, Bethesda, MD: National Association of School Psychologists.

Silver, A.A. and Hagin, R.A. (2002) *Disorders of Learning in Childhood* (2nd edn), New York: Wiley.

Vaughn, S., Bos, C.S. and Schumm, J. (2000) *Teaching Exceptional, Diverse and At-risk Students in the General Education Classroom* (2nd edn), Boston, MA: Allyn and Bacon.

Chapter 2

Students with intellectual disability and autism

Almost certainly, some of your students will have exceptionalities, and you will be expected to teach them as effectively as possible. Fortunately, changes that you'll need to make are more in how than in what you teach.

(Eggen and Kauchak 2001: 197)

The previous chapter explored a number of issues relating to children with general and specific learning difficulties. Students with general learning difficulties represent the largest population of children with special educational needs in mainstream schools. To this pool has been added in recent years an increasing number of students with disabilities who also require special consideration and extra support.

In the early days of 'integration' teachers often expressed grave doubts about the feasibility of placing students with disabilities in regular classrooms, particularly in relation to their own ability to meet the needs of these students. It was found that teachers' doubts and negative attitudes could be attributed in part to their lack of knowledge about disabilities and lack of previous experience in working with these children (Weisel and Tur-Kaspa 2002). The trend towards inclusion has made it essential now for all teachers to have at least a working knowledge of the effects a disability can have on a student's development, learning and social adjustment. Teachers also need to be aware of any priorities that need to be observed when working with these children and helping them participate in the mainstream curriculum.

This book is mainly concerned with methods for teaching students with mild disabilities and difficulties, but this chapter and the next provide important background information on children with more significant disabilities, impairments or disorders and highlight some of their specific needs in terms of teaching methods and management.

Guiding principles for the mainstream teacher

It is essential first to stress two basic principles that should underpin teachers' beliefs and actions in relation to students with disabilities:

- Students with disabilities are *more like all other children than they are different from them*. A lack of awareness of this fact is what contributes to teachers' fear of the unknown.
- Students with a particular disability (e.g. Down's Syndrome) as a group are *just as diverse* in their personal characteristics, behaviour, interests, and learning aptitudes as any other group of students. The assumption that they are all the same is a main cause of negative stereoptying of particular disability groups (Smith 2001).

The following statement should be read in conjunction with the main sections in this chapter and the next:

> The student with disability in your class is first and foremost another student – just like all the others in your class. As far as possible, treat him or her in exactly the same way that you treat all other students. He or she has the same basic need for your friendship, respect, assistance, stimulation and good quality teaching as every other student in your class. Don't lower your expectations. It is particularly important to remember that students with disabilities are not necessarily lacking in ability or motivation, and often they can learn effectively if they can gain access to the normal curriculum through appropriate support. Some students may need assistive technology and some may require a modified curriculum; but in general students with disabilities need the same experiences as are encountered by all other students in your class. Many of the following suggestions to support students with disabilities will also be helpful to some of the other students with learning problems in your classroom.

Students with intellectual disability

Individuals with intellectual disability comprise a very heterogeneous group, including some very low-functioning individuals who require almost complete and continuous care and management, and others (the majority) with only mild difficulties often not detected until they are required to learn in a school setting. As a group, children with *mild* intellectual disability comprise the largest group of students with disabilities. They tend to be indistinguishable in many ways from students who have been described in the past as 'slow learners'. In most countries where inclusive education practices have been established many children with mild intellectual disability attend mainstream schools and receive additional support in that setting.

Children with moderate to severe intellectual disability are more commonly accommodated in special schools or special classes – although in America, Canada, Australia and some parts of Europe there is a belief that children with even this degree of intellectual impairment should be integrated in mainstream schools. In those countries some students with moderate intellectual disability are already being integrated, mainly in the preschool and early primary years. It is argued that degree of disability should not act as a barrier to children attending their local school, and should not be a reason for forcing them into segregated education.

Regardless of where they are placed, students with moderate to severe disability require very high levels of support. Many individuals with severe intellectual disability also have additional difficulties or impairments (physical, sensory, emotional, behavioural) and are frequently described as having 'high support needs' (Orelove and Sobsey 1996). Moderate to severe intellectual disability often results in significant limitations of development in most of the following areas:

- communication skills;
- self-care and daily living skills;
- social skills;
- basic academic skills (literacy and numeracy);
- self-regulation and self-direction;
- independent functioning in the community;
- employability.

Over the years, individuals with impaired intellectual abilities have been given different descriptive labels. In America the term *mental retardation* is still in fairly common use (but is being replaced gradually by *cognitive impairment*). In parts of Asia the term *mental handicap* is still used. In Australia and New Zealand the current term is *intellectual disability*. *Moderate or severe learning difficulties* (MLD or SLD) is the description used in Britain.

Traditionally, for an individual to be identified as having an intellectual disability he or she obtained a measured intelligence quotient (IQ) below 70 and exhibited obvious delays in acquiring normal adaptive behaviours (Sukumaran 2000). In recent years attention in many countries has moved away from the importance of IQ for the identification of intellectual disability, and now the emphasis is more on assessing how well the individual can function and what skills he or she has already acquired. In the case of children with intellectual disability it is much more important for teachers to focus on the relative strengths that a child has, rather than any so-called impairments or deficits (Nind 2000). If one places too much importance on deficits there tends to be a lowering of expectations for the student's future progress. Positive expectations are more likely to lead to a stimulating curriculum. Students with intellectual disability can and will learn if provided with an appropriate instructional programme, adequate support and teaching methods oriented to their individual needs (Drew and Hardman 2000; Fisher and Frey 2001).

> Students with cognitive impairments require special and intensive instruction, and this instruction needs to begin early. When the target of instruction is specifically identified and is taught directly, and progress is evaluated systematically and consistently, students with mental retardation achieve well.
>
> (Smith 2001: 251)

Ashman (1998) suggests that for each student with intellectual disability we should ask:

- In what setting will the student learn most successfully?
- What skills does the student need to be taught?
- What are the most effective ways of teaching those skills?

The dilemma facing those who wish to educate all children with severe disabilities in the mainstream is how to meet their basic needs for training in self-care, communication and daily living skills once they are placed in an environment where a fairly standard academic curriculum prevails. Dymond and Orelove (2001) and Hockenbury *et al.* (2000) have queried whether the potential benefits of socialisation and normalisation in the mainstream should outweigh all the problems involved in supporting these children in a curriculum that is not necessarily very relevant to them. They observe, 'Functional skills, which were once widely accepted as the basis for curriculum development, have received limited attention as the field has moved to a more inclusive service delivery model' (Dymond and Orelove 2001: 111). For some students with disabilities a segregated education setting may still offer the best environment to meet their special needs.

Learning characteristics of students with intellectual disability

The most obvious characteristic of many individuals with intellectual disability is that they experience significant difficulties in learning almost everything that other children can learn with ease. From a practical viewpoint, intellectual disability presents itself as an inability to think as quickly, reason as deeply, remember as easily, or adapt as rapidly to new situations, when compared with so-called normal children. Children with intellectual disability appear to be much less mature than their age peers, exhibiting general behaviours typical of much younger children. Their behaviour patterns, skills and general knowledge are related more closely to their developmental age than to their chronological age.

Children who are developmentally delayed will be slower at acquiring cognitive skills. For them, interpreting information, thinking, reasoning and problem-solving are very difficult processes. In most aspects of concept development and reasoning, school-age children with mild to moderate intellectual disability tend to be functioning at what Piaget referred to as the 'concrete operational' level (Jenkinson, Sparrow and Shinkfield 1996). They understand and remember only those things and situations that they can directly experience; teaching for them has to be reality-based. Students with severe to profound disability may be at an even early Piagetian stage of 'sensori-motor' or 'pre-operational' level of cognitive development. It is generally accepted that children with intellectual disability pass through the same sequence of stages in cognitive development as other children (from sensori-motor, through pre-operational to concrete operational, and finally formal operational) but at a much slower rate. It is also clear that some intellectually disabled individuals even as adults never reach the highest level of formal operational thinking and reasoning.

The main messages that educators need to take from Piaget's work are these:

- Cognitive development comes from action and reflection, so students 'learn by doing'.
- The child needs to be active in order to develop intellectually.
- The child needs someone to interact with who will help to interpret (or *mediate*) learning experiences.

These three principles should guide the teaching of students with intellectual disability.

Specific difficulties

Attention: Individuals with intellectual disability appear often to have problems in *attending* to the relevant aspects of a learning situation. For example, when a teacher is showing the student how to form the numeral 5 with a pencil, or how to use scissors to cut paper, the student is attracted perhaps to the ring on the teacher's finger or to a picture on the paper, rather than the task itself (Taylor, Sternberg and Richards 1995). This tendency to focus on irrelevant detail, or to be distracted easily from a learning task, is potentially a major problem for the child with intellectual disability when integrated into mainstream programmes without close supervision. The teacher will need to think of many ways of helping a child with intellectual disability to focus on a learning task. Without adequate attention to task any student will fail to learn or remember what the teacher is trying to teach.

Memory: Many students with intellectual disability also have difficulty in *storing* information in long-term memory (Hallahan and Kauffman 2000). This problem may, in part, be linked with the failure to attend to the learning task as discussed above. It may also indicate that the lower the intellectual ability of the student the greater the amount of repetition and practice necessary to ensure that information and skills are eventually stored. Many students with intellectual disability do not develop effective learning strategies to aid memorisation, so the message for the teacher is to provide even more opportunities for guided and independent practice in every area of the curriculum. Very frequent revision and overlearning also need to be key parts of the teaching programme for students with intellectual disability.

Generalisation: It is typical of many students with intellectual disability that they have major problems in generalising what they learn (Meese 2001; Taylor *et al.* 1995). For any learner the most difficult stage of acquiring new learning is that of *generalisation.* In order to master information, skills or strategies a stage must be reached when the student can apply that learning to new situations not directly linked with the context in which it was first taught. Many students with intellectual disability are particularly weak in making these links for themselves; they may learn a particular skill or strategy in one context but fail to transfer it to a different situation. It is generally recommended that teachers should consider ways of facilitating generalisation when planning lessons for students with special needs by, for example, reteaching the same skills or strategies in different contexts, gradually increasing the range of contexts, challenging students to decide whether a skill or strategy could be used to solve a new problem, and reinforcing any evidence of students' spontaneous generalisation of previous learning.

Language delay in children with intellectual disability

One of the main characteristics of children with moderate and severe intellectual disability is the very slow rate at which many of them acquire speech and language. Even the child with mild retardation is likely to be behind the normal milestones for language development. Some individuals with severe and multiple disabilities never develop speech – for them alternative methods of communication may need to be developed (e.g. sign language; picture or symbol communication systems).

Language is important for both cognitive and social development. Communication skills are necessary for the following purposes:

- Language enables an individual to make his or her needs, opinions and ideas known to others.
- Language is important for cognitive development; without language one lacks much of the raw material with which to think and reason.

- Concepts are more effectively stored in memory if they have a mental representation in words as well as in sensations and perceptions.
- Language is the main medium through which school learning is mediated.
- Positive social interactions with other persons are heavily dependent upon effective language and communication skills.
- Language is important for regulating one's own behaviour and responses (self-talk).

The development of speaking and listening skills in students with intellectual disability is given high priority in special school curricula. Language stimulation will continue to be of vital importance for these students in mainstream settings. While language is best acquired naturally – through using it to express needs, obtain information, and interact socially – for some disabled students a more direct instructional approach may also be necessary (Beirne-Smith, Ittenbach and Patton 1998). Where possible, naturally occurring opportunities within the school day and at home are used to teach and reinforce new vocabulary and language patterns. This 'milieu approach' is found to be more productive in terms of generalisation and transfer of learning to everyday use than are the more clinical approaches to teaching language in isolation (Kaiser 2000). Two obvious benefits of placing a child with intellectual disability in a mainstream class are immersion in a naturally enriched language environment and the increased need for the student to communicate with others.

Many students with intellectual disability require the services of a speech therapist; but improvement can be very slow indeed with the intellectually disabled population. This is because the individuals receiving help may not appreciate the need for it and may therefore have no motivation to practise what is taught. There is also the usual problem of lack of generalization – what is taught in a clinical setting does not necessarily transfer to the person's everyday speech.

Social development of students with intellectual disability

The presence or absence of social skills in students with intellectual disability tends to be related to the extent to which they have had the opportunity to socialise in the home and other environments. Within the family, the social interactions between a child with intellectual disability and others are likely to be mainly positive, but the same assumption cannot be made for contacts within the community and at school. Although community attitudes towards people with disabilities are changing, there is still a likelihood that the child with intellectual disability will have experienced difficulty in making friends and gaining acceptance – particularly if he or she has some irritating or challenging behaviours (Snell and Brown 2000). In such cases he or she may experience rejection and teasing from other children.

Taylor *et al.* (1995) report studies indicating that some students with intellectual disability are rejected by their peers more on the basis of their irritating behaviour than because they are disabled; for example, the occasional presence of inappropriate responses such as aggression, shouting, or temper tantrums makes it difficult for a few of these children to be socially accepted. Intervention is needed to eliminate the negative behaviours and replace them with pro-social behaviours. If the student with a disability is to make friends and be accepted in the peer group, social skills training must be given a high priority in the programme. Strategies for developing social skills are described in Chapter 6.

While stressing the need to increase social interaction with others, students with intellectual disability (male and female) also need to be taught *protective behaviours* to reduce the possibility that they become the victims of sexual abuse. The lack of social judgement of some teenagers and young adults with intellectual disability causes them to be rather naïve and trusting. They may not really comprehend right from wrong in matters of physical contact and are therefore at risk. For their own protection they need to be taught the danger of going anywhere with a stranger, accepting rides in a car, or taking gifts for favours. They need to know that some forms of touching are wrong, and they also need to know that they can tell some trusted adult if they feel they are at risk from some other person. These matters must be dealt with openly in schools and also stressed as important by parents.

Teaching approaches for students with intellectual disability

The main priority in teaching children with intellectual disability is to make the curriculum reality-based. It has already been mentioned that for both cognitive development and for the acquisition of skills, these children need to experience things at first hand, and have others help them interpret these experiences. Children with intellectual disability are usually at the concrete operational stage in terms of cognitive development so the age-old principle of 'learning by doing' certainly applies in their case (Reddy, Ramar and Kusuma 2000). If they are to learn important number skills, for example, they should learn them not only from books, computer games and other instructional materials but also from real situations such as shopping, stocktaking, measuring, estimating, counting, grouping, recording data and comparing quantities. Reading skills should be developed and practised using real books, real instruction cards, real recipes, real brochures and real comic books, as well as through graded readers, games and flashcards. As far as possible the '4 R Test' should be applied when selecting curriculum content – is the content you are going to teach *real, relevant, realistic* and *rational*? (Brennan 1985).

In addition to reality-based learning, children with intellectual disability also need some high-quality direct teaching. Direct instruction is based to a large extent on behavioural views of learning (applied behaviour analysis).

- A relevant learning goal is set.
- Correct responses or skills are modelled by the teacher.
- Students imitate the response or skill.
- Students' responses are rewarded and shaped.
- Guided and independent practice lead to mastery and automaticity.

The approach is very teacher-directed with the content to be taught broken down into very simple steps to ensure high success rates. It has been found that direct instruction using these principles is extremely effective for students with disabilities, particularly for teaching basic skills and functional academics (Reddy *et al*. 2000; Turnbull *et al*. 2002).

In some contexts the teaching programme also involves the recording of baseline data (what the student could do before the direct instruction begins) and daily measurement and recording of the progress made. In instances where daily measurement of student responses is taken, the approach is sometimes referred to as *precision teaching*.

Lessons that employ direct instructional methods aim to use a fast pace of teaching with as many successful responses from the students as possible in the time available. There is heavy emphasis on practice, but lessons are made enjoyable and entertaining (Hallahan and Kauffman 2000). Direct instruction is among the most frequently researched teaching methods and has consistently proved that it is more effective for some types of learning than the student-centred, independent learning approaches.

Other basic principles to consider when working with students with intellectual disability include the following:

- Provide plentiful cues and prompts to enable the learner to manage each step in a task.
- Make all possible use of cooperative group work, and teach the child the necessary group-working skills.
- Frequently assess the learning that has taken place against the child's objectives in the curriculum.
- Use additional helpers to assist with the teaching (aides, volunteers, parents).
- Involve parents in the educational programme when possible.
- Most importantly, do not sell the students short by expecting too little from them.

In recent years, much emphasis has been placed on trying to increase the self-regulation and self-monitoring strategies of students with intellectual disability, using cognitive methods and metacognitive training. While this approach is proving very useful for students with mild disabilities it is very difficult indeed to employ cognitive training with low-functioning students for reasons that will be discussed in connection with autism. The teaching of self-regulation is discussed in Chapter 4.

Sensory stimulation for students with severe and multiple disabilities

In the case of young children with severe and multiple disabilities, sensory stimulation is important. Great interest has been shown in an approach called *Snoezelen* developed in Holland (Cuvo, May and Post 2001; Hutchinson and Kewin 1994). The approach is being adopted in a number of special schools in Europe and Australasia and is designed to provide both sensory stimulation and relaxation for severely or profoundly disabled individuals. The approach is therapeutic and educational, using structured sensory environments containing lights, textures, aromas, sounds and movement. It is reported to have particular benefits for individuals who have emotional and behavioural problems combined with their intellectual disability, and also for helping autistic children. In some cases Snoezelen has proved useful in reducing self-injurious behaviour (SIB) and self-stimulating behaviour (SSB) (Shapiro *et al.* 1997).

While Snoezelen rooms are unlikely ever to be developed in mainstream schools, teachers in preschools do need to note the potential value of sensory stimulation for young children with intellectual disability.

Students with autistic spectrum disorders

Children with autism remain among the most difficult students to place successfully in mainstream classrooms (Turnbull *et al.* 2002; Waterhouse 2000). Those with severe autism are usually functioning intellectually at a level too low even to cope with the demands of an adapted curriculum. Coupled with lowered intellectual functioning are the added problems of poor social development and significant communication difficulties (Pierangelo and Giuliani 2001; Wing 1996). In US only about 12 per cent of children with diagnosed autism receive their education in mainstream classes while the majority attend special schools or centres (Smith 2001). The same percentage would apply in Australasia and Britain. However, most higher-functioning students with Asperger Syndrome attend mainstream schools, as will be described later.

Characteristics of students with autism

Autism is a severe form of developmental disorder in which the most obvious characteristics are:

- major impairment of social interactions – lack of normal emotional relationship with others;
- impairment of communication;
- reduced ability to learn, particularly through observation and imitation;
- the presence of stereotyped behaviour patterns (e.g. rocking, hand flapping, spinning);
- obsessive interests, ritualised activities, and the desire to preserve 'sameness' in surroundings and daily routines;
- lack of imaginative and creative play.

Sue, Sue and Sue (2000: 480) describe typical autistic children thus: 'Children with autism often sit for hours, engaging mostly in unusual repetitive habits such as spinning objects, flapping arms, or just staring at their hands. Many exhibit self-injurious behaviours.' However, individuals with autism vary greatly and any single child diagnosed as autistic may not show all the above characteristics. Some students with 'autistic tendencies' or 'autistic features' are close to normal in many facets of their behaviour, while others may be very low functioning in terms of cognitive and social development (Sewell 2000).

Current thinking on the nature of autism embodies the notion of a *continuum* of autistic characteristics, implying that there is no clearly defined single syndrome (Wing 1996). Included at the upper level within this continuum are all the atypical children who are difficult to diagnose and do not necessarily conform to the typical pattern of autism. A significant number of children with autism exhibit overtly bizarre behaviour and are viewed by other children and adults as 'odd, quirky or eccentric'.

To be diagnosed as autistic a child must show symptoms of abnormal social and interpersonal development before the age of 3 years, and must meet at least 6 of the 12 criteria listed in the *Diagnostic and Statistical Manual of Mental Disorders* (APA 1994). The list helps to delineate in more detail the key areas of abnormal development typical of children with autistic spectrum disorders. The 12 diagnostic criteria are:

- marked impairment of nonverbal behaviours used in social interaction (e.g. eye contact, facial expression, posture, use of gestures, etc.);
- failure to develop peer relationships;
- no spontaneous interest in, or enjoyment of, other persons;
- no desire to return social or emotional contacts;
- delay (or total lack) of verbal communication skills;

- in individuals with speech, no obvious ability or desire to converse with others;
- the use of stereotyped and repetitive language (often echolalic);
- absence of imaginative play;
- preoccupation with one or more stereotyped patterns of behaviour or interest;
- inflexible adherence to specific rituals and routines;
- repetitive movements such as hand flapping, body rocking;
- obsessive preoccupation with tiny parts or details of objects.

The characteristics described in the *DSM IV* are evident in autistic children identified in all parts of the world and do not appear to be culturally determined (Wing 1996). Although autism has been found to occur in children at all levels of intelligence, a degree of intellectual disability ranging from mild to severe retardation is found in the majority of cases. As many as three-quarters of children with autistic disorders have IQ scores below 70 (Sue *et al.* 2000) and on-going special education is usually required to address their learning needs.

Autism is a low-incidence disability with approximately 4 to 10 cases per 10,000 in the population. The lower figure represents the more severe cases; the upper figure includes those children with mild autistic tendencies. The ratio of males to females is 4 to 1. Autism is actually one of several disorders referred to under a general category of *Pervasive Developmental Disorders* (PDD). Asperger Syndrome and Rett Syndrome are other examples of PDDs (Sue *et al.* 2000). These developmental disorders impair verbal and non-verbal communication and social interactions.

Interventions for autism

According to Rutter (1985) treatment for children with autism must have the following five general aims:

- to foster further development in the child;
- to promote learning;
- to reduce rigid and stereotypic behaviours;
- to eliminate maladaptive behaviours, such as self-injury;
- to alleviate family distress.

Many different approaches have been used to control or reduce the negative behaviours often associated with autism. A brief summary is provided here.

Pharmacological treatments

The belief that autism may be caused by some form of neuro-chemical dysfunction led researchers to use various forms of medication to try to influence the child's behaviour and responsiveness (Woodward and Hogenboom 2000). The general conclusion has been that drugs make very little difference to the overall syndrome of autism, although they are of some value in reducing any associated hyperactivity or aggression and for treating sleep disturbances. Disappointing results have been found for treatments that involve diet control.

Psychotherapy

Those who believe that autism stems from an underlying emotional cause have used psychotherapy with autistic children (e.g. Tustin 1992). Given the poor communication skills and lowered intelligence of children with severe autism, psychotherapy is not an effective treatment because it requires adequate language and an ability to reflect upon one's own actions and thoughts. On the other hand, family therapy or counselling to help brothers and sisters as well as parents understand the behaviour of the autistic child, has proved valuable in many cases (Waterhouse 2000).

Cognitive self-management training

The development of ability to self-monitor and self-regulate is a viable goal with high-functioning autistic individuals. Its use with low-functioning children is problematic, for the same reason that psychotherapy is difficult. Monitoring and controlling one's own behaviour or applying metacognition requires a level of self-awareness and a desire to change rarely found in severely autistic children.

Behaviour modification

The most effective intervention used to date has been behaviour modification. Traditional behaviour change programmes have been used extensively with autistic children, with generally positive effects in reducing some of their more unacceptable and potentially harmful behaviours, and for teaching new skills (Dempsey and Foreman 2001; Sue et al. 2000). Many hours of consistent application of the procedures are required in order for them to have any impact. The successful use of the behavioural approach has combined positive reinforcement (rewarding and shaping desirable responses) with the withdrawal of reinforcement through planned ignoring or time out. Often, however, it is not possible to ignore some of the self-injurious or potentially dangerous behaviours of children with autism. Eaves (1992) comments that aversive management techniques (punishment), although frowned upon for good reason by many psychologists, can often produce dramatic results quite quickly. Rutter (1985) advises that while aversive treatment may occasionally be both justified and necessary it should not be used frequently as it can have considerable negative outcomes in terms of relationship between caregiver and child.

Other interventions

Many other approaches have been tried with autistic children, including sensory-integration training, music therapy, play therapy, holding therapy, Snoezelen, facilitated communication, speech and language training, and social skills coaching. For a comprehensive description of these approaches see Waterhouse (2000) or Dempsey and Foreman (2001).

Teaching and training approaches: general principles

While some short-term gains from teaching programmes are reported in studies of autistic children, longer-term benefits are much more difficult to prove. Children with the most severe forms of autism often appear to make minimal gains, despite many hours of careful stimulation and teaching (Bibby *et al.* 2001). However, the benefits reported for a number of children with autism are positive enough to make the investment of time and effort worthwhile (Sue *et al.* 2000). Sewell (2000: 23) writes, 'Remember – everything you teach children with autism to do for themselves will be one more skill they will not have to depend on someone else to do for them the rest of their lives.'

A number of approaches to intervention for children with autism can lead to improved outcomes, even though the underlying causes of the problem cannot be identified or remedied. Evidence has proved that the most effective intervention strategies are *highly structured* and *delivered with intensity* (Waterhouse 2000). Teaching sessions for children with autism generally need to be implemented according to a predictable schedule. They need to teach new information, skills or behaviours in small increments through consistent, systematic and direct methods (Smith 2001).

There is general agreement that the focus of any intervention programme should attempt to:

- stimulate cognitive development;
- facilitate language acquisition;
- promote social development.

Each child's programme must be based on a very careful and detailed appraisal of the child's current developmental level and existing skills and responses. It is essential to assess the strengths of each individual child and to set intervention programme goals that will help to build on these strengths. All teachers, parents and other caregivers must know the precise goals and objectives of the programme and must collaborate closely on the methods to be used with the child. It is essential that parents also be trained in the teaching strategies to be used in any intervention programme as the child spends more time at home than at school (Bibby *et al.* 2001).

Sewell (2000) suggest the following ten top priorities when working with autistic children:

- Seek early behavioural and educational intervention.
- Be consistent in your management of the child (firmness plus affection).
- Maintain intensity and aid generalisation by extending the teaching into all environments.
- Build up the child's attention to task.
- Speak clearly and concisely to facilitate comprehension.
- Ignore attention-seeking behaviours but reward appropriate and compliant behaviours.
- Be firm but fair in making sure the child carries out requests.
- Ensure that all caregivers are aware of the objectives and targets for behaviour.
- Challenge the child enough to encourage progress towards new learning goals.
- Apply the '3 Ps': planning, patience and perseverance.

Objectives are best achieved by using both direct instructional methods and by maximising the naturally occurring opportunities in the child's daily life (Nind 1999, 2000). The most effective interventions involve the child's family as well as teachers and therapists. Home-based intervention programmes (or programmes combining both school- or clinic-based intervention with home programmes) produce better results than purely clinical programmes (Lovaas 1993).

Specific programmes and methods

TEACCH

One approach that has become popular in recent years is TEACCH (meaning 'Treatment and Education of Autistic and Communication-handicapped Children'). This approach stresses the need for a high degree of structure in the autistic child's programme, and uses a combination of cognitive and behavioural-change strategies, coupled with direct teaching of specific skills (Connor 1999). Importance is also placed on training parents to work with their own children and to make effective use of support services. An important feature of the approach is that it tries to capitalise on autistic children's preference for visual modes of communication (e.g. sign language and pictures) rather than the verbal mode.

Augmentative or alternative communication

For non-verbal autistic children the intensive use of visual cues (hand signing, pointing, pictures, symbols) is usually necessary in most teaching situations. Some programmes have been based on teaching a basic vocabulary of signs to autistic children who lack speech (Webb 1999). For a few students with autism, communication boards and other forms of augmentative communication aids can be useful.

Lovaas's 'Young Autism Program'

One very intensive programme for autistic children is that devised by Lovaas (1993). The programme begins with the child at age 2 years, and involves language development, social behaviours and the stimulation of play activity. Emphasis is also given to the elimination of excessive ritualistic behaviour, temper tantrums and aggression. The second year of treatment focuses on higher levels of language stimulation, and on cooperative play and interaction with peers. Lovaas claims high success rates for the programme, including increases in IQ. He claims that almost half of the intensively treated group of children reached 'normal' functioning levels. The fact that this programme takes 40 hours per week, using one-to-one teaching for two years, makes it very labour-intensive and expensive (Kirk et al. 2000). While the general principles are undoubtedly sound, it is difficult if not impossible to replicate the approach in the average special preschool.

Asperger's Syndrome

Individuals with Asperger Syndrome have some of the behavioural and social difficulties associated with other degrees of autism but they tend to have language and cognitive skills in the average or even above average range. Some researchers argue that Asperger's Syndrome is simply a subgroup within the autistic disorders spectrum, but others believe it is a different form of disability representing a discrete group of higher-functioning individuals with only a few autistic tendencies. Most students with this type of disorder are in mainstream schools. Their unusual behaviour patterns may cause them to be regarded as strange by peers and teachers, and they may have difficulty in making friends (Attwood 1998).

Students with Asperger's Syndrome may exhibit the following characteristics:

- unusual features in their oral language (e.g. repeatedly asking the same question of the same person, even though it has been answered; using a strangely pedantic style of speech; the overuse of stereotypic phrases);
- a lack of commonsense in their daily encounters with the physical environment;
- naïve and inappropriate social approaches to others;
- narrow, obsessive interests;
- sometimes motor coordination may be poor and the student appears physically awkward.

A few high-functioning students with this syndrome exhibit certain areas of very great talent or knowledge. The areas of outstanding performance have included such things as music, art, mental calculation and recall of factual information with amazing accuracy. Students with these highly developed abilities are sometimes referred to as 'autistic savants'.

The key educational considerations for these students include:

- strategic seating in the classroom so that they can be monitored closely and kept on task;
- great clarity in setting a task for the student to attempt;
- using direct, literal questioning, rather than open-ended questioning;
- avoiding the over-use of complex language that requires deeper interpretation (e.g. metaphors; idioms);
- trying to establish a reasonably predictable routine and structure to all lessons;
- using visual aids during lessons wherever possible;
- if necessary, using a student's obsessive interests as a focus for schoolwork, but at the same time trying to extend and vary the student's range of interests over time.

Some students with this form of autism may benefit from personal counselling to discuss such issues as the feelings of others, social interactions, dealing with their own problems, how to avoid trouble with other students and teachers. The student's own inability to understand the emotional world of others will not easily be overcome, but at least he or she can be taught some coping strategies (Attwood 1998). Children with Asperger's Syndrome are stronger candidates for social-skills training than are autistic children with intellectual disability.

Further reading

Drew, C.J. and Hardman, M.L. (2000) *Mental Retardation: A Life Cycle Approach* (7th edn), Upper Saddle River, NJ: Merrill.

Jordon, R. and Jones, G. (1999) *Meeting the Needs of Children with Autistic Spectrum Disorders*, London: Fulton.

Kirk, S., Gallagher, J.J. and Anastasiow, N.J. (2000) *Educating Exceptional Children* (9th edn), Boston, MA: Houghton Mifflin.

Nielsen, L.B. (2002) *Brief Reference of Students' Disabilities*, Thousand Oaks, CA: Corwin Press.

Sands, D.J. and Doll, B. (2000) *Teaching Goal Setting and Decision Making to Students with Developmental Disabilities*, Washington, DC: American Association on Mental Retardation.

Smith, D.D. (2001) *Introduction to Special Education* (4th edn), Boston, MA: Allyn and Bacon.

Turnbull, R., Turnbull, A., Shank, M., Smith, S. and Leal, D. (2002) *Exceptional Lives: Special Education in Today's Schools* (3rd edn), Upper Saddle River, NJ: Merrill-Prentice Hall.

Waterhouse, S. (2000) *A Positive Approach to Autism*, London: Jessica Kingsley.

Chapter 3

Students with physical disabilities and sensory impairments

Sometimes the enrolment of a child with a disability will require considerable effort on the teacher's part. Teachers and principals frequently express concerns that they will not have the teaching competencies or physical resources needed to integrate children with disabilities . . . There are children who will require individual programs and others who will require various levels of personal assistance.

(Foreman 2001:7)

Unlike the disabilities described in the previous chapter the learning difficulties considered in this chapter do not necessarily arise from a student's impaired intellectual functioning. Some students with physical disabilities or with impaired sight or hearing may be of average or better than average intelligence. Many of these students can cope well with the mainstream curriculum if specific teaching approaches are used to motivate and support them. In the case of students with physical disabilities or sensory impairment their greatest need may be help in accessing normal learning environments, instructional resources, and classroom experiences.

Students with physical disabilities

Students with physical disabilities comprise a relatively small but diverse group. Their disabilities can range from those that have little or no influence on a child's learning and development, through to other conditions that may involve neurological impairment affecting both fine and gross motor skills and intelligence. It is important for teachers to realise that a physical disability does not automatically cause a student to have intellectual disability or to experience learning problems. While it is true that some students with physical impairment do have learning problems, assumptions should never be made about an individual's capacity to learn on the basis of an apparent physical disability. Even severe types of physical impairment sometimes have no impact on intellectual ability and the intelligence levels for students with physical disabilities cover the full range from gifted to severely intellectually disabled (Heller *et al.*1996; Stieler 1998).

The education of students with physical disabilities needs to focus on providing these individuals with opportunities to access the same range of experiences as those available to students without handicaps. This may require adaptations to be made to the environment, to the ways in which these students move (or are moved) around the environment, and to the teaching methods and instructional resources used. In the case of students with milder forms of disability, and those with average or above learning aptitude, there is usually no reason why they should not attend ordinary schools and access the mainstream curriculum. For those with more severe disabilities and high support needs special schools may still offer the best placement. The special school can offer a curriculum, resources, methods of instruction and therapies tailored to meet their needs.

The problem for many severely disabled students with normal intelligence is to find ways of communicating with others in order to interact socially. It is also necessary to find alternative ways of accessing the school curriculum. Even those physically disabled students with good learning skills may need a great deal of support in order to achieve their potential. They, like many other students with disabilities, may also need to draw upon outside services in order to function successfully and to maintain a good quality of life (Snell and Brown 2000).

It is beyond the scope of this book to provide details of each and every physical disability or health problem. Readers will find such information in Batshaw (1997), Bigge, Best and Heller (2001), and Heller *et al.* (2000). Attention here will be devoted only to cerebral palsy (CP), spina bifida (SB) and traumatic brain injury (TBI).

Cerebral palsy (CP)

Cerebral palsy (CP) is a disorder of posture, muscle tone and movement resulting from damage to the motor areas of the brain occurring before, during or soon after birth (Turnbull *et al.* 2002). CP exists in several different forms (*spasticity*, *athetosis*, *ataxia*) and at several levels of severity from mild to severe. Type and severity of the condition are related to the particular area or areas of the brain that have been damaged and the extent of that damage. CP is not curable but its negative impact on the individual's physical coordination, mobility, learning capacity and communication skills can be reduced through appropriate intensive therapy, training and education. The use of assistive technology such as electronically controlled wheelchairs, communication aids and modified equipment can also help to ensure that the individual with CP is able to participate to the optimum degree in daily activities and to enjoy a better quality of life.

Students with CP often have additional disabilities. At least 10 to 16 per cent of cases have impaired hearing or vision. Major difficulties with eye-muscle control can lead the children who find close-focus tasks such as looking at pictures or attempting to read print physically exhausting and stressful, and they will tend to try to avoid engaging in such activity. Epilepsy is evident in up to 30 per cent of cases of CP (Capute and Accardo 1996) and a significant number of the children are on regular medication to control seizures. Medication can often have the effect of reducing individuals' level of arousal or alertness, thus adding to their problems in learning.

Some children with CP may not develop speech, although their receptive language may be quite normal. In their attempts to vocalise they may produce unintelligible sounds and their laughter may be loud and distorted. In addition they may exhibit other symptoms of inability to control their tongue, jaw and face muscles, resulting in drooling or facial contortions. These problems are beyond the individual's control but they can create potential barriers for easy social integration.

It is reported that approximately 60 per cent of individuals with CP also have some degree of intellectual disability (Turnbull *et al.* 2002), but some persons with quite severe CP are highly intelligent. There is a danger that the potential of some non-verbal students will not be recognised because of their inability to communicate. One of the main priorities for these individuals is to be provided with an alternative method of communication.

Cerebral palsy is one of the more frequently occurring physical disabilities with a prevalence rate of approximately 2 cases per 1000 live births. There has been no significant decline in the prevalence rate of CP, even though there have been major advances in prenatal and antenatal care (Heller *et al.*1996).

The instructional needs of students with cerebral palsy

Academic instruction for children with CP will depend mainly upon their cognitive ability. Students with mild cerebral palsy and normal intelligence may simply be slower at completing assignments and need more time. Allowance may need to be made for large and poorly coordinated handwriting. Some students may need to use a keyboard to type or word-process their assignments. For some, adapted devices such as pencil grips and page-turners may be required. Papers may need to be taped firmly to the desktop. Computers with adaptations such as switches or touch panels, rather than a keyboard or a 'mouse', are useful both for presenting academic work and as a medium for communication with others.

In addition to the problems with movement and speech many children with CP tend to:

- tire easily and have difficulty in attending to tasks for more than brief periods of time;
- take a very long time to perform basic physical actions (e.g. pointing at or

picking up an object; eating). Many need to be fed and toileted by parent or aide;

- require special physical positioning in order to make best use of their coordinated movements;
- require padded 'wedges' or other specially constructed cushions to enable them to be positioned correctly for work;
- rely on the teacher or an aide to lift and move them.

Useful advice for teachers and paraprofessionals on lifting, handling and management of physically disabled children can be found in Leigh (1996).

Spina bifida (SB)

Spina bifida is a congenital disorder, possibly of genetic origin. The condition results in a failure of certain bones in the spine to close over before birth to seal in the spinal cord. Spina bifida is referred to as a 'neural tube defect'. Spina bifida presents with different degrees of severity. The milder forms may have no significant influence on learning.

The most serious form of spina bifida with the greatest impact on the individual's development is *myelomeningocele*. In this condition, the spinal cord itself is exposed at birth and protrudes from a gap in the spine. The cord is often damaged and bodily functions below this point may be seriously disrupted. There may be no use of lower limbs. The individual may need to use a wheelchair or leg braces. Control of bladder and bowel function may be impaired necessitating the use of a catheter tube to drain the bladder and the implementation of a careful diet and bowel-emptying routine. The management of incontinence presents the greatest social problem for individuals with SB.

In some cases the individual with spina bifida may have learning difficulties due to minor perceptual problems. Some may have had a restricted range of experiences prior to schooling, and this adds to their difficulty in understanding some aspects of the curriculum. Their lack of mobility may have also reduced their range of social interactions.

Approximately 60 to 70 per cent of children with myelomeningocele may also have some degree of *hydrocephalus*. The normal circulation and drainage of cerebrospinal fluid within the skull is impaired, resulting in increased intra-cranial pressure. Treatment for hydrocephalus involves the surgical implanting of a catheter into the ventricle in the brain to drain the excess fluid to the abdominal cavity. A valve is implanted below the skin behind the child's ear to prevent any back flow of cerebrospinal fluid. Teachers need to be aware that shunts and valves can become blocked, or the site can become infected. If the child with treated hydrocephalus complains of headache or earache, or if he or she appears feverish and irritable, medical advice should be obtained.

Children with spina bifida and hydrocephalus tend to be hospitalised at regular intervals during their school lives for such events as replacing shunts and valves, treating urinary infections or controlling respiratory problems. This frequent hospitalisation can significantly interrupt the child's schooling, with subjects such as mathematics being most affected by lost instructional time. Many students in this situation require intensive remedial assistance with their schoolwork.

Some students with SB exhibit what is termed the 'cocktail party syndrome'. They appear at first meeting to have extremely advanced verbal skills and can converse in a very adult way. This may come about in part from their time spent in the company of adults (e.g. in hospital). They pick up the conversational style and patterns of adult speech without having any real depth to the matters they discuss. The potential problem in school is that teachers may judge them to be far more academically capable than they really are and demand more from them than is reasonable; or they may fail to recommend additional learning support for the student when it is actually needed.

Traumatic brain injury (TBI)

The term *traumatic brain injury* (TBI) is used to describe any acquired brain damage resulting from such events as car accidents, falls, blows to the head, unsuccessful suicide attempts, sports injury, the 'shaken infant syndrome', and recovery after drowning. An increasing number of school-age individuals acquire brain injury from falls, car accidents, blows to the head and partial drowning.

The effects of TBI can include:

- memory problems;
- attention difficulties;
- inability to solve problems and plan strategies;
- speech and language functions disrupted temporarily or permanently;
- impairment of general motor patterns such as walking, balancing;
- onset of epilepsy;
- unpredictable and irrational behaviour (aggressive, restless, apathetic, lacking in self-management).

It is beyond the scope of this chapter to provide details of all the classroom instructional considerations that may be necessary when working with students with TBI. The book by Bigge *et al.* (2001) contains a section on this subject. The main challenges for the teacher are:

- finding ways of maximising the individual's attention to the learning task (remove distractions; provide cues; limit the amount of information presented);

- helping to compensate for memory loss and poor recall (presenting visual cues to aid recall of information; encouraging visual imagery; rehearsing information more than would be necessary with other learners; teaching self-help strategies such as keeping reminder notes in your pocket; checking the daily time table);
- helping the individual plan ahead and monitor own progress, set goals and work towards them.

Additional useful information on this topic will be found in Glang, Singer and Todis (1997) *Students with Acquired Brain Injury: The School's Response.*

Augmentative and alternative communication

It has been mentioned above that many students with severe and multiple disabilities, whether congenital or acquired, may have no oral–verbal method of communication. This can lead others to judge them wrongly as functioning at a low cognitive level. The priority need for severely disabled persons without speech is to develop an alternative method of communicating.

Alternative communication modes include:

- sign language, finger-spelling and gesture;
- the use of a picture and symbol system that the person may access by pointing, or in some cases by eye glance;
- computer-aided communication.

The simplest form of alternative communication is the communication board, comprising a small set of pictures or symbols that are personally relevant to the child's life and context. For example, the board may have pictures of a tv set, a glass, a knife and fork or plate, a toilet, a toy, and a cross for 'no' and a tick for 'yes'. The child can communicate his or her wishes or needs by pointing to or looking at the appropriate picture.

The ultimate aim of any augmentative or alternative communication system is to allow the child to 'talk' about the same range of things that other children of that age would discuss (Hallahan and Kauffman 2000).

General points for the mainstream teacher

- For students in wheelchairs or walking with leg-braces and sticks, it may be necessary to rearrange the classroom desks and chairs slightly to give easier access (wider corridor for movement).
- Some students with physical disabilities may have a high absence rate due to (a) the need to attend therapy or treatment appointments during school hours; (b) frequent health problems. Frequent absence means that the teacher may need to provide the student with work to do at home,

and may need to enlist the help of the support teacher to provide some short-term remedial assistance for the student.

- Some students with physical disabilities (especially cerebral palsy) may also have epilepsy. To control the epilepsy the student may be on medication that tends to lower their level of arousal and responsiveness in class.
- While applying all commonsense safety procedures teachers should try to not overprotect students with physical disabilities. Whenever possible these students should be encouraged to take part in the same activities enjoyed by other students. Teachers of PE and sport need to get practical advice on ways in which these physical activities can be modified to include students with disabilities. Physically disabled students should never be left on the sidelines as mere spectators.
- Some students with physical disabilities will need to use modified desks or chairs. It is the teacher's responsibility to ensure that the student makes use of the equipment.
- Some students with physical disabilities will have great difficulty in writing and taking notes. Their fine-motor movements may be slow and their coordination very poor and inaccurate. The teacher needs to establish a peer support network and also allow the student to photocopy the notes of other students or use a tape recorder to record lessons. Sometimes the teacher may need to allow the student to submit an assignment as an audiotape rather than an essay.

Additional information on teaching and management of students with physical disabilities will be found in Heller *et al.* (2000) and Bigge *et al.* (2001).

Students with impaired vision

In some countries the term *vision impairment* is replacing the older term *visually impaired* – often at the request of adults who have this disability. When a child is described as vision impaired it does not necessarily mean that he or she is blind; it means that the child has a serious defect of vision that cannot be corrected by wearing spectacles. In the population of children with impaired vision there are those who are totally blind, those who are 'legally' blind, and those with varying degrees of partial sight.

While impaired vision represents the lowest-incidence disability category, it is important to note that it is also a common secondary handicap present in many cases of severe and multiple disability (Hoon 1996). For example, many students with cerebral palsy also have serious problems with vision, as do many individuals with traumatic brain injury.

Impaired vision has multiple causes, including structural defects or damage, for example, to the retina, lens, or optic nerve, inefficiency in the way the brain interprets and stores visual information or an inability of the retina to transmit images to the brain. Some vision problems are inherited, including those associated with albinism, congenital cataracts and degeneration of the retina, while others may be due to disease or to medical conditions such as diabetes or tumours. Prematurity and very low birth weight can contribute to vision problems, with 'retinopathy of prematurity' (ROP) being reported as one of the most common causes of impaired vision in the very young child.

It is not necessary to describe in detail the various conditions that lead to impaired vision. Teachers are referred to the relevant chapters in Batshaw (1997) or Silverstone *et al.* (2000). The book by Arter *et al.* (1999) contains excellent information on the learning characteristics and instructional needs of children with impaired vision.

The special educational needs of children with impaired vision

There are at least three areas in which blind children and those with seriously impaired vision may need to be taught additional skills. These areas are mobility, orientation, and the use of Braille.

Mobility

Blind students and those with very limited sight need to be taught mobility skills to enable them to move safely and purposefully in their environment. The skills include:

- self-protection techniques: for example, in unfamiliar environments holding the hand and forearm in front of the face for protection while trailing the other hand along the wall or rail;
- checking for doorways, steps, stairs and obstacles;
- using auditory information to locate objects: for example, the air-conditioner, an open doorway; traffic noise;
- long-cane skills: moving about the environment with the aid of a long cane swept lightly on the ground ahead to locate hazards and to check surface textures;
- using electronic travel aids such as 'sonic spectacles' with a sound warning built into the frame;
- using a sighted guide.

The person with impaired vision needs sufficient mobility skills and confidence to negotiate the outside environment, including crossing the road, catching buses or trains, and locating shops. Increased mobility adds significantly to the quality of life for persons with impaired vision. Mobility training is usually regarded as a specialist area of instruction. While the classroom teacher and parents can certainly assist with the development of mobility skills, a mobility-training expert usually carries out the planning and implementation of the programme.

Orientation

Orientation is the term used to indicate that a person with impaired vision is familiar with a particular environment and at any time knows his or her own position in relation to objects such as furniture, barriers, open doors or steps. Teachers should realise that for the safety and convenience of students with vision impairment the physical classroom environment should remain fairly constant and predictable. If furniture has to be moved or some new object is introduced into the room, the blind student needs to be informed of that fact and given the opportunity to locate it in relation to other objects. In classrooms it is necessary to avoid placing overhanging obstacles at head height, and to make sure that equipment such as boxes and books are not left scattered on the floor. Doors should not be left half open, with a hard edge projecting into the room.

Mobility and orientation together are two of the primary goals in helping the blind student towards increased independence. Without these skills the quality of life of the blind person is seriously restricted.

Braille

Braille is of tremendous value as an alternative communication medium for those students who are blind or whose remaining vision does not enable them to perceive enlarged print. Braille is a complex code so its use with students who are below average in intelligence is not always successful. Obviously if an individual's cognitive level is such that he or she would experience difficulties in learning to read and write with conventional print, Braille is not going to be an easier code to master. Surveys suggest that only about 10 to 15 per cent of the blind population reads primarily by Braille (Reddy *et al.* 2000). The notion that all legally blind and totally blind students use Braille is false. However, if a child's intelligence is adequate the younger he or she begins to develop some Braille skills the better, as this will prepare the child to benefit from later schooling.

Assistive devices

In the same way that students with physical disabilities can be helped to access the curriculum and participate more effectively in daily life through the use of assistive technology so too children with partial sight impaired can be assisted. Many devices have been designed to enable the student to cope with the medium of print. The devices include magnification aids, closed-circuit television (used to enlarge an image), microfiche readers, talking calculators, speaking clocks, dictionaries with speech outputs, 'compressed speech' recordings, and thermoform duplicators used to reproduce Braille pages or embossed pictures and maps. *Low vision aids* are magnification devices or instruments that help the individual with some residual sight to work with maximum visual efficiency. Some students with impaired vision benefit from modified furniture such as desks with bookstands or angled tops to bring materials closer to the child's eyes without the need to lean over, or with lamp attachments for increased illumination of the page.

Instructing students with low vision

The following suggestions are adapted from many sources. Useful advice can also be found in Best (1992) and Silverstone *et al.* (2000).

- Allow the partially sighted students when writing to use a fibre-tip black ink pen that will produce clear, bold writing.
- Prepare exercise paper with dark ruled lines.
- Enlarge all text, notes and handouts to 24, 36, or even 48 point size.
- Allow much more time for students with impaired vision to complete their work.
- Read written instructions to students with impaired vision to reduce the amount of time required to begin a task and to ensure that the work is understood.
- Use very clear descriptions and explanations; verbal explanation will have to compensate for what the student cannot see.
- Train other students, and any classroom aide or assistant you may have, to support the student with impaired vision (e.g. for note taking, repeating explanations).
- Speak to blind students frequently by name during lessons to engage them fully in the group-learning processes. Make sure they contribute. Value their contributions.
- Call upon other students clearly by name so that the blind student knows who is responding.
- Get all the advice you can from the visiting support teacher and other advisory personnel.
- Make sure that any specialised assistive equipment is always at hand and in good order.
- Note that almost all students with impaired vision in mainstream classes will have partial sight rather than total or legal blindness. It is essential

to encourage them to use their residual vision effectively. Using the remaining vision is helpful, not harmful to these students.

- If the student with impaired vision uses assistive equipment such as magnification aids, lamps, or adjustable bookstand, make sure that (a) you know when and how the equipment needs to be used; (b) you ensure that the student does not avoid using the equipment.

- Use a photocopier when necessary to make enlarged versions of notes, diagrams and other handouts for the student. Use large type size when preparing materials on the word processor or for Powerpoint presentations.

- Seat the student in the most advantageous position to be able to see the blackboard or screen.

- Ensure that your own material on the blackboard or screen is neat and clear, using larger script than usual. Keep the blackboard surface clean to ensure clarity of words against background.

- Avoid overloading worksheets with too much information and heavy density of print.

- Some forms of vision impairment respond well to brighter illumination, but in some other conditions very bright light is undesirable. Obtain advice on illumination from the visiting teacher or other support personnel who are aware of the student's characteristics.

- If the student has extremely limited vision, make sure that any changes to the physical arrangement of the room are explained and experienced by the student to avoid accidents. The student needs to develop fresh orientation each time an environment is changed.

- Try to ensure that the student establishes a network of friends within the class. Social interaction is often not easily achieved without assistance.

Students with impaired hearing

Hearing impairment is a general term used to describe all degrees and types of hearing loss and deafness. Individuals are usually referred to as *deaf* if they are unable to perceive speech sounds and if their own language development is disordered. In some countries, those who can hear some sounds and can make reasonable use of their residual hearing are either termed *hard of hearing* or *partially hearing.*

Hearing impairment can be classified as one of three basic types: conductive, sensori-neural, or central deafness. The key features of each type of hearing problem are summarised below.

Conductive hearing loss

Conductive hearing loss indicates that the individual's hearing problem is due to the fact that sounds are not reaching the middle ear or the inner ear (the cochlear) because of some physical malformation, blockage or damage to the ear canal or middle ear. Common causes are excessive build-up of wax in the outer ear canal, a ruptured eardrum, abnormality of the ear canal, infections in the middle ear (e.g. otitis media), or dislocation or damage to the tiny bones of the middle ear. Hearing loss due to middle-ear infection is usually temporary and will improve when the infection is treated successfully. If infections are allowed to continue untreated, damage may be done to the middle ear resulting in permanent hearing loss. The use of a hearing aid may significantly help an individual with conductive hearing loss.

Sensori-neural loss

Sensori-neural loss is related to the inner ear and the auditory nerve. The most serious hearing losses are often of this type. As well as being unable to hear many sounds, even those that are heard may be distorted. This problem of distortion means that the wearing of a hearing aid may not always help because amplifying a distorted sound does not make it any clearer. It is reported that in some cases individuals with sensori-neural loss are particularly sensitive to loud noises, perceiving them to be painfully loud (Owens 1995).

Central deafness

Central deafness is a rare condition in which sound signals can reach the brain but are not interpreted within the auditory processing areas of the cortex. The hearing mechanisms of the outer, middle and inner ear may be perfectly normal. Central deafness is regarded as a major receptive language disorder.

Many students with impaired hearing have no other disability, but hearing impairment is often present as a secondary disability in children with intellectual disability, cerebral palsy, or language disorders.

Degrees of hearing loss

Acuity of hearing is measured in units called decibels (dB). Zero dB is the point at which people with normal hearing can begin to detect the faintest sounds. Normal conversation is usually carried out at an overall sound level of between 40 and 50dB (Steinberg and Knightly 1997). Loss of hearing is expressed in terms of the amplification required before the individual can hear each sound. The greater the degree of impairment the less likely it is that the child will develop normal speech and language, and the more likely it is that they will need special education services (Power 1998).

Individuals with a hearing loss above 95dB are usually categorised as 'deaf' or 'profoundly deaf'. Other categories are:

slight loss: 15–25dB*. Vowel sounds still heard clearly. Some consonants may be missed.

mild loss: 25–40dB*. Can hear only loud speech sounds. Usually requires hearing aid. May need speech therapy. Some difficulty with normal conversation.

moderate loss: 40–65dB*. Misses almost all speech at normal conversational level. Requires hearing aid. Serious impact on language development. Speech therapy and special education often required.

severe loss: 65–95dB*. Unable to hear normal speech. Major problems with language development. Hearing aid required (but may not help in some cases). Language training and other special services required.

profound loss: Above 95dB*. Cannot hear speech or other environmental sounds. Severe problems in language acquisition. Normal conversation impossible. Alternative forms of communication usually required (e.g. sign language). Special class placement often indicated.

* Note: The specific dB range varies slightly from country to country.

The impact of deafness on development

An inability to hear places a young child at risk of delay in many areas, including the acquisition of spoken language, literacy skills and social development. For example, the speech of children with impaired hearing often has very poor rhythm and phrasing, together with a flat and monotonous tone of voice. A priority goal in the education of all children with impaired hearing is to advance their language skills as much as possible. Any improvement in language will allow each child to make better use of his or her intellectual potential, understand much more of the curriculum, and develop socially.

Helping the deaf child acquire intelligible speech can be a long and difficult process. Early intervention and active parental involvement are essential elements in language stimulation. In some cases speech training and auditory training are advocated for hearing-impaired students (Reddy *et al.* 2000). Speech therapists or language teachers may, for example, use speech and articulation coaching, based mainly on behavioural principles of modelling, imitation, rewarding, and shaping. In recent years, however, speech therapists and teachers have placed even more importance on trying to stimulate language development through the use of naturally occurring activities in the classroom ('milieu teaching': Kaiser 2000). Such teaching is thought to result in better transfer and generalisation of vocabulary, language patterns and skills to the child's everyday life.

The inability to hear language from an early age not only creates a major problem in developing speech but can also have a negative impact on some aspects of intellectual development. It is often said that the deaf students' lack of words slows down development of cognitive skills necessary for learning in school. In recent years there has been some criticism of this viewpoint and it is now suggested that although deaf children may lack depth in *spoken* language they still encode and store information and experience in other ways (Hallahan and Kauffman 2000). They often have some other more visual style of language, such as signing and gesture, that enables them to express their ideas. Turnbull *et al.* (2002) state categorically that deaf children have the same intellectual abilities as children who can hear; and Barnes (2001) believes students with severe and profound hearing loss are capable of achieving as much as their hearing peers.

Over the past two decades the movement towards integration of children with disabilities into ordinary schools has stressed the value of including hearing-impaired children in mainstream classes. It is argued that these children will experience the maximum social interaction and communication by mixing with other students using normal spoken language. They will be exposed to more accurate language models than they might hear in a class for deaf students. It is believed that regular class placement increases the need and motivation for the deaf child to communicate. It is also hoped that students with normal hearing will develop improved understanding and tolerance for individuals who are slightly different from others in the peer group.

Basic academic skills

Careful attention must be given to the explicit teaching of reading and spelling skills to students with impaired hearing. It is typical of students with impaired hearing that as they progress through primary school they fall three to four years behind the peer group in terms of reading ability. This reading lag has a detrimental impact on their performance in all subjects across the curriculum.

Many of their difficulties in reading and spelling are thought to stem from their problem in perceiving speech sounds within spoken words (phonemic awareness). Limited phonemic awareness results in difficulty in learning phonic decoding and encoding skills. While the beginning stages of reading instruction can focus on building a basic sight vocabulary by visual methods, later the teaching of word-analysis skills must also be stressed for students with hearing loss. Without some phonic knowledge their ability to read and spell unfamiliar words will remain seriously deficient. It is also essential when providing reading instruction for hearing-impaired children that due attention be given to developing comprehension skills. Their restricted vocabulary and reduced proficiency in recognising sentence structure can cause major problems in reading fluency and comprehension.

The written expression of deaf children is often reported to be a problem

(Power 1998). Their difficulties often include inaccurate sentence structure, incorrect verb tenses, difficulties in representing plurals correctly, and inconsistencies in using correct pronouns. The written work of older deaf students has many of the characteristics of the writing of younger children, and may also contain *deafisms* involving incorrect word order (e.g. 'She got black hair long', instead of 'She has long black hair'). In a later chapter reference is made to activities involving sentence building and sentence transformations; such activities are particularly valuable for students with impaired hearing.

Spelling instruction needs to be systematic rather than incidental. For deaf children, it is likely that more than usual attention will need to be given to the development of visual memory processes to enable them to spell and check by eye rather than ear. The 'look-say-cover-write-check' strategy is particularly helpful and needs to be taught thoroughly (see Chapter 11). The book by Stewart and Kluwin (2001) contains much valuable advice on teaching different school subjects to students with impaired hearing.

Modes of communication

While listening and speaking remain the preferred methods of communication for students with mild and moderate degrees of impairment, for those who are severely to profoundly deaf, alternative manual methods may be needed. These methods include gesture, sign language and finger-spelling. There are different forms of sign language (e.g. Signed English, Auslan, American Sign Language) sharing obvious characteristics in common but also having some unique features. Deaf children from deaf families will almost certainly have been exposed to, and become competent in, manual communication even before entering formal education.

Sign language

Plant (1990: 200) states, 'There is almost certainly no topic that generates greater controversy in the field of deaf children than the use of sign language.' If an individual becomes dependent upon manual rather than verbal methods of communication, he or she will be less able to interact successfully with other members of the community. The individual who uses gesture, signs or finger-spelling will be able to communicate easily with only those who know manual communication.

Often the use of sign language is the only thing that attracts the attention of others to the fact that the person is deaf. Many parents and some teachers feel that to encourage manual forms of communication will cause the child to be accepted only in the deaf community rather than in the wider community of hearing persons. They also believe that the use of signs will retard the development of speech, thus isolating the child even further. Experts suggest however that sign language should be respected as a language in its own right, with its own vocabulary, grammar and semantics, and it should be valued and encouraged as an effective mode of communication. There is no evidence to support the notion that if you use sign language you will not learn to speak.

Oral–aural approach (oralism)

The opposing school of thought is based on the notion that the individual with impaired hearing must learn to communicate by oral–aural means (Steinberg and Knightly 1997). The approach termed *oralism* virtually places a ban on manual communication and stresses instead the use of residual hearing, supplemented by lip reading and speech training. The feasibility of lip reading for many hearing-impaired individuals is often greatly overestimated; it is an extremely difficult and inaccurate method of interpreting the communication of others (Reddy *et al.* 2000). The belief underpinning oralism is that to be accepted and to succeed in a hearing world you need to be able to communicate through oral–verbal methods. The relative popularity of manualism versus oralism ebbs and flows from decade to decade.

Total communication approach

Total communication (TC) or Simultaneous Communication (SC) deliberately combines oralism with manualism. Advocates for TC incorporate the aural–oral processes of listening and speaking, together with some use of signing, gesture, finger-spelling, mime, and virtually anything else that will help the deaf child comprehend and express ideas and opinions clearly to others (Steinberg and Knightly 1997).

Assistive technology

Hearing aids

Hearing aids are of various types, including the typical 'behind the ear' or 'in the ear' aids, and radio frequency (FM) aids. An audiologist assesses the specific needs of the child and a hearing aid is prescribed to suit the individual's sound-loss profile. The aid is adjusted as far as possible to give amplification of the specific frequency of sounds needed by the child. No hearing aid fully compensates for hearing loss, even when carefully tailored to the user's characteristics.

The great limitation of the conventional type of hearing aid is that it amplifies all sound, including noise in the environment. The advantage of the radio frequency (FM) aid is that it allows the teacher's voice to be received with minimum interference from environmental noise. The teacher wears a small microphone and the child's hearing aid receives the sounds in the same way that a radio receives a broadcast transmission. The child can be any-where in the classroom, and does not need to be close to or facing the teacher, as with the conventional aid.

A valuable chapter on integrating technology into teaching of students with impaired hearing appears in the text by Stewart and Kluwin (2001). See Pagliano (2002) for information on hearing aids and methods of communication.

Cochlear implants

A cochlear implant is a device used to produce the sensation of sound by electrically stimulating the auditory nerve (Turnbull *et al.* 2002). The device has two main parts, the internal component (electrodes implanted into or on the cochlear) and an external receiver embedded in the temporal bone. Many developed countries are now carrying out the surgery required to implant this form of assistive device at a very young age.

Cochlear implants are normally recommended only for children who are profoundly deaf and cannot benefit at all from other forms of hearing aid. However, there are signs that the procedure is now extending to some indi-viduals with severe hearing loss (Stewart and Ritter 2001). While the child can begin to perceive the electrical stimulation soon after surgery it normally takes at least a year for gains in the child's language skills to become evident. The child's effective adaptation to the cochlear implant needs support and encouragement from the parents.

Additional advice on cochlear implants can be found in the text by Watson, Gregory and Powers (1999). Some of the ethical issues involved in cochlear implantation are discussed in Beattie (2001).

General strategies for the teacher

Using some of the following basic strategies will also be helpful often to students with other types of learning difficulty in the classroom. It is recom-mended that teachers:

- Make greater use of visual methods of presenting information whenever possible.
- Use clear and simple language when explaining new concepts. Don't be afraid to introduce new terminology but teach the new words thoroughly.
- Write new vocabulary on the blackboard. Ensure the student with hear-ing impairment hears the word, sees the word, and says the word. Revise new vocabulary regularly. Revise new language patterns (e.g. 'Twice the size of . . .'; 'Mix the ingredients . . .'; 'Invert and multiply . . .').
- Repeat instructions clearly while facing the student with impaired hearing.

- Don't give instructions while there is noise in the classroom.
- Where possible, write instructions in short statements on the blackboard.
- Attract the student's attention when you are about to ask a question or give out information.
- Check frequently that the student is on task and has understood what he or she is required to do.
- Where possible, provide the student with printed notes to ensure that key lesson content is available (it may not have been heard during the lesson).
- When group discussion is taking place make sure the deaf student can see the other students who are speaking or answering questions.
- Repeat the answer that another student has given if you think the deaf student may not have heard it.
- Make sure you involve the deaf student in the lesson as much as possible.
- Ensure that the student has a partner for group or pair activities and assignments.
- Encourage other students when necessary to assist the deaf student to complete any work that is set – without doing the work for the student!
- Don't talk while facing the blackboard; the deaf student needs to see your mouth and facial expression. When explaining while using overhead projector, face the class and not the screen.
- Don't walk to the back of the room while talking and giving out important information.
- Try to reduce background noise when listening activities are conducted.
- Don't seat the student with impaired hearing near to sources of noise (e.g. fan, open window, generator).
- Do seat the student where he or she can see you easily, can see the blackboard, and can observe the other students.
- Make sure that you know how to check the student's hearing aid, and check it on a regular basis. The student won't always tell you when a battery needs replacing or a connection is broken.
- Seek advice from the visiting teacher of the deaf and from the support teacher. Use such advice in your programme.

Further reading

Arter, C., Mason, H.L., McCall, S., McLinden, M. and Stone, J. (1999) *Children with Visual Impairment in Mainstream Settings*, London: Fulton.

Bigge, J.L., Best, S.J. and Heller, K.W. (2001) *Teaching Individuals with Physical, Health, or Multiple Disabilities* (4th edn), Upper Saddle River, NJ: Merrill-Prentice Hall.

Heller, K.W., Forney, P.E., Alberto, P.A., Schwartzman, M.N. and Goeckel, T.M. (2000) *Meeting Physical and Health Needs of Children with Disabilities*, Belmont, CA: Wadsworth.

Marschark, M., Lang, H.G. and Albertini, J.A. (2002) *Educating Deaf Students: From Research to Practice*, New York: Oxford University Press.

Paul, P.V. (2001) *Language and Deafness* (3rd edn), San Diego, CA: Singular.

Sacks, S.Z. and Silberman, R.K. (eds) (1998) *Educating Students who have Visual Impairments with Other Disabilities*, Baltimore, MD: Brookes.

Stewart, D.A. and Kluwin, T.N. (2001) *Teaching Deaf and Hard of Hearing Students: Content, Strategies and Curriculum*, Boston, MA: Allyn and Bacon.

Turnbull, R., Turnbull, A., Shank, M., Smith, S. and Leal, D. (2002) *Exceptional Lives: Special Education in Today's Schools* (3rd edn), Upper Saddle River, NJ: Merrill-Prentice Hall.

Chapter 4

Teaching children self-management and self-regulation

> Students should assume as much responsibility for self-management as they can handle . . . The goal of classroom socialization should be to help all students become as autonomous and as adaptive as possible.
>
> (Good and Brophy 2000: 150)

Self-control, self-regulation and self-management are all essential capacities that children need to develop if they are to become fully autonomous learners. In the case of students with intellectual disability, emotional disturbance or learning disability, the skills and strategies involved in self-management and self-regulation may need to be taught. When children acquire adequate self-management skills it is much easier for them to be accommodated effectively in inclusive classrooms (Agran *et al.* 2001).

Definition of terms

The terms self-control, self-regulation and self-management are often used interchangeably in educational discourse, but in the field of psychology each has its own precise meaning.

- *Self-control* refers to an individual's ability to monitor his or her own behaviour; to exercise appropriate restraint over impulses, or exert extra effort when necessary in order to accomplish particular goals and to maintain positive social interactions (Mazur 1998).
- *Self-regulation* is a term more commonly used in relation to an individual's ability to monitor his or her own approach to learning tasks and to modify thinking processes or strategies as necessary (Eggen and Kauchak 2001). Self-regulation in learning involves a significant amount of *metacognition* – the ability to monitor and control one's own cognitive processes such as attention, rehearsal, recall, checking for understanding, self-correction and strategy application. Self-regulation in learning will be discussed fully later in the chapter.

- *Self-management* refers to an individual's ability to function independently in any given learning environment, without the need for constant supervision, prompting or direction (Agran 1997). In the classroom, for example, it relates to such behaviours as knowing how to organise one's materials, knowing what to do when work is completed, recognising when to seek help from the teacher or a peer, understanding how to check one's own work for careless errors, how to maintain attention to task, how to observe the well-established routines such as ordering lunch, having sports equipment or books ready for a specific lesson, knowing when a change of lesson or room is to occur, and so on.

Self-management in children

The specific self-management skills required by a child in school will tend to differ slightly from classroom to classroom according to a particular teacher's management style, routines and expectations. For example, in some classrooms a premium is placed upon passive listening, note-taking and sustained on-task behaviour, while in other classrooms initiative, group-working skills and cooperation with other children are essential prerequisites for success. The self-management skills required in an informal classroom setting tend to be different from those needed in a more formal or highly structured setting. Knowing how to respond to the demands and constraints of different lessons or settings is an important aspect of a student's growth towards independence.

The type of classroom learning environment created by the teacher and the instructional approach used can both markedly influence the development of self-management and independence in children. Some teachers seem to operate with students in ways that foster their *dependence* rather than encourage their independence. For example, they may offer too much help and guidance for children with special needs in an attempt to prevent possible difficulties and failures. They may virtually spoon-feed the children using individualised support programmes that offer few challenges and call for no initiative on the child's part. Too much of this support restricts the opportunities for a child to become autonomous and may operate in such a way as to segregate the child from the mainstream curriculum or from the peer group for too much of the day.

Why are self-management skills important? The answer to this question is simple: the possession of self-management skills by a child with a disability or a learning problem seems to be one of the most important factors contributing to the successful inclusion of that child in a regular classroom (Choate 1997; Salend 1998). It is essential that students with special needs, whether placed in special settings or in the regular classroom, be helped to develop adequate levels of independence in their work habits, self-control, social skills and readiness for basic academic learning. Self-management shares much in common with what some psychologists term 'self-determination' (Browder *et al.* 2001), which in turn is related to feelings of 'self-efficacy'.

Some students, for example those with intellectual disability, or with social, emotional or psychological disorders, frequently exhibit poor self-management and adaptive behaviour (Carver and Scheier 1999). One of the major goals of intervention with such students is to increase their independence by improving their skills in self-management and self-regulation. Even students with milder forms of disability or learning difficulty often display ineffective self-management or self-regulation strategies and need positive help to become more independent learners (Bartlett, Weisenstein and Etscheidt 2002; Moore *et al.* 2001).

Self-management can be taught

Evidence is accumulating to support the view that deliberate training in self-management and self-regulation can be effective in promoting students' independence (Bartlett *et al.* 2002; Meese 2001). Cole (2000: 1616) concludes, 'Although total self-management is not possible for many special education students, most can be taught to be more self-reliant.' When students are able to manage the routines in the classroom and look after their own needs during a lesson the teacher is able to devote much more time to teaching rather than managing the group.

What can be done to teach self-management? First, teachers must believe that such teaching is important and that it is possible to teach self-management skills to children who lack them. Second, teachers need to consider precisely which skills or behaviours are lacking in the students but are required in order to function independently in their particular classrooms – for example, staying on task without close supervision, using resource materials appropriately, or seeking help from a peer.

For students with special needs a five-step procedure can be used to teach self-management. The steps are:

- *Explanation*: Discuss with the student why a particular self-management behaviour is important. Help the student recognise when other students are exhibiting examples of the target behaviour.
- *Demonstration*: Teacher or a peer can model the behaviour.
- *Role play*: The student practises the behaviour, with descriptive feedback.
- *Cueing*: Prompt the student when necessary to carry out the behaviour in the classroom. Praise examples of the student remembering the behaviour without prompting.
- *Maintenance*: Check at regular intervals to ensure that the student has maintained the behaviour over time.

In some situations a teacher might employ a 'star chart' or other visual recording system to reward at regular intervals all those students who demonstrate the specific self-management skills expected of them. Rewarding would be most frequent immediately after the teaching of the behaviour, and would be phased out after several weeks once the behaviour is established and maintained.

It is important to develop the idea of maintaining the appropriate behaviour *without prompting*. When teachers are constantly reminding the class of what to do (e.g. 'I've told you before, if you have finished your work, please put it on my desk and start on your activity book') they are maintaining the students' dependence. Teachers may need to remind children with special needs rather more frequently than other students, and may have to reward them more frequently for their correct responses, but the long-term aim is to help these children function independently. When they do display improved self-management they have become more like other children in the class. Teaching self-management skills as part of an inclusive programme should have a high priority in all classrooms, particularly with young children and those with developmental delay (Agran 1997).

Locus of control

Self-management, and the notion of learned helplessness (Chapter 1), link quite closely with the personality construct known as *locus of control*. To explain locus of control one needs to understand that individuals attribute what happens to them in a particular situation either to internal factors (e.g. their own ability, efforts or actions) or to external factors (e.g. luck, chance, things outside their control). Children with an internal locus of control recognise that they can influence events by their own actions and believe that they do to some extent control their own destiny. Appreciating the fact that outcomes are under one's personal control is also a key component of one's feelings of 'self-efficacy' (Ormrod 2000). At classroom level an example of internality might be when students recognise that if they concentrate and work carefully they get much better results.

The internalisation of locus of control usually increases steadily with age if a child experiences normal satisfaction and reinforcement from his or her efforts and responses in school and in daily life outside school. However, it has been found that many children with learning problems and with negative school experiences may remain markedly external in their locus of control in relation to school learning, believing that their efforts have little impact on their progress, that they lack ability, and that what happens to them in learning tasks is unrelated to their own actions (Bender 2001; Marrone and Schutz 2000). Young children enter school with highly positive views of their own capabilities, but this confidence rapidly wanes if they experience early failures and frustrations (Paris, Byrnes and Paris 2001).

The child who remains largely external in locus is likely to be the child who fails to assume normal self-management in class and is prepared to be managed or controlled by powerful others such as the teacher, parent, teacher's aide or more confident peers. There exists a vicious circle wherein the child feels inadequate, is not prepared to take a risk, seems to require support, gets it, and develops even more dependence upon others. The teacher's task is one of breaking into this circle and causing the child to recognise the extent to which he or she has control over events and can influence outcomes. It is natural for a teacher or aide to wish to help and support a child with special needs, but it should not be done to the extent that all challenge and possibility of failure are eliminated. Failure must be possible and children must be helped to see the causal relationship between their own efforts and the outcomes. Children will become more internal in their locus of control, and much more involved in learning tasks, when they recognise that effort and persistence can overcome failure (Bender 2001).

It is important that teachers and parents publicly acknowledge and praise children's positive efforts, rather than emphasising lack of effort or difficulties. Teachers' use of praise has been well researched. Good and Brophy (2000) reviewed studies in this area and concluded that praise does seem particularly important for low-ability, anxious, dependent students, provided that it is genuine and deserved, and that praiseworthy aspects of the performance are specified. A child should know precisely why he or she is being praised if appropriate connections are to be made in the child's mind between effort and outcome. Trivial or redundant praise is very quickly detected by children and serves no useful purpose. *Descriptive* praise, however, can be extremely helpful:

> 'That's beautiful handwriting, Leanne. I really like the way you have taken care to keep your letters all the same size.'

> 'Good, David! You used your own words instead of simply copying from the reference book'.

In general, teachers' use of praise has a strong positive influence on children's beliefs about their own ability and the importance of effort (Paris *et al.* 2001). When descriptive praise is perceived by children to be genuine and credible it appears to enhance the children's motivation and feelings of self-efficacy.

Attribution retraining

An external locus of control can have a negative impact upon a student's willingness to persist in the face of a difficult task. It is easier for the child to give up and develop avoidance strategies rather than persist if the expectation of failure is high (Carver and Scheier 1999). In the instructional approach known as *attribution retraining* (McInerney and McInerney 1998) students are taught to appraise carefully the results of their own efforts when a task is completed. They are taught to verbalise their conclusions aloud. 'I did that well because I took my time and read the question twice'; 'I listened carefully and I asked myself questions'; or 'I didn't get that problem correct because I didn't check the example in the book. Now I can do it. It's easy!' The main purpose in getting students to verbalise such attribution statements is to change their perception of the cause of their successes or failures in school-work. Verbalising helps to focus their attention on the real relationship between their efforts and the observed outcomes.

Grainger and Frazer (1999) have discussed the negative attributional styles of students with reading disabilities, many of whom have developed learned helplessness in relation to their own ability to improve. They suggest that these children may not respond to remedial teaching if the intervention focuses only on skill development. They recommend first helping the child explore his or her feelings, beliefs and attitudes linked to their reading difficulty, and then to teach the child to use positive self-talk to overcome personal reluctance and to restore some feeling of self-efficacy.

In most cases, attributional retraining seems to have maximum value when it is combined with the direct teaching of effective task-approach strategies necessary for accomplishing particular tasks. Evidence suggests that strategy training does produce definite improvement in learning for students with special needs (Paris and Paris, 2001; Swanson 2000b).

Teaching task-approach strategies

Pressley and McCormick (1995) have observed that often task-approach strategies are not taught explicitly in classrooms and they may therefore remain obscure to many students. Some teachers add to students' learning problems by failing to demonstrate the most effective ways of approaching each new task. A teacher needs to provide clear modelling of an appropriate strategy to maximise the chances of early success. A teacher who says, 'Watch and listen. This is how I do it – and this is what I say to myself as I do it', is providing the learner with a secure starting point. The teacher who simply says, 'Get on with it', is often providing an invitation to failure and frustration.

It was noted in Chapter 1 that many students with learning difficulties appear to lack appropriate task-approach strategies. They seem not to under-stand that school tasks can be carried out effectively if approached with a suitable plan of action in mind (Meese 2001). For example, attempting to solve a routine word problem in mathematics usually requires careful reading of the problem, identification of what one is required to find out, recognition of the relevant figures to use, selection of the appropriate process, completion of the calculation, and a final checking of the reasonableness of the answer. This approach to solving the mathematical problem involves application of a *strategy* (an overall plan of action) and utilisation of *procedural knowledge* (knowing how to carry out the specific calculation and record the result) and *declarative knowledge* (an understanding of the information presented in the problem) (Frieman 2002).

Learning strategies are techniques, principles or rules that help students solve problems, complete tasks, and self-regulate. Cole and Chan (1990) have referred to the process of instructing students in how best to carry out classroom learning tasks as *attack strategy training*. They describe it as a structured method to teach students to apply step-by-step procedures when completing particular learning tasks. The approach involves explicit teaching of procedural knowledge through teacher demonstration, imitation by the students, feedback, practice and application. The initial stages of teaching and learning will often involve 'thinking aloud' and directing actions through verbal self-instruction.

Maintenance and generalisation of strategy training have always been problematic, particularly for students with learning difficulties. Students may learn successfully how to apply a given strategy to a specific task but not recognise how the same approach could be used more widely in other contexts. To help overcome this problem teachers might:

- provide strategy training that makes use of a variety of different authentic task from across the curriculum;
- discuss situations in which a particular strategy could be applied; and
- involve students as much as possible in creating or adapting strategies to the demands of particular tasks.

It is important to ensure that the specific strategies taught to students are actually needed in the daily curriculum to facilitate their immediate application. Students will find most relevance in strategies they can use regularly to accomplish classroom tasks and homework more successfully.

Effective strategy training incorporates elements of cognitive and meta-cognitive instruction that enable the students not only to complete tasks independently but also to monitor and control their own performance. It is this attention to *metacognition* that brings strategy training and strategy use clearly into the realm of self-regulated learning.

One of the common observations concerning many students with learning problems is that they have become passive learners (or even non-learners). They show little confidence in their own ability to control learning events, or to bring about improvement through their own efforts or initiative. Teaching a student how to learn and how to regulate and monitor his or her own performance in the classroom must be a major focus in any intervention programme. Studies over many years have yielded data indicating that self-regulated students tend to do well in school. They are more confident, diligent and resourceful, and they tend to have a stable internal locus of control (Gettinger and Stoiber 1999). One of the goals of education should be to help all students to achieve a similar level of self-efficacy.

The development of self-regulation in learning

There is a difference between task-approach strategy training and meta-cognitive instruction. Task-approach training involves teaching the student procedural knowledge – the specific steps to follow and skills to use when working on a particular task, for example, the exchanging rule in subtraction, the 'look-cover-write-check' method of learning to spell an irregular word, or the appropriate way to read a six-figure reference to locate a point on a map. Metacognitive instruction goes far beyond this, focusing on tactics that require the learner to monitor the appropriateness of his or her responses and to weigh up whether or not a particular strategy needs to be applied in full, in part, or not at all in a given situation.

Reading comprehension and mathematics problem solving are often cited as examples of academic areas that can be improved by task-approach and metacognitive strategy training. Students can be taught how to approach printed information and mathematical problems strategically, and then given abundant opportunity to practise the application of the strategies on a wide variety of texts and problems (Coyne, Kameenui and Simmons 2001). Several practical examples of strategies are provided in later chapters.

Self-regulation in learning requires that students play an active role in monitoring closely the effects of various actions they take and decisions they make while engaging in learning activities. This involves the capacity to think about their thought processes (metacognition) and to modify a learning strategy if necessary while tackling a particular problem. This self-management of thinking includes mental activities such as pre-planning, monitoring, regulating, evaluating, and modifying a response. It is considered that metacognition helps a learner recognise that he or she is either doing well or is having difficulty learning or understanding something. A learner who is monitoring his or her own on-going performance will detect the need to pause, to double-check, perhaps begin again before moving on, to weigh up possible alternatives, or to seek outside help.

Metacognition often involves inner verbal self-instruction and self-questioning – talking to one's self in order to focus, reflect, control or review. Training in self-regulation involves teaching students to tell themselves specifically what they need to do and how they need to monitor and self-correct. Part of the scaffolding that teachers provide is the modelling of thinking aloud that later influences the student's own use of inner language. The teaching of verbal self-instruction is considered to be very important in helping all students become better self-regulated in terms of both learning and behaviour (see *cognitive behaviour modification* below).

The view is now widely held that many learning problems that students exhibit are related to inefficient use of metacognition, that is, the learners lack the ability to monitor or regulate their responses appropriately. Some students undoubtedly develop their own efficient strategies without assistance; others do not. For self-regulated learning to develop teachers need to demonstrate convincingly how to use appropriate strategies, explain in ways that students can understand, and make frequent and consistent use of metacognition and strategy training in all parts of the school curriculum (Zimmerman *et al.* 1996). It is essential that teachers realise the need to devote time and effort to encourage students to think about their own thinking in a variety of learning situations. Paris *et al.* (2001) recommend that strategy use can be fostered by scaffolded support, discussions about strategies and how to apply them, and making visible the tactics used by effective learners. Once the basics of strategic learning have been established, Gettinger and Stoiber (1999) suggest that cooperative learning activities, peer tutoring, sharing views on how problems can be solved or task accomplished, may help to foster, generalise, and maintain self-regulation.

Cognitive behaviour modification (CBM)

Cognitive behaviour modification is a closely related approach to metacognitive training. It involves the application of a set of procedures designed to teach the students to gain better personal control over a learning situation (or of their own behaviour) by use of self-talk which guides their thoughts and actions. The students are taught an action plan or mental 'script' in which they talk themselves through a task or a problem situation in order to control their performance, modify their responses and monitor their results. Cognitive behaviour modification is different from other forms of behaviour management in that the students themselves, rather than teachers or powerful others, are the agents for change.

The training procedure for a typical cognitive behaviour modification programme usually follows this sequence:

1   *Modelling*: The teacher performs the task or carries out the new procedure while thinking aloud. This modelling involves the teacher self-questioning, giving self-directions, making overt decisions, and evaluating the results.
2   *Overt external guidance*: The student copies the teacher's model and completes the task, with the teacher still providing verbal directions and exercising control.
3   *Overt self-guidance*: The learner repeats the performance while using self-talk as modelled by the teacher.

4   *Faded self-guidance*: The learner repeats the performance while whispering the instructions.
5   *Covert self-instruction*: The learner performs the task while guiding his or her responses and decisions using inner speech.

Typical self-questions and directions a student might use at steps 3, 4 and 5 would include: *What do I have to do? Where do I start? I will have to think carefully about this. I must look at only one problem at a time. Don't rush. That's good. I know that answer is correct. I'll need to come back and check this part. Does this make sense? I think I made a mistake here, but I can come back and work it again. I can correct it.* These self-questions and directions cover problem definition, focusing attention, planning, checking, self-reinforcement, self-appraisal, error detection and self-correction. They are applicable across a fairly wide range of academic tasks.

Sometimes the instructions, cue words or symbols to represent each step in the procedure may be printed on a prompt card displayed on the student's desk while the lesson is in progress. Training in self-instruction techniques of this type is considered to be particularly useful for students with mild intellectual disability to improve their self-management (Meese 2001). The application of cognitive behaviour modification to cases of chronic behaviour disorder is discussed in the next chapter. Cole (2000: 1616) concludes, 'Evidence suggests that self-management procedures are at least as effective as similar externally managed procedures in facilitating positive behavior change and in ensuring maintenance of the behavior change.'

Further reading

Agran, M. (1997) *Student Directed Learning: Teaching Self-determination Skills*, Pacific Grove, CA: Brooks-Cole.
Block, C.C. and Pressley, M. (2002) *Comprehension Instruction*, New York: Guilford.
Dorn, L.J. and Soffos, C. (2001) *Shaping Literate Minds: Developing Self-regulated Learners*, Portland, ME: Stenhouse.
Frieman, J. (2002) *Learning and Adaptive Behavior*, Belmont, CA: Wadsworth.
Hogan, K. and Pressley, M. (1997) *Scaffolding Students' Learning*, Cambridge, MA: Brookline.
Kaplan, J.S. (1998) *Beyond Behavior Modification* (3rd edn), Austin, TX: ProEd.
Lindberg, J.A. and Swick, A.M. (2002) *Common-sense Classroom Management*, Thousand Oaks, CA: Corwin Press.
Meltzer, L.J. (ed.) (1993) *Strategy Assessment and Instruction for Students with Learning Disabilities*, Austin, TX: Pro-Ed.
Pressley, M. and Woloshyn, V. (1995) *Cognitive Strategy Instruction that Really Improves Children's Academic Performance* (2nd edn), Cambridge, MA: Brookline.
Zimmerman, B.J. and Schunk, D.H. (2001) *Self-regulated Learning and Academic Achievement*, Mahwah, NJ: Erlbaum.

Chapter 5

The management of behaviour

> Effective behaviour management is essential to the smooth running of a
> school and in the creation of an environment where everyone's rights and
> responsibilities are addressed. A balance between fundamental rights and
> responsibilities is at the heart of behaviour management.
>
> (Rogers 1995: 12)

Many teachers report that one of their main concerns in the regular classroom is the child who disrupts lessons, seeks too much attention from the
teacher or peers and who fails to cooperate when attempts are made to
provide extra help. The teachers feel that although they may know what the
child needs in terms of basic instruction it proves impossible to deliver
appropriate teaching because the child is unreceptive. Some writers suggest
that the inclusion of students with behavioural disorders in regular classes
will continue to present the biggest challenge to teachers now and in the
future (Visser 2000).

Teachers with emotionally disturbed children, or children with behaviour
disorders, in their classes need the moral and professional support of their
colleagues. In particular they need acknowledgement and understanding
from colleagues that the student's behaviour is not due to their own inability
to exercise effective classroom control. There is a tendency in some schools to
see the management of a student's problem behaviour as being the responsibility only of the teacher in whose class the child is enrolled, rather than
accepting it as a whole-school matter.

Unless a school adopts a collaborative approach to the management
of difficult and disruptive behaviour certain problems tend to arise. These
problems include:

- Individual teachers feeling that they are isolated and unsupported by
  their colleagues.
- Teachers feeling increasingly stressed by the daily conflict with some
  students.

- The problem becoming worse over time.

This chapter presents an overview of some of the approaches to preventing behaviour problems in school through effective use of proactive strategies. Consideration is also given to methods for intervention that might be used if problems do occur.

Preventing behaviour problems

Algozzine and Kay (2002: 2) have written:

> A school that adopts a comprehensive system of prevention strategies has the potential to reduce the development of both new and current cases, or the incidence and prevalence of school-related problems. A well-crafted approach to prevention improves the efficiency and effectiveness with which schoolwide, classroom and individual behavior support systems operate.

It is generally agreed that the first step in prevention of problem behaviour is to have a clear school policy on behaviour management issues, leading to consistent implementation and practice by all staff (Cowley 2001). The school policy will describe ways in which individual teachers and the whole school staff should approach general matters of discipline and classroom control. The policy may also make specific reference to the management of students with significant emotional or behavioural disorders, and to students with disabilities (Taylor and Baker 2002).

A school policy document must be much more than a set of rules and consequences. A good policy will make clear to students, teachers, parents and administrators that schools should be safe, friendly, and supportive environments in which to work. In many ways, a school policy on student behaviour should be seen as dealing more with matters of welfare, safety and social harmony, rather than procedures for punishment and enforcing discipline. The heart of any behaviour management policy should be the stated aim of teaching all students responsible and effective ways of managing their own behaviour and making appropriate choices. A good policy in action will protect not only teachers' rights to teach and students' rights to feel safe and to learn, but will also help students recognise the personal and group benefits that self-control and responsible behaviour can bring (Powell *et al.* 2001).

Classroom behaviour

While it is true that some students exhibit behavioural problems in school that may be a reflection of stresses or difficulties outside school it is also evident in some school situations that disruptive behaviour can result directly from factors within the learning environment. Large classes can contribute to problem behaviour. Research has shown that smaller classes seem to have fewer discipline problems, are friendlier, and can produce higher achievement in the students (Biddle and Berliner 2002). Even the seating arrangement in classrooms seems to influence behaviour and achievement. For example, on-task behaviour is significantly better and students are more productive when they are seated in rows rather than grouped (Hastings and Schwieso 1995), yet the common practice in many schools is to have children seated in groups to facilitate cooperative learning.

The curriculum can also be a contributing factor of poor behaviour in some cases. Any student who is bored by work that lacks interest and challenge may well become troublesome. The atmosphere in some schools, together with the teaching style used by some teachers, tends to alienate certain students. Unfortunately, teachers are more likely to see the problem as lying within the student and his or her background than within the school curriculum or the methods used.

When cases of disruptive or challenging behaviour are reported, particularly in secondary schools, it is important to consult with other teachers to discover whether the student is also a problem when in their classes. All teachers who have contact with the student will usually need to get together to agree upon a consistent approach to be used in dealing with the problem behaviour. In some schools it has proved valuable to create a Behaviour Support Team, comprising staff with experience in behaviour management who can be available to other teachers for advice and problem solving (Hill and Parsons 2000). There has to be a whole-school recognition that behaviour problems are best dealt with from a shared perspective and tackled with a team approach.

One of the factors adding to a student's problems in secondary school is the frequent change of teachers for different subjects. Within the course of one day a student may encounter quite different and inconsistent treatment, ranging from authoritarian to permissive. This lack of consistency can have a destabilising effect on students who may have emotional or behavioural difficulties. In an attempt to minimise the adverse effects of meeting too many different teachers some large schools have established sub-schools, each with a smaller pool of teachers to cater for specific groups of students. With younger children the problem of inconsistent management is reduced somewhat since most of the curriculum is planned and implemented by one teacher who gets to know the children well. In senior schools many more difficulties can arise.

Occasionally of course it is necessary to seek expert advice when a child's behaviour does not respond to standard forms of effective management; but in many cases behaviour can be modified successfully within the school setting. When possible, teachers need to adopt a proactive rather than a reactive approach to classroom control (Jacobsen, Eggen and Kauchak 2002). A sound starting point is the establishment of positive classroom rules, building upon sound principles set out in the school policy.

Classroom rules

Classroom rules are essential for the smooth running of any lesson and should be formulated jointly by the children and the teacher very early in the school year. Rules should be few in number, clearly expressed, displayed where all students can see them and expressed in positive terms (what the students *will do*, rather than *must not do*). Students should appreciate why the rules are necessary and must agree on appropriate consequences if a rule is broken. Clear, consistent rules and consequences must be negotiated with all members of the class, based on the rights of others and on personal responsibility. While the actual rights and the rules that protect them are important, the process by which they are developed is just as important. Students should feel ownership for rules through contributing to their formulation. Rules might include matters like classroom communication, treatment of others' ideas (e.g. listening and praising), movement in the room, noise level, safety, personal property, and use of equipment.

Classroom-based research on the management style of teachers has yielded a clear indication that the most effective teachers establish rules and procedures as a top priority at the beginning of the year. They discuss the rules with the students and apply them systematically and fairly. Such teachers are also more vigilant in the classroom, use more eye contact, are more proactive to prevent behaviour problems arising, set appropriate and achievable tasks for students to attempt, avoid 'dead spots' in lessons, keep track of student progress, check work regularly and provide feedback to the whole class and to individuals (Lovitt 2000).

Classroom procedures

Rogers (1995) suggests that all teachers should develop their own discipline plan to enable them to know in advance what to do when classroom behaviour is disruptive. The plan gives a teacher confidence when the pressure is on. Corrective actions a teacher might decide to use include:

- tactical ignoring of the student and the behaviour (low-level disruptions);
- simple directions ('Ann, get back to your work please');
- positive reinforcement ('Good, Ann');
- question and feedback ('What are you doing, Mark? I'll come and help you');
- rule reminders ('David, you know our rule about noise. Please work quietly');

- simple choices ('Excuse me, Joanne. You can either work quietly here, or I'll have to ask you to work at the carrel – OK?');
- isolation from peers (take the student aside and discuss the problem, then place him or her in a quiet area to do the work);
- removal from class (time out under supervision in a different room may sometimes be needed).

Teachers may also use strategies such as deflection and diffusion to take the heat out of a potential confrontation. Teacher: 'Sally, I can see you're upset. Cool off now and we'll talk about it later; but I want you to start work please.' The judicious use of humour can also help to defuse a situation, without putting the student down.

In Rogers's (1995) approach three steps are taken when any problem arises:

- Give a warning in the form of a rule reminder.
- Give time out for five minutes.
- Student gives an apology to the class.

Sometimes it is appropriate to ask senior students to write a self-reflection about an incident of inappropriate behaviour in which they have been involved. They must say what they did, what they should have done, and what they are going to do to remedy the situation. This written paper might then become the basis of a discussion with the teacher or school counsellor, and might be used as a starting point from which to formulate a plan of action for behaviour change.

Identifying the problem

According to Levin and Nolan (2000) a discipline problem exists whenever a behaviour interrupts the teaching process, interferes with the rights of others to learn, and results in lost instructional time. Children who are constantly seeking attention, interrupting the flow of a lesson and distracting other children are often very troubling to teachers. Naturally, teachers may feel professionally threatened by children who constantly challenge their discipline. The feeling of threat can cause the situation to get out of hand, and a teacher can get trapped into confrontations with a child, rather than looking for possible solutions that will provide responsible choices and save face for the child and the teacher (Lindberg and Swick 2002).

All too often teachers react overtly to undesirable behaviour, thus reinforcing it. Many behaviour problems in the classroom, particularly disruptive and attention-seeking behaviours, are rewarded by the adult's constant reaction to them (McNamara and Moreton 2001). For example, the teacher who spends a lot of time reprimanding children is in fact giving them a lot of individual attention at a time when they are behaving in a deviant manner. This amounts to a misapplication of social reinforcement, and the teacher unintentionally encourages what he or she is trying to prevent. Some control techniques used by teachers (e.g. public rebuke) can have the effect of strengthening a child's tough self-image and status in the peer group.

If a teacher has a student who presents a problem in terms of behaviour in the classroom it would be useful to analyse possible reasons for this behaviour in the context in which it is occurring. The following questions may be helpful when teachers attempt to analyse a case of disruptive behaviour.

- How frequently is the behaviour occurring?
- In which lesson is the behaviour less frequent (e.g. the more highly structured sessions, or the freer activities)?
- At what time of day does the behaviour tend to occur (a.m. or p.m.)?
- How is the class organised at the time (groups, individual assignments, etc.)?
- What am I (the teacher) doing at the time?
- How is the child in question occupied at the time?
- What is my immediate response to the behaviour?
- What is the child's initial reaction to my response?
- How do other children respond to the situation?
- What strategies have I used in the past to deal successfully with a similar problem?

The analysis deals with issues that are immediately observable in the classroom. Behaviour analysis does not need to examine the child's past history or search for deep-seated psychological problems as causal explanations for the child's behaviour.

Sparzo and Poteet (1997) present a nine-step plan for setting up a behaviour-change intervention. They point out that in many cases it is not necessary to apply all nine steps; often it is sufficient merely to specify the target behaviour to be changed, apply an appropriate change strategy and assess the outcome. The steps in Sparzo and Poteet's programme are described below:

- define the target behaviour to be changed;
- observe and record the current frequency and duration of the behaviour;
- set attainable goals, involving the student in this process if possible;
- identify potential reinforcers by observing what this student finds rewarding;
- select teaching procedures, such as modelling, prompting, role play;
- plan to have the child rehearse the target behaviour;
- implement the programme over time, providing feedback to the child;
- monitor the programme through on-going observation, and by comparing frequency and duration measures with those evident before the intervention;

- once the change in behaviour has occurred make sure it is maintained, and take every opportunity to help the child generalise the behaviour to different settings and contexts.

Changing behaviour

There are said to be at least four ingredients necessary for changing behaviour (McGrath 2000):

- The child should *desire* to change.
- He or she should *know*, or be shown, *how* to change (i.e. have an action plan to establish alternative behaviour).
- The child must *practise* the alternative behaviour frequently.
- He or she will need to *persevere*, even in the event of temptations or occasional regressions to old habits.

It should be understood that changing a student's behaviour is often difficult. Sometimes the behaviour we regard as inappropriate has proved to be quite effective for the child in attaining certain personal goals. It has been practised frequently and has become very well established.

In order to change undesirable behaviour in a specific student it is usually necessary to consider all factors that may be supporting the behaviour both directly and indirectly. For example, a girl who openly defies a teacher's request to work quietly on an assignment and not disturb those around her may actually be seeking peer group approval for provoking and standing up to the teacher. She may also be successfully avoiding a situation where she is forced to admit that she cannot do the work that has been set. She may later gain more attention (albeit criticism) from her parents if a letter of complaint is sent home from school.

These factors combine to reinforce the *status quo*. In addition, the girl may be preoccupied with the outcome of a confrontation she had with another teacher in the previous lesson or with another student at lunchtime. Finally, if the work appears to her to have no real significance for her there is little motivation to attempt it. In order to bring about change the teacher must work to ameliorate the influence of as many of these factors as possible. This type of multi-perspective attack on the problem – an attempt to manipulate variables within the total context in which the child operates – has been termed the 'ecological approach' by Hallahan and Kauffman (2000).

Behaviour modification

One approach that is commonly used in conjunction with the ecological approach for maximum impact is the behavioural approach, more often referred to as *behaviour modification*. It is based on principles of applied behaviour analysis (ABA) (Alberto and Troutman 1999). In this approach three assumptions are made:

- all behaviour is learned;
- behaviour can be changed by altering its consequences;
- factors in the environment (in this case the classroom) can be engineered to target specific behaviours to be rewarded.

Typically, a problematic behaviour is observed and analysed. The factors that are possibly causing the behaviour, and the factors maintaining it, are identified. A programme is devised to reshape this behaviour into something more acceptable and more productive through a consistent system of reward, ignoring or punishment. Often, in cases of very persistent behaviours such as aggression or severe disruptiveness, reinforcement procedures may not be sufficient alone to bring about change. In such cases it may be necessary to introduce negative consequences and reductive procedures, such as loss of privileges, loss of points, or time out. Attention must also be given to improving the student's own self-monitoring and decision-making in order to increase self-control over the problem behaviour.

Criticism is sometimes levelled at a behaviour modification approach on the basis that the control is exercised by powerful others from outside the individual. It is suggested that the manipulation of the individual's behaviour is somehow out of keeping with humanistic views on the value of interpersonal relationships, the social nature of learning, and the need for personal autonomy. However, the very precise planning and management of a behaviour modification programme requires careful observation of how the child, the teacher and other children are interacting with one another and influencing each other's behaviour. Far from being impersonal the techniques used to bring about and maintain change are usually highly interpersonal. It is also noted that when the behaviour of some students improves as a result of ABA they become more socially acceptable, thus increasing their chances of successful inclusion (Porter 2000).

Regardless of criticisms that have been made the behavioural approach has proved its value in an impressive number of research studies over a long period of time, and there can be no doubting the power of behaviour modification techniques in changing students' behaviour and enhancing learning (Kavale and Forness 1999; Turnbull *et al.* 2002). In particular, ABA is of great practical value for use by parents, carers, and teachers working with students who have severe disabilities, autism, or challenging behaviour.

Additional information on behaviour modification techniques can be found in Alberto and Troutman (1999), Porter (2000) and Zirpoli (2001).

Strategies for reducing disruptive behaviour

Levin and Nolan (2000) define disruptive behaviour as the upsetting of orderly conduct of teaching. Disruptions often prevent a teacher from achieving the objectives for a particular lesson and may also impair the quality of personal and social interaction within the group. Frequent disruptions have a ripple effect and can cause major reduction in the overall quality of learning and teaching occurring in that classroom, as well as destroying a positive classroom atmosphere. It is reported that teachers can lose about half of their teaching time in some classrooms due to students' disruptive behaviour (Charles and Senter 2002).

Sometimes changes as simple as modifying the seating arrangements, restructuring the working groups, reducing noise level in general, and monitoring more closely the work in progress will significantly reduce the occurrence of disruptive behaviour. The following strategies are also recommended.

Deliberate ignoring

The tactic of ignoring a child who is acting inappropriately can be used far more frequently than most teachers realise (Levin and Nolan 2000). If a child begins some form of disruptive behaviour (e.g. calling out to gain attention) the teacher ignores that child's response, and instead turns away and gives attention to another student who is responding appropriately. When the first student is acting appropriately the teacher will ensure that he or she is noticed and called upon. If the peer group can also be taught to ignore a disruptive student and not reinforce the behaviour by acknowledging it and reacting to it, planned ignoring technique will be even more successful.

Clearly it is not sufficient merely to ignore disruptive behaviour. It is essential that planned ignoring be combined with a deliberate effort to praise descriptively and reinforce the child for appropriate behaviours at other times in the lesson – 'catch the child being good'. While it is common to view the frequency of undesirable behaviour in a child as something to reduce, it is more positive to regard the non-disruptive (appropriate) behaviours as something to reward and thus increase. It is a golden rule to be much more positive and encouraging than to be critical and negative in interactions with students.

A teacher cannot ignore extremely disruptive behaviour when there is a danger that someone will be hurt or damage will be done. Nor can a teacher go on ignoring disruptive behaviour if it is putting other children at educational risk through lost learning time. The teacher must intervene to prevent physical danger but should do so quickly, quietly and privately. Private reprimands coupled if necessary with 'time out' are less likely to bring the inappropriate behaviour to the attention and approval of other children.

Reinforcement and rewards

In order to modify behaviour according to ABA principles, particularly in young or immature children, it may be necessary to introduce a reward system (Lindberg and Swick 2002). If social reinforcers like praise, smiles and overt approval are not effective, it will be necessary to apply more tangible rewards, selected according to students' personal preferences. Children are different in their preferences for rewards – what one child may find rewarding another may not. It may be that one child likes a stamp, a sticker or coloured star, another child will work hard or behave well for a chance to play a particular game on the computer or build a model, yet another may like to listen to a taped story on a cassette, or may even crave the privilege of cleaning the blackboard!

Some teachers use tokens to reinforce behaviour or academic work in class. Tokens are simply a means of providing an immediate concrete reward. Tokens are usually effective because of their immediacy and students can see them accumulating on the desk as visible evidence of achievement. Tokens can be traded later for back-up reinforcers such as time on a preferred activity, being dismissed early, or receiving a positive report to take home to parents. While not themselves sensitive to individual preferences for particular types of reinforcement, tokens can be exchanged for what is personally reinforcing. Most textbooks on educational psychology provide some general rules for using reinforcement (e.g. Eggen and Kauchak 2001). It is worth repeating them here:

- Reinforcement must be given immediately after the desired behaviour is shown and must be given first at very frequent intervals.
- Once the desired behaviours are established, reinforcement should be given only at carefully spaced intervals after several correct responses have been made.
- The teacher must gradually shift to unpredictable reinforcement so that the newly acquired behaviour can be sustained for longer and longer periods of time without reward.

Time out

This refers to the removal of a student completely from the group situation to some other part of the room or even to a separate but safe setting for short periods of isolation. While time out may appear to be directly punishing it is really an extreme form of ignoring. The procedure ensures that the child is not being socially reinforced for misbehaviour.

It is important that every instance of the child's disruptive behaviour be followed by social isolation if the time out technique is being used. The appropriate behaviour will not be established if sometimes the inappropriate behaviour is tolerated, sometimes responded to by punishment, and at other times the child is removed from the group. It is essential to be consistent.

Avoid placing a student outside the classroom for time out if in that situation he or she gets other interesting rewards – being able to peer through the window and attract the attention of other students in the room, making contact with other students in the corridor, watching more interesting events in other parts of the school. Bartlett *et al.* (2002) warn that removing a student frequently from a lesson or activity that he or she does not like becomes negatively reinforcing rather than punitive, and the student is likely to continue to misbehave in order to be removed.

Cooling off

Explosive situations may develop with some disturbed children and a cooling-off period will be necessary. A set place should be nominated for this (e.g. a corner of the school library where worksheets may be stored for use by the student). The student should be under supervision for all of the time spent out of the classroom. The student will not return to that particular lesson until he or she is in a fit emotional state to be reasoned with and some form of behaviour contract can be entered into between teacher and student. Following a period of time out it is usually beneficial to have the child participate in a debriefing session in which he or she is encouraged to discuss the incident, reflect upon the behaviour, identify behaviour that might have been more effective, and set a goal for improvement. Useful advice on debriefing procedures will be found in Nelson *et al.* (1998).

Behavioural contracts

A behavioural contract is a written agreement signed by all parties involved in a behaviour-change programme (Bartlett *et al.* 2002; Salend 1998). After rational discussion and negotiation the student agrees to behave in certain ways and carry out certain obligations. The staff and parents agree to do certain things in return. For example, a student may agree to arrive on time for lessons and not disrupt the class. In return the teacher will sign the student's contract sheet indicating that he or she has met the requirement in that particular lesson, and adding positive comments. The contract sheet accompanies the student to each lesson throughout the day. At the end of each day and the end of each week, progress is monitored and any necessary changes are made to the agreement. If possible, the school negotiates parental involvement in the implementation of the contract, and the parents agree to provide some specific privileges if the goals are met for two consecutive weeks, or loss of privileges if it is broken. When behaviour contracts are to be set up it is essential that all teachers and school support staff are kept fully informed of the details.

The contract system is strongly advocated by Lovitt (2000) who suggests that the daily report card can specify precisely which features of behaviour are to be appraised each lesson by the teacher. A simple yes/no response column makes the recording task quick and easy for a teacher to complete at change of lesson. For example:

Arrived on time	Y	N
Remembered to bring books	Y	N
Followed instructions	Y	N
Stayed on task	Y	N
Did not disturb others	Y	N
Completed all class work	Y	N
Completed homework	Y	N

Lovitt (2000) also suggests sending a copy of the report home, and liaising regularly with parents by telephone or letter.

Punishment

Punishment represents yet another way of eliminating undesirable behaviours – but the use of punishment in schools is a contentious issue. The principal objection to punishment or *aversive control* is that while it may temporarily suppress certain behaviours, it may also evoke a variety of undesirable outcomes (fear, a feeling of alienation, resentment, an association between punishment and schooling, a breakdown in the relationship between teacher and student). Punishment may also suppress a child's general responsiveness in a classroom situation as well as eliminating the negative behaviour. Porter (2000) provides a comprehensive summary of these and other disadvantages of punishment as an approach to changing behaviour – including the observation that punishment is fundamentally ineffective because it is retroactive rather than proactive; it has to be delivered after inappropriate behaviour has occurred.

If it is absolutely necessary to punish a child (and of course there are occasions when mild punishment is appropriate) the punishment should be administered as soon as the inappropriate behaviour is exhibited. Delayed punishment is virtually useless. Punishment needs always to be combined with positive reinforcement and other tactics to rebuild the child's self-esteem. The goal of intervention should be to help students gain control over their own emotions and behaviour, but this goal will not be achieved if ongoing aversive control is imposed by powerful others.

Aggressive behaviour

Teachers are bothered most by aggressive behaviour in children (Hart 2002). Increases in acting-out and aggressive behaviour in schools are possibly linked to reported increases in work-related stress among teachers. Blum (2001) states that anger is a daily feature of school life and its presence can impair the teaching process. He suggests that teachers must be trained in simple strategies for dealing with students' anger. Similarly, McGrath (1998: 92) has remarked, 'If you can manage angry pupils and your own anger confidently, your teaching skills will be greatly enhanced and life will simply be much easier.'

It is reported that less aggression is found in schools where a caring and supportive environment has been nurtured and where curricular demands are realistic. Schools where there is constant frustration and discouragement seem to breed disaffection and stimulate more aggressive and anti-social behaviour in students (Cowley 2001; Hart 2002; Levin and Nolan 2000). Effective schools honour their responsibility of meeting students' emotional needs.

Bullying

While bullying may have been evident for as long as schools have existed, this fact does not make it any less serious. It is crucial not to ignore bullying in schools, as this problem will not cease of its own accord (Hazler 1996). The lives of too many children are made miserable if they become the victims of bullying. Some estimates put the prevalence of bullying at about one child in every ten, but self-report studies reveal many more students who indicate that they were bullied when they were at school but did not report the problem to teachers or parents. For the victim, bullying is known to cause absenteeism, psychosomatic illnesses, low self-esteem, impaired social skills, feelings of isolation, learning problems and depression. From the number of adults who report the impact that bullying had on them, it is clear that the experience frequently has lasting effects.

Bullying may take several different forms – direct physical attacks, verbal attacks, or indirect attacks such as spreading hurtful rumours or by excluding someone from a social group. Boys are more likely to be physically violent, while girls tend to use more indirect ways to make life unpleasant for their victims (although reports suggest that there has been an increase in aggression and violence among girls).

Bullying is different from generally aggressive behaviour because bullies pick their targets very selectively. Olweus (1993) suggests that there are often characteristics of victims that make them targets for bullies; for example, they may appear to be vulnerable, weaker, shy, nervous, overweight, of different ethnic background, or 'teacher's pet'. Bullies are typically needing to feel powerful, sometimes to cover their own feelings of inadequacy. They are generally older or more physically advanced than their victims. Four out of five bullies come from homes where physical and emotional abuse are used frequently, and are therefore victims themselves to some degree (Hazler 1996). They appear to have less empathy than non-bullies. When bullying is carried out by gangs of students factors come into play such as the importance of roles and status within the group. Some individuals feel that they are demonstrating their power by repressing the victim. Even those who are not themselves bullies get carried along with the behaviour and do not object to it or report it. Few would ever intervene to help the victim.

Within a school's behaviour management policy there should be agreed procedures for handling incidents of bullying so that all staff approach the problem with similar strategies. Much bullying occurs in the schoolyard, particularly if supervision is poor. Increased supervision is one intervention that schools can introduce to reduce bullying. Obviously the behaviour of the bully or the gang members needs to be addressed with direct intervention; but in addition, the issues of consideration and respect for others and the right of every student to feel safe also need to be discussed. It is suggested that issues of bullying and aggressive behaviour should become the focus of attention within the school curriculum – perhaps under the general heading 'human relationships' (Porter 2000).

Cognitive approaches to self-control

The main goal of any type of behaviour-change intervention should be the eventual handing-over of control to the individual concerned so that he or she is responsible for managing the behaviour. A self-control programme developed by Wragg (1989) is a good example of a cognitive behaviour modification programme (see also Chapter 4). The programme *Talk Sense to Yourself* uses individual coaching and rehearsal to establish self-talk strategies in the student. These self-instructions are used to help the student monitor his or her own reactions to daily problems and control and manage such situations more effectively.

The first stage in intervention is to help the students analyse their own inappropriate behaviour and to understand that what they are doing is not helping them in any way (e.g. lashing out at others, arguing with staff). Next the student is helped to establish both the *desire to change* and the *goals* to be aimed for over the following week (to stop doing the negative behaviour and to start doing the more positive behaviour).

Over a number of sessions the student is helped to change negative thoughts and beliefs to more appropriate positive perspectives. A key ingredient in the programme is teaching the student to use covert self-talk statements that serve to inhibit inappropriate thoughts or responses, allowing time for substitution of more acceptable responses – for example, to be assertive but not aggressive; to approach another student in a friendly rather than confrontational manner.

Cognitive approaches overlap significantly with what is known as cognitive behaviour therapy (CBT). Psychologists may use cognitive behaviour therapy to help a student overcome irrational thoughts, depression, anxieties or phobias. The various forms of CBT are associated more with clinical treatment rather than classroom-based interventions, so are outside the scope of this book. Information is available in Lane, Gresham and O'Shaughnessy (2002).

Helping withdrawn or timid children

Teachers are much more likely to notice and respond to aggressive and disturbing behaviour than they are to passive and withdrawn behaviour in the average classroom. Quiet children who cause no problem to the teacher may easily be overlooked. They are likely to go unnoticed because their behaviour never disrupts the classroom routine and they do not constantly come to the teacher's attention. In recent years, however, teachers are becoming more aware of the significance of extreme withdrawal as a sign of possible unhappiness or depression. However, quiet children are not necessarily emotionally disturbed and may have no problems at all; for example, children reared in families where parents are quiet and reflective are themselves likely to learn similar patterns of behaviour. Reticent and quiet children may be quite happy, and it is a questionable practice to force such children to be overly assertive.

If a child does have a genuine problem of withdrawal from social interaction with other children, the teacher does need to intervene. This may apply particularly to children with intellectual disabilities where social acceptance in a mainstream school may sometimes be a problem. Some of the strategies for teaching social skills described in the next chapter will be very important in such cases. Let it suffice here to suggest that lonely or rejected children may need to be helped to establish a friendship within the class by judicious selection of partners for specific activities, and by planning frequent opportunities for all children to experience some very positive outcomes from working closely with and helping other children.

When a child suffers social isolation it may be the result of lack of social skills on the child's part, from a history of rejection, from childhood depression, or from some combination of these factors. In such cases verbal communication can be minimal and even eye contact may be avoided. In extreme cases the self-imposed social isolation may be maintained by negative reinforcement – the behaviour is continued because it avoids unpleasant contact such as teasing or ridicule from other children.

Currently the number of students reported to be suffering from chronic depression has increased very significantly. This situation has signalled alarm in the mental health and counselling professions as some depressed students take their own lives (Robbins 1998). On this issue Salend (1998: 113) has urged, 'If teachers suspect that a student is depressed or suicidal they should work with other professionals and parents to help the student receive the services of mental health professionals.'

The starting point for helping socially isolated children is usually observation within the classroom and in the schoolyard to find the point at which some cautious intervention might be attempted (e.g. getting the child to engage in some parallel play alongside other children as a preliminary step to later joining the play of others, taking a turn). The teacher or teacher assistant will need to guide, support, prompt and reinforce the child through these various stages. In all cases the cooperation of the peer group may need to be enlisted if the child is to become an accepted member of that group.

Studies that have focused upon the inclusion of children with disabilities in regular classes have indicated that social acceptance of these children into the peer group does not occur spontaneously. Most children with disabilities need to be taught how to relate to others – how to greet them, how to talk with them, how to share things – just as the students without disabilities need to develop tolerance of those who are different from themselves and learn how they can help them in class.

Attention-deficit hyperactivity disorder (ADHD)

Some students display severe problems in maintaining attention to any task, both in and out of school. These children have been classified as having Attention Deficit Disorder (ADD). Often these students also exhibit hyperactive behaviour so the term Attention-Deficit Hyperactivity Disorder (ADHD) has been coined to describe this form of learning difficulty (American Psychiatric Association 1994). Children with ADD and ADHD display diminished persistence of effort, have difficulty sustaining attention to task, are overactive, and do not seem able to inhibit impulsive actions or responses (Lowe and Reynolds 2000). To be diagnosed as ADHD the child must exhibit six or more of the nine symptoms described under 'inattention' and 'hyperactivity' sections in the *Diagnostic and Statistical Manual of Mental Disorder*, *DSM IV* (APA 1994). No single test or checklist exists that can lead to certain identification; usually information from several sources is combined to help the doctor or psychologist reach a conclusion.

It is considered by experts that approximately 3–5 per cent of school-age children present symptoms of ADD or ADHD, but in the past ten years there has been an increase in the number of students being diagnosed (correctly or incorrectly) as having ADHD, resulting in suggestions that as many as 12 children in every 100 might have the disorder. This is unlikely to be the case, and estimates of 12 per cent prevalence rate are probably too high. The labels ADD and ADHD are often misused and applied to children who are merely bored and restless, or who are placed in a class where the teacher lacks good management skills. However, there are genuine cases of attention deficit and hyperactivity where the children do experience great difficulty in controlling their motor responses and exhibit high levels of inappropriate activity throughout the day. Hyperactivity is also present sometimes as an additional problem in certain disabilities (e.g. cerebral palsy, acquired brain injury, specific learning disability, and emotional disturbance).

No single cause for ADHD has been identified, although the following have all been put forward as possible explanations: central nervous system dysfunction (perhaps due to slow maturation of the motor cortex of the brain), subtle forms of brain damage too slight to be confirmed by neurological testing, allergy to specific substances (e.g. food additives), adverse reactions to environmental stimuli (e.g. fluorescent lighting), inappropriate management of the child at home, maternal alcohol consumption during pregnancy (causing Foetal Alcohol Syndrome: FAS). Most investigators now tend to agree that the hyperactivity syndrome encompasses a heterogeneous group of behaviour disorders with multiple causes of possibly neuropsychological origin. Lowe and Reynolds (2000) suggest that psychosocial factors such as parenting style, child–parent relationships and home environment probably play a secondary role to genetic and neurological causes.

ADHD children, while not necessarily below average in intelligence, usually exhibit poor achievement in most school subjects. Impaired concentration span and restlessness associated with ADHD have usually seriously impaired the child's learning during the important early years of schooling. They may also have other identifiable behaviour problems, such as Oppositional Defiant Disorder (ODD) and Conduct Disorder (CD), both described fully in *DSM IV* (APA 1994). They may also be poorly co-ordinated. Some have problems with peer relationships. The literature indicates that most hyperactivity diminishes with age even without treatment, but in a few cases the problems persist into adult life (Wender 2000).

Interventions for ADHD

Owing to the possibility that ADHD is caused by different factors in different individuals, it is not surprising to find that quite different forms of treatment are advocated; and what works for one child may not work for another. Treatments have included diet control, medication, psychotherapy, behaviour modification and cognitive behaviour modification. The conclusion must be that any approach to the treatment of ADHD needs to attend to *all* factors that may be maintaining the behaviour. Evans (1995: 210) has concluded that 'Current best practice indicates that behaviour management principles, cognitive-behavioural strategies for self-management, and effective instruction in both academic and social skills assist these students substantially.'

Teaching children with ADHD

There is strong agreement among experts that children with ADHD need structure and predictability in the learning environment and within the teaching method (Alban-Metcalfe and Alban-Metcalfe 2001). The principles of effective teaching described in Chapter 1 apply particularly to the education of children with ADHD. These children need to be engaged as much as possible in interesting work, at a successful level, in a predictable environment. Stevens (2000: 70) writes:

> [Teachers who manage ADHD children effectively] are keenly aware of the fact that youngsters who are not actively involved in learning will get into trouble. They prevent difficulties from arising by maintaining a quiet, productive classroom environment and by ensuring that all students can fully participate in class activities.

Other suggestions for enhancing the learning of children with ADHD include:

* Providing strong visual input that holds attention.
* Using computer-assisted learning (CAL).
* Teaching the student better self-management and organisational skills.
* Devising interesting and motivating activities and tasks in all lessons.
* Monitoring children with ADHD closely during lessons and finding as many opportunities as possible to praise them descriptively when they are on task and productive.

Additional advice on teaching modifications for children with ADHD can be found in Kewley (2001) and Alban-Metcalfe and Alban-Metcalfe (2001).

Further reading

Algozzine, B. and Kay, P. (eds) (2002) *Preventing Problem Behaviors*, Thousand Oaks, CA: Corwin Press.

Barkley, R.A. (2000) *Taking Charge of ADHD* (2nd edn), New York: Guilford Press.

Davis-Johnson, S.P. (2001) *Seven Essentials for Character Discipline*, Thousand Oaks, CA: Corwin Press.

Lane, K.L., Gresham, F.M. and O'Shaughnessy, T.E. (eds) (2002) *Interventions for Children with or at risk for Emotional and Behavioral Disorders*, Boston, MA: Allyn and Bacon.

Lindberg, J.A. and Swick, A.M. (2002) *Common-sense Classroom Management*, Thousand Oaks, CA: Corwin Press.

Mathieson, K. and Price, M. (2002) *Better Behaviour in Classrooms: A Framework for Inclusive Behaviour Management*, London: RoutledgeFalmer.

Newell, S. and Jeffery, D. (2002) *Behaviour Management in the Classroom*, London: Fulton.

Porter, L. (2000) *Behaviour in Schools: Theory and Practice for Teachers*, Buckingham: Open University Press.

Zirpoli, T.J. (2001) *Behavior Management Applications for Teachers* (3rd edn), Upper Saddle River, NJ: Merrill.

Chapter 6

Improving social skills and peer group acceptance

> Many students with mild disabilities demonstrate difficulties in developing social relationships with adults and peers in their environment. These students often evidence reduced social perceptiveness, finding it challenging to read verbal and nonverbal social cues and appropriately interpret these cues within a social and cultural context. Such difficulties inhibit social behavior that facilitates the development of friendships and peer relationships, and increases feelings of loneliness and social isolation.
>
> (Pavri and Monda-Amaya 2001: 392)

The quotation above reminds us of the need to address the issue of how best to enhance the social acceptance of children with special needs when placed in a regular class. Inclusive educational settings create a situation where children with disabilities can increase their social competence – but it is important to note that such an increase in social competence certainly does not always occur automatically. The situation is most problematic for children who have an emotional or behavioural disorder (Gresham 2002). There is a danger that such children will be marginalised, ignored or even openly rejected by the peer group

The results of most studies of integration and inclusion do not support the belief that merely placing a child with a disability in the mainstream spontaneously improves the social status of that child (Csoti 2001; Turnbull *et al.* 2002; Vaughn, Gersten and Chard 2001). Wilkins (2001: ix) observes, 'Many students in special education programs have difficulty relating to others and interacting with peers. When interactions are negative, students are often prevented from working or playing together.' It is evident that poor peer relationships during the school years can have a lasting detrimental impact on social and personal competence in later years. It is for this reason that establishing good social relationships with other children has been described as one of the most important goals of education (Elksnin and Elksnin 2001).

Opportunities for social interaction

At least three conditions must be present for positive social interaction and the development of friendships among children with and without disabilities. These conditions include:

- *Opportunity*: That is, being within proximity of other children frequently enough for meaningful contacts to be made.
- *Continuity*: Being involved with the same group of children over a relatively long period of time, for example, several consecutive years; and also seeing some of the same children in your own neighbourhood out of school hours.
- *Support*: Being helped to make contact with other children in order to work and play with them; and if possible being directly supported in maintaining friendships out of school hours.

Inclusive schooling provides the opportunity for friendships to develop in terms of proximity and frequency of contact, and has potential for continuity. It creates the best possible chances for children with disabilities to observe and imitate the social interactions and behaviours of others. What inclusive classrooms must also provide is the necessary support for positive social interactions to occur (Sparzo and Poteet 1997). This is particularly important for students who are low in self-esteem and confidence and who are missing some of the basic social skills.

When students with disabilities are placed in regular settings without adequate preparation or on-going support, three basic problems may become evident:

- Children without disabilities do not readily demonstrate high levels of acceptance of those with disabilities.
- Children with disabilities, contrary to popular belief, do not automatically observe and imitate the social models which are around them.
- Some teachers do not intervene positively to promote social interaction on the disabled child's behalf.

In relation to the last of the three points above it seems that teachers in general are becoming much more aware of the need to assist children in establishing friendships in class. Strategies for encouraging social interaction among children feature frequently now in training and development programmes for teachers.

Identification of children with peer relationship problems

Naturalistic observation

The most obvious strategy for identifying children with particular problems is the informal observation of social interactions within and outside the classroom. Naturalistic observation is probably the most valuable method of identification for the teacher to use since it focuses on the child within the dynamics of peer-group interactions and can thus indicate a number of factors that might be modified. A teacher who takes the trouble to note the ways in which children play and work together will quickly identify children who are neglected by their peers or who are openly rejected and become an object of ridicule and teasing. It is very important also to try to identify any obvious reasons that give rise to this situation. For example, is the child in question openly obnoxious to others through aggression, hurtful comments, spoiling games or interfering with work? Or at the other extreme, does the child seem to lack motivation, confidence and skills to initiate contact with others, remaining very much on the outside of any action?

Sociometric survey

Naturalistic observation tends to identify the most obvious cases of popularity or rejection. It may not pick up some of the subtleties of social interactions in the class. For this reason some teachers find it useful to carry out a whole-class survey in order to get all the children to indicate, in confidence, their main friendship choices (Sheridan and Walker 1999). The teacher may interview each child privately or, if the children can write, may give out slips of paper with the numerals 1 to 3 printed on them. The teacher then requests that each child write down first the name of the person he or she would most like to play with or work with as a partner in a classroom activity or at lunchtime. The teacher may then say, 'If that person was away from school who would you choose next?' and that name is listed second. When the papers are collected the teacher calculates the score for each child on the basis of two points for a first choice and one point for a second choice. For example, Susan obtains a total score of eight points if other children choose her three times as first preference and twice as second preference. The results for each individual in the class can then be tabulated for the teacher's use. The information gained from a survey of this type may help a teacher identify children who are of low sociometric status, and may also be used to determine the composition of certain working groups in the class.

Peer ratings

This procedure ensures that some children are not forgotten or overlooked, as may happen with a traditional sociometric survey of the type described above. The children are provided with a list of the names of all children in the class and required in confidence to place a score from 1 (not liked very much) to 5 (liked a lot) against each name. Summation of the completed scores will reveal the children who are not well liked by class members as well as showing the general level of acceptance of all children. The result may sometimes correlate highly with naturalistic observation, but occasionally quite subtle positive or negative attitudes appear that are not immediately obvious to outside observation.

Teacher ratings

The use of checklists that specify important indicators of social competence can be helpful in providing a clear focus for teachers' observations of children. The items in the checklist would normally be those responses and behaviours considered to comprise 'social skills', such as greeting, interacting with others, sharing, and avoiding conflict.

Parent nomination

Sometimes a child's social relationship problems at school may be brought to the teacher's attention first by the parent who says 'I'm worried about Paul. He doesn't bring any friends home and doesn't play with other children after school'; or 'Marion has been coming home from school saying that the other girls are making fun of her in the yard and on the bus'. This type of information should be treated in a sensitive manner and followed up by the teacher.

Creating a supportive environment

To facilitate social interaction for children with special needs in regular classrooms three conditions are necessary:

- The general attitude of the teacher and the peer group towards students with special needs must be made as positive and accepting as possible.
- The environment should be arranged so that the child with a disability has the maximum opportunity to spend time socially involved in a group or pair activity, during recess and during academic work in the classroom.
- The child needs to be taught the specific skills that may enhance social contact with peers.

Sheridan and Walker (1999: 701) refer to manipulation of these conditions as providing 'contextual enhancement' to support the development and maintenance of social relationships.

Influencing attitudes

It has long been acknowledged that one of the key factors influencing the effectiveness of integrated and inclusive education is the *attitude* of those involved in the process – teachers, children and parents (e.g. Cook 2001; Smith 2000). Teachers and classmates tend to become more accepting of children with disabilities when they gain experience in working with them and acquire a better understanding of the nature of disabilities. Studies have shown that a combination of information about, and direct contact with, disabled children provides the most powerful positive influence for attitude change in both teachers and in the peer group. It is also evident that attitude change tends to be a gradual process.

Children's attitudes are likely to be influenced most when teachers work to build a climate of concern for others in the classroom. This can be achieved in part by the teacher's own example, and also by the open discussion and resolution of problems that may arise from time to time. Consideration of 'individual differences' can be an on-going theme within the taught curriculum. Facilitating and encouraging peer assistance and buddy systems in the classroom can be useful in increasing non-disabled students' close contact with others who have difficulties in learning.

The following approaches, particularly when used in combination, have all been beneficial in improving attitudes towards children with disabilities. Throughout these awareness-raising techniques the stress should be upon 'How will we help students with disabilities fit into our class activities?' 'How will we respond positively and supportively to someone with a difficulty in our class?' 'How will we help to make these students feel happy and productive?' Attention should also be drawn to various strengths possessed by every person with a disability or learning difficulty. Highlight the 'sameness' as well as any 'differences'.

- Viewing films or videos depicting children and adults with disabilities coping well and doing everyday things. Many videos and VCDs are available showing inclusive classroom environments and the accommodations made for students with special needs.
- Conducting factual lessons and discussion about particular disabilities.
- Having persons with disabilities as visitors to the classroom or as guest speakers.
- Producing simulation activities, e.g. simulating deafness, or vision impairment or being confined to a wheelchair. (Note that two conditions that cannot be simulated are intellectual disability and emotional

disturbance. These are also the two disabilities that produce the greatest problems in terms of social isolation and rejection in the peer group.)
- Reading and discussing stories about disabled persons and their achievements.
- Organising regular visits as helpers to special schools or centres.

Creating opportunities

If optimum social learning is to take place it is essential that all children have the opportunity to be involved regularly in group activities both inside and outside the classroom. To aid the social integration of children with disabilities they need to be included fully within all group activities.

To enhance social development, teachers must first create classroom environments where competition is not a dominant element. They must then use group activities frequently enough to encourage cooperation among students (Johnson and Johnson 2000).

Organisation for group work

Careful planning is required if group work is to achieve the desired educational and social outcomes. The success of collaborative group work depends on the composition of the working groups and the nature of the tasks set for the students. Group work often becomes disorganised because the group tasks are poorly defined or too complex. Other problems arise if the students are not well versed in group-working skills, or if the room is not set up to facilitate easy access to resources. It is essential that all tasks have a very clear structure and purposes that are understood by all.

When utilising group work as an organisational strategy it is important to consider the following basic principles:

- Initially there is some merit in having groups of children working cooperatively on the same task at the same time. The procedure makes it much easier to prepare resources and to manage the time effectively. When each of several groups are undertaking quite different tasks it can become a major management problem for the teacher, unless the students concerned are already very competent and experienced in group work.
- Choice of tasks for group work is very important. Tasks have to be selected which *require* collaboration and teamwork. Lyle (1996) comments that children are often seated in groups in the classroom but are expected to work on individual assignments. This does not involve collaboration, and the physical arrangement often creates difficulties for the individual student in terms of interruptions and distractions.
- It is not enough merely to establish groups and to set them to work. Group members may have to be taught how to work together. They may

need to be shown behaviours that encourage or enable cooperation – listening to the views of others, sharing, praising each other, and offering help to others. If the task involves the learning of specific curriculum content, teach the children how to rehearse and test one another on the material.

- The way in which individual tasks are allotted needs to be carefully planned (division of labour); the way in which each child can assist another must also be made explicit, e.g. 'John, you can help Craig with his writing then he can help you with the lettering for your title board.' Contingent praise for interacting with others should be descriptive. 'Well done, Sue. That's nice of you to help Sharon with that recording.'

- Teachers should monitor closely what is going on during group activities and must intervene when necessary to provide suggestions, encourage the sharing of a task, praise examples of cooperation and teamwork and model cooperative behaviour themselves. Many groups can be helped to function efficiently if the teacher (or the aide or a parent helper) works as a group member without dominating or controlling the activity.

- The size of the group is also important. Often children working in pairs is a good starting point. Select the composition of the group carefully to avoid obvious incompatibility among students' personalities. Information from a sociometric survey may help to determine appropriate partners.

- When groups contain students with special needs it is vital that the specific tasks and duties to be undertaken by these students are clearly delineated. It can be useful to establish a system whereby the results of the group's efforts are rewarded not merely by what individuals produce, but also by the way in which they have worked together positively and supportively. Under this structure, group members have a vested interest in ensuring that all members learn, because the group's success depends on the achievement of all. Helping each other, sharing, and tutoring within the group are behaviours that must be modelled and supported.

- Talking should be encouraged during group activities. It is interesting to note that sub-grouping in the class has the effect of increasing transactional talk (talk specifically directed to another person and requiring a reply) by almost three times the level present under whole-class conditions.

- Seating and work arrangements are important. Group members should be in close proximity but still have space to work on materials without getting in each other's way.

- Group work must be used frequently enough for the children to learn the skills and routines. Infrequent group work results in children taking too long to settle down.

Facilitating social interaction

The following strategies can be used to increase the chances of positive social integrations for students with disabilities:

- Greater use of games and play activities of a non-academic type can place the disabled child in situations where he or she can more easily fit in and work with others.
- 'Peer tutoring', 'buddy systems' and other helping relationships have all been found effective to a greater or lesser degree.
- Make a particular topic – for example, 'friends' or 'working together' – the basis for class discussion. 'If you want someone to play with you at lunchtime how would you make that happen?' 'If you saw two children in the schoolyard who had just started at the school today how would you make them feel welcome?' Sometimes teachers prepare follow-up material in the form of worksheets with simple cartoon-type drawings and speech balloons into which the children write the appropriate greetings or comments for the various characters. Much of this can be incorporated into a social education programme.
- Peer-group members can be encouraged to maintain and reinforce social interactions with less-able or less-popular children. Often they are unaware of the ways in which they can help. They, too, may need to be shown how to initiate contact, how to invite the child with special needs to join in an activity, or how to help that classmate with particular school assignments.

What are social skills?

Social skills are the specific behaviours an individual uses to perform effective interpersonal communication and interaction. According to Kavale *et al.* (1997) social skills are defined as a set of competencies that allow children or adolescents to initiate and maintain positive social interactions with others, establish peer acceptance, and cope effectively and adaptively with the larger social environment.

Positive social relationships also appear to be related to satisfactory academic progress in school. Many students with learning disabilities (LD), although not labelled as emotionally or behaviourally disturbed, exhibit problems in developing effective social skills. In recent years remedial interventions for LD students have tended to include attention to both social and academic skill deficits.

Many lists of important pro-social behaviours have been created (e.g. Caldarella and Merrell 1997) as have many checklists allowing teachers, parents and psychologists to assess a child's social skill level (e.g. Elksnin and Elksnin 1995). Guidelines have also been published to give teachers suggestions for what to teach and how to teach it in the domain of social skill development (e.g. Begun 1996).

Social skills training interventions usually include some or all of the following behaviours:

- making eye contact;
- greeting others by name;
- gaining attention in appropriate ways;
- talking in a tone of voice that is acceptable;
- initiating a conversation;
- maintaining conversations;
- answering questions;
- listening to others and showing interest;
- sharing with others;
- saying please and thank you;
- helping someone;
- making apologies when necessary;
- taking one's turn;
- smiling;
- accepting praise;
- giving praise;
- accepting correction without anger;
- coping with frustration;
- managing conflict.

The basic list above is similar to that found in most texts on social skills training. Each skill can be broken down further into smaller sub-skills if necessary, and each skill or behaviour needs to be considered relative to the particular child's age and specific deficits (Merrell 2001). For example, the conversational skills needed to function adequately in an adolescent peer group are obviously far more complex and subtle than those required by the young child just starting school. Similarly, the skills needed to deal with conflict situations become more complex as a child gets older.

Social skills training

Some children with disabilities or with emotional and behavioural difficulties are particularly at risk of social isolation (Gresham, Sugai and Horner 2001) – although it is important to stress here that some students with disabilities are popular with classmates in the mainstream, particularly if they have a pleasant personality.

One of the main reasons why certain children are unpopular is that they lack appropriate social skills that might make them more acceptable. They are in a Catch-22 situation since friendless students have fewer opportunities to practise social skills, and those who don't develop adequate social skills are unable to form friendships.

There is no shortage of social skills training programmes and curricula available to schools (e.g. Waksman 1998; Walker 1983) and their advocates firmly believe that teaching of social skills can have lasting positive effects, particularly for students with milder degrees of socialisation difficulty. These experts believe that social skills training for students with special needs can be effective if (a) it targets the precise skills and knowledge an individual lacks; (b) it is intensive and long term in nature; (c) the programme is implemented in such a way as to promote the maintenance, generalisation and transfer of new skills outside the training context and into the individual's daily life (Gresham 2002). While most social skills training programmes do produce positive short-term effects, there is usually a significant problem with maintenance and generalisation of the trained skills over time.

Some researchers warn against over-optimism in regard to the longer-term efficacy of social skills training. For example, Kavale *et al.* (1997) and Quinn *et al.* (1999) carried out meta-analyses of a large number of group and single-subject interventions and discovered only modest effect sizes. In particular, they suggest that social skills training appears to have limited effect when applied to seriously behaviourally disordered children. The main problem appears to be lack of maintenance and generalisation of the taught skills to everyday life (Gresham *et al.* 2001). It must also be noted that even when children with disabilities are specifically trained in social skills, some may still not find it any easier to make friends. For example, Margalit (1995) found that students with intellectual disability reported on-going feelings of loneliness even after successfully participating in a social skills programme. Unexpected outcomes may also occur, for example, Elliott, Pring and Bunning (2002) found that students with intellectual disability may feel *less competent* in social skills after training because the training has made them more aware of their own difficulties and deficiencies.

The failure of many social skills programmes to bring about lasting measurable change in students may be due to:

- A mismatch between the exact social deficits a child displays and the activities provided in the training programme (with some programmes reportedly being much too generic and not based on an accurate assessment of the student's specific needs) (Merrell 2001).
- Poor or inconsistent quality of the training provided in some programmes (Gresham *et al.* 2001).
- Training sessions too infrequent and too lacking in intensity to have any lasting impact (Bullis, Walker and Sprague 2001).
- A failure to plan for and support generalisation from the training or coaching context to natural social environments (Gresham *et al.* 2001).

As pointed out in the previous chapter, often the training is not a matter of teaching a child something that is missing from his or her repertoire of social behaviour, but rather it involves replacing an undesirable behaviour that is already strongly established with a new alternative behaviour. Gresham *et al.* (2001) suggest that the negative behaviours we often take as indicative of lack of social skill in some children (e.g. aggression, non-compliance, verbal abuse) may actually be very rewarding behaviours for the individuals concerned and represent more powerful and effective forces than the new pro-social skills we attempt to teach. This residual influence of pre-existing behaviours is one of the reasons why skills taught during training are often not maintained – they are competing with powerful behaviours that have already proved to work well for the child.

Even given the cautionary comments above it is still a high priority in inclusive settings for any students who lack specific social skills to be provided with every opportunity (including specific training) in order to acquire them.

Social competence

Social skills contribute significantly to a somewhat broader domain of human behaviour termed *social competence*. Social competence goes beyond essential age-appropriate social skills. It includes knowing how to behave and respond in the acceptable manner in different social contexts. For example, when shopping in a supermarket there are behaviours that are acceptable and others that are totally inappropriate; similarly, the way that you behave when attending the cinema is different from the way you behave when attending a sporting event. The socially competent individual behaves appropriately in all social settings because he or she knows the social 'rules' that apply in those contexts.

Warger and Rutherford (1996) state that a person is socially competent when he or she is able to:

- recognise social rules and expectations;
- perform socially appropriate behaviours;
- perceive social situations accurately and identify the relevant skills to use;
- correctly interpret information and cues from others;
- initiate social interaction appropriately;
- communicate effectively in different social situations;
- perform social skills in a consistent and generalised manner;
- establish and maintain friendships;
- solve interpersonal or social problems as they arise;
- negotiate tactfully and successfully with others.

Most special schools for students with intellectual disability usually give high priority within their objectives and curricula to helping students develop social competence. Without social competence individuals tend to draw adverse attention to themselves and thus have difficulty in gaining acceptance in the community. In special school curricula, social competence training overlaps and integrates with other key areas of development such as communication, self-care, daily living skills and adaptive behaviour.

As well as having appropriate positive pro-social skills, a socially competent individual must also *avoid* having negative behavioural characteristics that prevent easy acceptance by others – for example, high levels of irritating behaviour (interrupting, poking, shouting, etc.), impulsive and unpredictable reactions, temper tantrums, abusive language, or cheating at games. In most cases these undesirable behaviours need to be eliminated by behaviour modification or through cognitive behaviour management training.

Teaching approaches

Most programmes for training social skills have been based on a combination of modelling, coaching, role-playing, rehearsing, feedback and counselling. At times, video recordings have also been used to provide examples of social behaviours to discuss, or to provide the trainee with feedback on his or her own performance or role-play.

In each individual case the first step is to decide what the priorities are for this child in terms of specific skills and behaviours to be taught. The skills to be targeted need to be of immediate functional value to the child in the social environment in which he or she operates. The most meaningful settings in which to enhance the child's skills are usually the classroom and schoolyard. It is pointless to teach skills that are not immediately useful in the child's regular environment.

At times a teacher needs to intervene to help a child gain entry to group activity or to work with a carefully chosen partner. The teacher must also praise and reinforce both the target child and the peer group for all instances of cooperative, helpful and friendly behaviour. In the case of children with extreme withdrawal or rejection, simply relying on milieu intervention is not always sufficient. Sometimes it may be necessary for a child to be removed from the classroom situation and coached intensively in a particular skill before that skill can be applied in the peer group setting. Franco *et al.* (1983) describe an excellent example of this in a case study of a very shy adolescent male. These practitioners focused on conversational skills as being the most important behaviours to establish in this youth. In a withdrawal room they worked on four areas: asking questions of others, making reinforcing comments and acknowledging what others say, showing affective warmth, and maintaining eye contact. Sessions were held twice weekly for 20 minutes over a fifteen-week period. After explanations and demonstrations from a tutor, the youth then practised these behaviours with the tutor and applied them in a series of ten-minute conversations with different male and female partners (as a method to aid generalisation). The partners were previously instructed to be warm and friendly but to refrain from asking questions of the subject unless he asked one first. They were also told to keep their responses brief so that the onus would be on the subject to maintain the conversation. The subject was instructed to adopt the strategy of finding out as much as possible about the other person's interests and to keep the conversation going. Observations were made at intervals after the coaching sessions had finished and significant and durable improvements were reported in his classroom interactions.

Typical steps in coaching social skills include:

- *Definition*: Describe the skill to be taught. Discuss why the particular skill is important and how its use helps social interactions to occur. The skill may be illustrated in action in a video, a picture or cartoon, a simulation using puppets, or pointed out to the child by reference to activities going on in the peer group. The teacher may say 'Watch how she helps him build the wall with the blocks'; 'Look at the two girls sharing the puzzle. Tell me what they might be saying to each other.'
- *Model the skill*: Break the skill down into simple components and demonstrate these clearly yourself, or get a selected child to do this.
- *Imitation and rehearsal*: The child tries out the same skill in a structured situation. For this to occur successfully the child must be motivated to perform the skill and must attend carefully and retain what has been demonstrated.
- *Feedback*: This should be informative. 'You've not quite got it yet. You need to look at her while you speak to her. Try it again.' 'That's better! You looked and smiled. Well done.' Feedback via a video recording may be appropriate in some situations.
- *Provide opportunity for the skill to be used*: Depending upon the skill taught, use small group work or pair work activities to allow the skill to be applied and generalised to the classroom or other natural setting.
- *Intermittent reinforcement*: Watch for instances of the child applying the skill without prompting at other times in the day and later in the week. Provide descriptive praise and reward. Aim for maintenance of the skill once it is acquired. To a large extent these behaviours, once established, are likely to be maintained by natural consequences, i.e. by a more satisfying interaction with peers.

There is much still to be discovered about how best to implement social skills training. Bullis, Walker and Sprague (2001: 89) are probably accurate in their conclusion:

Unfortunately we do not know the necessary intensity or duration for the social skills intervention to be effective, and we are uncertain of the precise combination of components that should be added to the treatment to achieve maximum effect.

Poor scholastic achievement seems to be one factor contributing to poor social acceptance, even after social skills have been taught. Unless achievement within the curriculum can also be increased, acceptance may remain a problem for some children. Attention is therefore focused in the following chapters on approaches for teaching basic academic skills to students with special needs.

Further reading

Csoti, M. (2001) *Social Awareness Skills for Children*, London: Jessica Kingsley.

Johnson, D.W and Johnson, R.T. (2000) *Joining Together: Group Theory and Group Skills* (7th edn), Boston, MA: Allyn and Bacon.

Jones, C.J. (2000) *Curriculum Development for Students with Mild Disabilities: Academic and Social Skills*, Springfield, IL: Thomas.

Putnam, J.W. (1998) *Cooperative Learning and Strategies for Inclusion* (2nd edn), Baltimore, MD: Brookes.

Richardson, R.C. and Evans, E.T. (1997) *Connecting with Others: Lessons for Teaching Social and Emotional Competence, Grades 6–8*, Champaign, IL: Research Press.

Taylor, G.R. (1998) *Curriculum Strategies for Teaching Social Skills to the Disabled*, Springfield, IL: Thomas.

Waksman, S. (1998) *The Waksman Social Skills Curriculum for Adolescents* (4th edn), Austin, TX: ProEd.

Wilkins, J. (2001) *Group Activities to Include Students with Special Needs*, Thousand Oaks, CA: Corwin Press.

Chapter 7

Developing early literacy skills: Principles and practices

> The acquisition of literacy skills is a developmental process. Teachers must plan the learning for pupils who do not acquire these skills readily, based on their individual learning needs. The teacher of pupils with special educational needs should use what children already know, coupled with a knowledge of how pupils learn, as a basis for planning their future learning.
>
> (Duncan and Parkhouse 2001: 1)

Learning to read is a complex task even for children of average intelligence. It can be a very difficult task indeed for children with disabilities. Yet despite the difficulties, almost all children can be helped to acquire skills in word recognition and comprehension through application of effective teaching methods (Butler and Silliman 2002; Conners 1992).

A balanced approach to literacy teaching

It has been said that there is no one method, medium, approach or philosophy that holds the key to the process of learning to read. From this it follows that the greater the variety of methods known to teachers the more likely it is that they will feel competent to provide appropriate help for children with learning difficulties.

Spiegel (1999: 11) has written:

> Because research does not support the idea that one size fits all, that one approach will work with all children for all aspects of literacy development for all curricula, a balanced approach must be flexible. Teachers must examine all the alternatives and strive each day to find the best ways to help each child develop as a reader and a writer. This means that few approaches or strategies are automatically assumed appropriate for all children. It also means that few approaches or strategies are automatically rejected as never appropriate.

In recent years much has been written about the need for 'balance' within the overall methodology used to teach reading – 'balance' implying a combination of explicit teaching of decoding skills and comprehension strategies on the one hand with 'whole-language' immersion in literature on the other. Balance also implies a combination of teacher-directed and student-centred activity within the reading curriculum (Blair-Larsen and Williams 1999; Pressley 1998). In the early stages of learning to read, the best curricula offer an amalgam of elements, including reading for meaning, reading for thinking, experience with high-quality literature, systematic instruction in phonics, development of sight vocabulary, and ample opportunities to read and write. As Cunningham *et al.* (2000) indicate, children *need* a balanced literacy programme if they are to develop all necessary skills and strategies for independence in reading and writing.

Differing perspectives on reading methodology

In the past 50 years the teaching of reading has been dominated at various periods either by what is termed a 'skills-based approach' or by the 'meaning-emphasis approach' (Hoffman and Duffy 2001). The former stresses the importance of teaching children the skills considered necessary for decoding and interpreting text; the other stresses that reading should be a thinking process and must be driven 'top down' by a search for meaning.

There continues to be heated argument between advocates of the two approaches concerning the superiority of one over the other – indeed, the debates have raged so strongly and antagonistically that they have been referred to as the 'reading wars' (Stanovich 2000). Those favouring a balanced approach to instruction believe that reading involves both a top down (search for meaning) and a bottom up (decoding) processing of text.

There have been attempts to fuse the skills approach with whole-language approach, building on the strengths in both (e.g. Harrison 2001); but extreme devotees of each approach remain sceptical. Pressley (1994: 211) makes a helpful comment when he writes:

> Experiencing more explicit instruction of reading skills and strategies in no way precludes the authentic reading and writing experiences emphasized in whole language. Rather, explicit instruction enables at-risk students to participate more fully in such literacy experiences.

It is important to consider the contribution that both meaning-emphasis and skills-based approaches can make to the creation of a balanced reading programme.

A skills-based approach to reading

A skills-based approach teaches students decoding skills to aid word identification. It also develops comprehension skills and strategies to facilitate processing of text for different purposes. The approach usually involves a high
degree of teacher direction in the early stages, using explicit instruction and a
carefully sequenced curriculum, rather than unstructured student-centred
discovery. Within the skills-based approach to reading there are many ways
of ensuring that children acquire an understanding of the alphabetic principle and apply appropriate strategies for comprehending what they read.
Later chapters provide coverage of some of these strategies. Research
strongly supports the direct teaching of phonic knowledge and skills by any
effective method, and there is no evidence that any one method is superior to
any other (Strickland 2000). Similarly, reading comprehension strategies may
be taught by several methods, as described later in the chapter.

On the issue of teaching decoding skills, research has given overwhelming
support to teaching beginning readers the alphabetic principle and how it can
be applied to reading and spelling of words (e.g. Adams 1990; Manset-
Williams *et al*. 2002). Without such information children are lacking a reliable strategy for unlocking unfamiliar words. In the earliest stages of learning
to read children have not yet built up a large vocabulary of words they know
instantly by sight, so they must use knowledge of letters and groups of letters
to help identify unfamiliar words. Children cannot really become independent readers unless they master the code. It is now generally accepted that
explicit instruction in phonic principles needs to be part of all early reading
programmes (Hoffman and McCarthey 2000; IRA 1997) – although some
voices are still raised in opposition (e.g. Meyer 2002). Evidence is also readily
at hand to indicate the value of directly teaching comprehension strategies
(e.g. Alvermann and Hruby 2001; Pressley 1999).

No teacher ever uses a skills-based approach *exclusively*; to do so would be
to teach reading and writing in the most unnatural and boring way, working
from parts to whole and only engaging in meaningful reading once all the
skills were in place. Valid criticisms have been made of some forms of
remedial teaching of reading that err on this side and involve nothing but
repetitive drilling of isolated skills (Moody *et al*. 2000). The teachers who
embed explicit instruction within their total literacy programme represent
the effective use of a skills-based approach best. They give due attention to
developing and applying skills in decoding, spelling and comprehending text,
but always with emphasis on *meaningful* reading and writing. The International Reading Association's position paper on the role of phonics in the
teaching of reading states:

> When phonics instruction is linked to children's reading and writing
> they are more likely to become strategic and independent in their use of

phonics than when phonics instruction is drilled and practised in isolation.

(IRA 1997: 2)

The criticism is sometimes made that phonic knowledge is of little value because of the irregularity of English spelling. This is true only if children's phonic knowledge is limited to single letter-to-sound correspondences. If students become proficient in identifying larger phonic units represented by clusters of letters (*orthographic units*) such as *pre–, str–, –tion, –eat, –ough, –ight, –oon*, they can decode many more words. When children equate strings of letters with pronounceable units such as syllables in spoken words, many inconsistencies in English spelling patterns are removed.

Osborn and Lehr (1998: 339) conclude that:

> The systematic and explicit instruction in decoding and comprehension skills has been neglected in recent years [but] the evidence that skills instruction is necessary is overwhelming. Particularly problematic is that many children do not acquire word recognition skills merely as a by-product of immersion in reading and writing . . . what is supported by evidence is that systematic and intensive decoding instruction provides an excellent start toward becoming a fluent reader.

More detailed information on the teaching of phonic skills will be found in Chapter 9.

The meaning-emphasis approach

Meaning-emphasis approaches are based on a belief that readers recognise words and interpret print mainly on the basis of the meaning conveyed by the text. It is suggested that readers pay very little attention to lower-level processes such as phonic decoding. Many years ago Goodman (1967) described reading as a psycholinguistic guessing game in which skilled readers use their knowledge of language (vocabulary and syntax), together with knowledge of the topic, to predict many of the words on the page. Only when the reader cannot predict a word, or when meaning is lost, does he or she have to resort to the use of phonic principle. This appears to be the way in which skilled readers operate – so the argument from the advocates of meaning-emphasis 'whole language' approach is that even beginning readers need to be encouraged to develop the same general 'guess-from-meaning' strategy.

Whole-language (meaning-emphasis) theory holds that authentic literacy experiences foster a child's understanding of the true nature and purposes of reading, whereas the teaching of component skills may fail to achieve this goal. A key belief underpinning whole language is that children acquire literacy skills in much the same way as they learned to use speech for purposes of communication – that is without having to be taught. Young learners immersed in a print-rich environment are considered capable of constructing meaning and developing skills for themselves by drawing on their experience of spoken language when engaging actively with print. The teacher's role is to provide opportunities for children to work with text and to support ('scaffold') their efforts. Through experimenting with written language – recognising some words, guessing others, and self-correcting when necessary – they begin to acquire basic reading skills without direct instruction. The teacher is there as a model and a resource, but also engages in much indirect and incidental teaching. This approach to literacy learning is one that is essentially child-centred and involves providing children with daily experiences in using reading and writing for real purposes, rather than engaging in exercises.

At classroom level, the implementation of whole-language approach usually embodies at least the following teaching strategies:

- reading good literature to students every day, and having 'real' literature available for students to read for themselves;
- providing time each day for shared reading;
- discussing and reflecting upon stories or other texts;
- encouraging silent reading;
- providing daily opportunities for children to read and write for real purposes;
- encouraging children to invent the spelling for words they do not know;
- adopting a conference-process approach to writing (drafting, sharing, editing and revising with feedback from teacher and peers);
- assisting children with any particular aspect of reading and writing at the time they require such guidance (the 'teachable moment');
- teaching specific skills always within the context of material being read or written;
- integrating language and literacy activities across all areas of the curriculum.

Pressley (1998) reviewed studies evaluating the effectiveness of the whole-language approach. He reached the conclusion that when whole-language practices are skilfully implemented they can:

- benefit children in the earliest stages of learning to read;
- increase children's awareness of the purposes and processes of reading and writing;
- build positive attitudes towards books and writing;
- help children develop strategies for interpreting text beyond the literal level (e.g. prediction, inference, critical reading, reflection);
- enrich a child's vocabulary and general knowledge;
- encourage risk-taking with invented spelling.

With these positive features in mind it is clear that the whole-language approach makes a major contribution to children's overall progress towards literacy. The question remains, however, whether whole-language practice is comprehensive and intensive enough to ensure that all children become knowledgeable and competent in every aspect of reading, writing and spelling. Whole language may not suit the learning characteristics of every student. It was remarked in Chapter 1 that teaching approaches lacking clear direction and structure might cause difficulties for some learners. It is also generally accepted that students with intellectual disability do not make effective progress if taught by immersion methods alone.

The study by Stahl and Miller (1989) suggests that while the whole-language approach produced encouraging results with the most able students, positive effects were much less evident in weaker students and in those students disadvantaged by low socioeconomic background. This finding is not surprising, as many studies have shown that readers with learning difficulties, or with sociocultural disadvantage, tend to need highly systematic, direct, and intensive instruction that matches their developmental level. Birsh (1999: xix) observes:

> Whole language instruction used in isolation has been found to be counterproductive with children with learning disabilities or children at risk of not learning to read, and has been found to produce fewer gains in word recognition and decoding skills than does instruction based on phonics.

It seems safe to assume that the best features of whole language create a *necessary but not sufficient* condition to ensure that all children become proficient readers.

The beginning-reading approaches described below encourage a combined application of skills-based and meaning-emphasis principles. Shared-book experience and language-experience approach are two approaches entirely compatible with modern theories of language acquisition and reading skill development. In both cases when used for remedial teaching purposes the approaches require a much greater degree of structuring than is necessary when applied to children without learning problems. Neither method precludes the teaching of word-attack skills. As explained later in the chapter, both approaches can complement the teaching strategy called 'guided reading'.

Shared-book experience

This approach owes much to the influence of the New Zealand educator Don Holdaway (1990) and has been developed further by other practitioners (e.g. Fisher and Medvic 2000). Shared-book approach has clear applications for young children in the first stages of learning to read, but the basic principles can also be applied to older children with learning difficulties if age-appropriate books are used. As a beginning-reading method the approach has proved equal or superior to other methods, and produces very positive attitudes towards reading, even in the slower children (Allington 2001). By their very nature, shared-book sessions are inclusive of all children in the group.

Shared-book experience aims to:

- develop children's enjoyment and interest in books and stories;
- develop concepts about books and print;
- focus on comprehension;
- build children's awareness of English language patterns (syntax);
- develop word-recognition skills;
- build phonic skills for decoding and spelling;
- provide opportunities for discussion, reflection and writing.

In shared-book approach children enjoy stories, poems, jingles and rhymes read to them by the teacher using a large-size book with enlarged print and colourful pictures. Sitting in a group close to the teacher all children can see the pages of the 'big book' easily. They can see the pictures and the words, and can follow the left-to-right direction of print as the teacher reads aloud. Holdaway says that the book should have the same visual impact from 10 feet away as a normal book would have in the hands of the child.

Children's attention is gained and maintained by the teacher's enjoyable and enthusiastic presentation of the story and discussion of the pictures. Familiarity with the language patterns in the story is developed and reinforced in a natural way. Stories that children may already know and love are useful in the early stages because they present an opportunity for the children to join in even if they cannot read the words.

The basic principles and procedures for implementing shared book include:

- *Before reading*

  1 read together the story title;
  2 refer to the cover picture or other pictorial material;
  3 stimulate discussion about the topic or the title;
  4 praise children's ideas.

- *During reading the teacher*

  5 reads the story aloud;
  6 maps the direction of print with finger or pointer;
  7 thinks aloud sometimes: 'I wonder if she is going to . . .'

8   pauses sometimes at predictable words to allow children to guess;
9   sometimes asks children 'What do you think will happen next?'

The first time the story is read, the teacher does not interrupt the reading with too many questions or teaching points. The main aim is to enjoy and understand the story.

- *After first reading*

    1   the children and teacher discuss the story;
    2   recall main information.

- *Second reading of the story the teacher*

    3   aims to develop word-recognition skills;
    4   covers certain words to encourage prediction from context (cloze procedure);
    5   increases children's phonic knowledge;
    6   encourages writing (spelling) of a few of the words.

- *Possible follow up*

    7   writing and drawing activities;
    8   word families;
    9   individual and partner reading of small books (same story);
    10 children can make up some questions about the story.

Shared-book experience embodies all the basic principles of effective teaching, particularly the elements of motivation, teacher demonstration, active student participation, feedback and successful practice. It also encourages cooperative learning and sharing of ideas between adult and child in a small group situation. The method can serve a valuable compensatory role for children with special needs who enter school lacking rich language and literacy experiences from the preschool years. The discussion of each story should not simply focus on low-level questions of fact and information, but rather should encourage children to make personal connections, think, feel, predict and extend ideas (Honig 2001). The study of the text should also facilitate vocabulary growth.

Language-experience approach

In both whole-class and remedial-group situations shared-book experience can operate in parallel with the individualised language-experience approach. Language-experience approach uses the child's own language to produce carefully controlled amounts of personalised reading material (Ruddell 2002). It could be described as a form of dictated-story approach. The principle of language-experience approach is summed up in the following statements:

- What I know about, I can talk about.
- What I say can be written down by someone.
- I can read what has been written.

Young children, or older children with literacy problems, are helped to write something that is relevant and personally meaningful to them. With assistance and practice they can read what they have written and can begin to store some of the words in long-term memory. From the language-experience recordings, and from activities conducted in parallel with the recordings, the children can also be taught important phonic knowledge and skills.

From the viewpoint of the failing reader the approach combines two major advantages: first, there is the possibility of utilising the child's own interests to generate material for reading and writing; and second, the teacher is able to work within the child's current level of language competence. This is of great value for children who are well below average in general language ability, due perhaps to restricted preschool language experience, hearing impairment or language disorder.

The work produced in the child's language-experience book (or language-experience wall chart) is usually relevant and motivating. Language-experience approach is considered to forge a clear connection between speech and print (Cramer 1998). The basic principles of the language-experience approach can also be used within intervention programmes for non-literate adults or those learning English as a second language (Rasinski and Padak 2000). The procedures for using language-experience approach in a remedial context are described in detail below. It is not necessary to follow such highly controlled steps when using language experience with normal learners in whole-class settings.

Step 1

The starting point for language experience with young children (or older children of limited ability) can be the labelling of some of the child's drawings.

'This is my cat, Moonbeam.'
'I can ride my BMX bike fast.'
'This is a photo of me and Wendy.'

The child and teacher together read the captions and review them regularly. At this stage the reading approach is holistic and attention is not drawn to individual letters or words. A little later, the written recordings can be cut into separate word cards and the child can be encouraged to build the sentences again using the word cards in the correct left-to-right sequence. The word cards can also be used separately to practise word recognition.

During this early stage of the programme the child can contribute a dictated sentence associated with an experience shared by the class – for example, a class excursion to the airport ('I saw a jumbo jet'). These sentences are added, along with others from the class, to the picture-map produced by the children as part of the follow-up to the excursion. Again, the recordings are not in any way analysed at the phonic level; they merely serve the purpose of establishing in the learner's mind the notion that 'What I say can be written down.'

Step 2

After a few weeks of this introductory work the child is ready to make his or her first book. A topic is carefully selected related to the child's personal interests, e.g. motorcycle speedway. The teacher produces some visual material that will provide the illustration for the first page, perhaps a picture of the child's favourite speedway rider from a magazine. Teacher and child talk together about the rider and from the discussion they agree upon one brief statement that can be written under the picture: 'This is Chris Copley.' The teacher prints the agreed statement for the child, who then copies it carefully under the teacher's version. If the child cannot copy due to perceptual-motor problems, he or she can trace over the words with a coloured pencil or wax crayon. Both teacher and child then read the statement together once or twice and the child is left to paste the picture carefully into the book. With older children they can be encouraged to type or word-process the same sentence on a sheet of paper and paste that into the book. When the student sees the same sentence in different styles and fonts it is an aid to generalisation from handwritten to printed form of the same words.

Step 3

Next day the child is presented with the same statement written on a strip of card: 'This is Chris Copley.' Without reference to the book the child is encouraged to read the words. He or she may have forgotten the material so some brief revision may be needed. The child then cuts the strip of card into separate word cards. These are placed at random on the desk and the child has to arrange them in correct left-to-right sequence. If the child cannot do this he or she must spend time matching the word cards against the original version in the book until the sequencing task can be performed correctly. At this point the teacher picks up one of the cards – perhaps the word 'is' – and using it as a small flashcard asks the child to pronounce the word. This procedure is continued until the child can recognise each word out of context as well as in context. The word cards are then placed in an envelope stapled in the back cover of the book, ready to be revised the following day.

Step 4

Over the next week the child continues to produce a page of his or her book with much guidance and encouragement from an adult. Regular revision of the previous day's words ensures repetition and overlearning to the point of mastery. The teacher's control over what is written will ensure that not too much is added to the book each day. If the child is allowed to dictate too much material this will result in failure to learn and loss of satisfaction.

Step 5

Once important sight words have been mastered these can be checked off or coloured in on a vocabulary list in the front cover of the child's book. Such charting of progress within the book gives the child visual evidence of progress, and also indicates to the teacher what has been covered so far and what still needs to be taught. If certain words seem to present particular problems for the child, games and activities can be introduced to repeat and overlearn these words (e.g. word bingo). Gradually the amount written can be increased, and after some months the child will need less and less direct help in constructing sentences. The use of language-experience approach in this way is highly structured and is based on mastery principles at each step. The approach may sound slow and tedious but it does result in progress in even the most resistant cases of reading failure. The growth in word recognition skills is cumulative.

Step 6

At some appropriate stage in the programme the teacher will help the child expand his or her word-attack skills. For example, perhaps the child has used the word 'crash' in writing about the speedway interest. In a separate booklet the teacher can help the child to learn the value of the blend /cr/ by collecting other /cr/ words (crab, crook, cross, cry, etc.). Similarly he or she can experiment with the unit /ash/ from the word 'crash' by building the appropriate word family (b-ash, d-ash, c-ash, r-ash, fl-ash, tr-ash, etc.). This incidental word study linked with meaningful material from the child's own book is important but will be inadequate on its own for developing functional decoding skills. It will be necessary to teach word-attack and spelling skills explicitly for certain students (see Chapter 9).

Step 7

Once a child has made a positive start using this language-experience approach he or she can be introduced to a carefully selected real book. It is wise to prepare the way for this transition by including in the child's language-experience book some of the new words that will be met in the real book.

Stauffer's (1980) text, *The Language-experience Approach to the Teaching of Reading*, remains one of the best sources of detailed information on this method. More recent summaries can be found in Rubin (2000) and Tompkins (2002).

Guided reading

In the literature on reading methodology 'guided reading' is most often presented as an approach to use with children after third or fourth year of schooling. It is described as an excellent way to develop a strategic, reflective and critical approach in children who are beyond the beginner stage. Most of the suggestions for providing guidance are, however, merely extensions of what should have been occurring from an early age during shared-book experience and in discussions stemming from students' language-experience material.

Fountas and Pinnell (1996: 2) describe guided reading as '. . . a context in which a teacher supports each reader's development of effective strategies for processing novel texts at increasingly challenging levels of difficulty'. For this reason guided reading is considered an essential part of any balanced approach to literacy. It addresses the need to help students become efficient in comprehending text of various levels of complexity. The guidance provided for the students may focus at times on specific sub-skills such as word identification and decoding, but its main emphasis is the development of a strategic approach to comprehension. The guided reading sessions are usually conducted by the teacher, but with heavy emphasis placed on students' active participation through discussion, cooperative learning, and sharing of ideas.

There are three main stages at which guidance from the teacher is provided: *before* reading the text, *during* the reading, and *after* reading the chosen text.

- *Before reading*: Guidance before reading prepares the reader to enter the text with some clear purpose and a plan of action in mind. At the 'before reading' stage the teacher may, for example, focus children's attention on their prior knowledge related to the topic, encourage them to generate questions or make predictions about information to be presented in the text, remind them of effective ways of reading the material, alert them to look out for certain points, and pre-teach some difficult vocabulary to be encountered later in the text.

- *During reading*: The guidance during reading may encourage the student to generate questions, look for cause–effect relationships, compare and contrast information, react critically, check for understanding and highlight main ideas.
- *After reading the text*: The guidance provided by the teacher may help the children summarise and retell, check for understanding and recall, and encourage critical reflection and evaluation.

The processes involved in guided reading sessions, while primarily serving a teaching function, also allow the teacher to observe and assess the students' comprehension strategies. This is a very important diagnostic function, enabling a teacher to adapt reading guidance to match students' specific needs.

One of the best sources for additional information on guided reading is the text by Fountas and Pinnell (1996). Yopp and Yopp (2001) describe a broad range of valuable ideas and activities to use within the pre-reading, during reading, and post-reading phases of literature-based lessons; their book is highly recommended. The text by Vacca, Vacca and Gove (2000) contains other useful ideas under the general heading 'Guiding interactions between reader and text'.

A focus on comprehension

Reading comprehension is not something that comes *after* learning the mechanics of reading; reading for meaning must be the focus of any literacy programme from the very beginning. When teachers read stories to children they can discuss the material and encourage children to think about and evaluate the ideas in the story. In guided reading activities, attention should be devoted to seeking and clarifying meaning, explaining, interpreting, and summarising.

Reading comprehension has been described as 'a complex intellectual process involving a number of abilities' (Rubin 2000: 171). Understanding text involves word identification skills, activating prior knowledge, and the application of cognitive strategies. Children who are good comprehenders use a variety of cognitive process as they read. For example, they may visualise as they read narrative material; they may pose questions to themselves; they reflect upon the relevance of what they are reading; they may challenge the accuracy of stated facts; and they monitor their own level of understanding.

As long ago as 1969 Nila Banton Smith identified four levels of comprehension, each level containing a cluster of component skills and each dependent upon competence at the previous level. The following summary is adapted from Smith's model.

- *Literal comprehension*: This is the most basic level of understanding, involving a grasp of the factual information presented in the text. Literal comprehension is dependent upon sub-skills such as understanding word meanings, recognition of main idea, grasp of sequence and order of detail or events. This level depends greatly upon the learner's own previous knowledge and experience. Even literal comprehension and recall will be difficult if concepts being presented are completely new to the reader.

- *Inferential*: This level of comprehension involves the reader in going beyond what is actually presented in the text, and 'reading between the lines' to predict and draw tentative conclusions. Sub-skills at this level include anticipating outcomes, making generalisations, reasoning cause-and-effect when these are not stated, and discovering real or possible relationships. Some reading experts prefer to call this *interpretive level*, believing that the skills involved cover more than prediction and inference.

- *Critical reading*: This level of comprehension involves judgements of the quality, value, accuracy and truthfulness of what is read, or detecting bias or overstatement. Critical reading requires a personal (and sometimes emotional) response from the reader.

- *Creative reading*: At this level the reader goes beyond the message of the text to generate new ideas or develop new insights related to the theme or topic, but not explicit in the text.

It is argued that in many classrooms comprehension activities rarely demand responses beyond the literal level (recall of facts). This level is important since it is basic to the other three levels, but a curriculum that sets out to develop comprehension skills in children should include questions that demand thinking at the interpretive, critical and creative levels. For example, following a short story about the crash of a passenger aircraft these questions might be posed:

- How many passengers escaped the crash? (literal)
- Why did failure of cabin pressure lead to the crash? (inferential)
- From the way he behaved before the crash what kind of man do you think the pilot was, and could his judgement be trusted? (interpretive/ inferential)
- A section of the extract contains information from eyewitness accounts summarised in a newspaper report. Why might this information not be entirely trustworthy? (critical)
- Many air crashes similar to this one occur each year. How might flight be made a safer method of transport? (creative)

Difficulties in comprehension

Sometimes comprehension difficulties stem from the student's limited vocabulary knowledge or lack of fluency (Tompkins 2002). If a student has difficulties in understanding what is read, it is worth considering whether there is a serious mismatch between the student's own vocabulary and the words used in the text. A student may be able to read a word correctly on the page but not know its meaning. In this situation there is a need to devote more time to word study and vocabulary building when comprehension activities are used in classroom. There is also a need sometimes to pre-teach difficult vocabulary before the text is read.

Obviously the readability level of the text is a major factor influencing whether or not material can be read easily with understanding – difficult text, in terms of concepts, vocabulary, sentence complexity and length, is not easy for any reader to process. Difficult text leads to high error rate, thus impairing comprehension and leading to frustration and loss of motivation. Matching the readability level of books to students' current reading ability level can do much to increase students' comprehension.

There appears to be an optimum rate of fluency in reading that allows for accurate processing of information. Automaticity in reading, based mainly on smooth and effortless word identification and contextual cueing, allows the reader to use all available cognitive capacity to focus on meaning (Carver 2000). Children who read very slowly – or much too fast – often comprehend poorly. Slow word-by-word reading makes it difficult for the reader to retain information in working memory long enough for meaning to be maintained. Slow reading also tends to restrict cognitive capacity to the low-level processing of letters and words, rather than allowing attention to higher-order ideas and concepts within the text. Fast reading may result in important detail being overlooked. Sometimes attention to rate of reading needs to be a specific focus in children's intervention programmes (Allington 2001).

Some children have difficulty recalling information after reading. Recall is dependent partly upon such factors as vividness and relevance of the information in the text; but it is also dependent upon a student giving adequate focused attention to the reading task and knowing that it is important to remember details. Recall is best when readers connect passage content to their own previous knowledge and experience, and when they rehearse key points from the text. These factors may provide clues to help identify why a particular child is having problems in remembering what he or she has read.

Improving comprehension

The reading comprehension skills of all children can be increased when teachers spend time modelling and demonstrating effective strategies for processing text. Such strategies must encompass:

- Previewing the material before it is read to gain an overview.
- Locating the main idea in a paragraph.
- Generating questions about the material by thinking aloud.
- Predicting what will happen, or suggesting possible cause-and-effect.
- Summarising or paraphrasing the main content.

A successful programme for the development of comprehension should include at least these components:

- Large amounts of time devoted to reading.
- Teacher-directed instruction in comprehension strategies.
- Using text as one source from which to obtain new information.
- Frequent occasions when students can talk with the teacher and with one another about their response to a particular text.

Strategy training to develop effective reading comprehension is one of the most promising areas of instructional intervention. Research has indicated that reading comprehension can be improved if students are taught to use effective text-processing strategies (Pressley 1999). In particular, teaching students how to use step-by-step plans of action when interacting with text has produced impressive results in various meta-analyses of training studies (e.g. Swanson 2000a). Strategies such as self-questioning, self-monitoring, rehearsing information, constructing story maps or graphic organisers, and creating mnemonics to assist recall, have all proved valuable.

One example of a simple reading comprehension strategy is *PQRS*, where each letter in the mnemonic signifies a step in the strategy. The four steps are:

P = Preview

First scan the chapter or paragraph, attending to headings, subheadings, diagrams and illustrations. Gain a very general impression of what the text is likely to cover. Ask yourself, 'What do I know already about this subject?'

Q = Question

Next generate some questions in your mind: What do I expect to find out from reading this material? For example, will it tell me how to make the object? Will it tell me how to use it? Will I need to read the text very carefully or can I skip this part?

R = Read

Then read the passage or chapter carefully for information. Read it again if necessary. Do I understand what I am reading? What does this word mean?

Do I need to read this section again? Are my questions answered? What else did I learn?

S = Summarise

Finally, identify the main ideas and state briefly in your own words the key points in the text.

The teacher models the application of the PQRS approach several times using different texts, demonstrating how to focus on important points in the chapter or article, how to check one's own understanding, how to back-track or scan ahead to gain contextual cues, and how to select the key points to summarise. This modelling helps students appreciate the value of having a plan of action for gaining meaning from text, and the value of self-questioning and self-monitoring while reading. The students are helped to practise and apply the same approach with corrective feedback from the teacher. To aid generalisation it is important to use different types of reading material used for different purposes and to remind students frequently to apply the strategy when reading texts in different curriculum areas.

Reading and study-skill strategies are best taught through dialogue between teacher and students working together to extract meaning from the text. Dialogue allows students and teachers to share their thoughts about the process of learning and to learn from the successful strategies used by others. Dialogue also serves a diagnostic purpose by allowing a teacher to appraise the students' existing strategies used for comprehending and summarising texts.

Peers can facilitate each other's learning of reading strategies in small groups. An approach known as *reciprocal teaching* has proved extremely useful in a group situation to facilitate dialogue and to teach specific cognitive strategies (Carter 2001; Rosenshine and Meister 1994). In this approach teachers and students work together, sharing and elaborating ideas, generating questions that may be answered from a specific text, predicting answers, checking for meaning, and finally collaborating on a summary. The teacher's role initially is to demonstrate effective ways of processing the text, to ask relevant questions, and to instruct the students in strategic reading; the long-term aim is to have students master these strategies for their own independent use across a variety of contexts.

The following general principles may also help to facilitate comprehension skill development for all students, including those with learning difficulties.

- Ensure that the reading material presented is interesting to the student and at an appropriate readability level.
- Always make sure students are aware of the goals in reading a particular text.

- Apply comprehension strategy training to real texts, read for genuine purposes; don't rely on contrived comprehension exercises for strategy training.
- Prepare students for entry into a new text. Ask, What might we find in this chapter? What do the illustrations tell us? What does this word mean? Let's read the subheadings before we begin.
- Read comprehension questions *before* the story or passage is read so that students enter the material knowing what to look for in terms of key information.
- After reading the text, encourage students to set comprehension questions for each other; then use these questions to discuss what is meant by literal level information, critical reading, inferring, predicting. This type of activity lends itself to the reciprocal teaching format described above.
- Devote time regularly to discussing how a particular sample of text can be summarised. Making a summary is an excellent way of ensuring that students have identified main ideas.
- Make frequent use of graphic organisers or story maps as advance organisers, or to summarise the relationships among key points after reading the text.
- Use newspapers and magazine articles sometimes as the basis for classroom discussion and comprehension activities. Highlighter pens can be used to focus upon key ideas, important terms, or facts to remember.
- In general, aim to *teach* comprehension skills and strategies, rather than simply *testing* comprehension.

Additional information on improving reading comprehension in students with learning difficulties can be found in Barr *et al.* (2002), Dymock and Nicholson (1999) and Strickland, Ganske and Monroe (2002).

Writing a summary

Students with learning difficulties often have problems when required to write a summary of something they have just read. Specific help is needed in this area and one or more of the following procedures can be helpful to such students.

- The teacher provides a set of 'true/false' statements based on the text just read. The statements are presented on the sheet in random order. The student must read each statement and place a tick against those that are true. The student then decides the most logical sequence in which to arrange the true statements. When copied into the student's exercise book these statements provide a brief summary of the text.
- The teacher provides some sentence 'starters' in a sequence that will provide a framework for the summary. For example: 'The first thing most

travellers notice when they arrive at the airport is . . .'; 'When they travel by taxi to the city they notice . . .'. The student completes the unfinished sentences and in doing so writes the summary.

- The teacher provides a summary with key words or phrases omitted (cloze passage). The words may be presented below the passage in random order, or clues may be given in terms of initial letters of word required, or dashes to represent each letter of the word. The student completes the passage by supplying the missing words.
- Simple multiple-choice questions can be presented. The questions may deal with the main ideas from the text and with supporting detail. By selecting appropriate responses and writing these down the student creates a brief summary.

It is important now to consider what else is necessary for students who are failing to learn to read despite good quality teaching and adequate opportunities to learn. In the following chapters more specific advice is provided on teaching and assessing aspects of reading, writing and spelling for students with learning difficulties.

Further reading

Allington, R.L. (2001) *What Really Matters for Struggling Reader?* New York: Longman.

Barr, R., Blachowicz, C., Katz, C. and Kaufman, B. (2002) *Reading Diagnosis for Teachers* (4th edn), Boston, MA: Allyn and Bacon.

Crawley, S.J. and Merritt, K. (2000) *Remediating Reading Difficulties* (3rd edn), New York: McGraw Hill.

Heald-Taylor, G. (2001) *The Beginning Reading Handbook*, Portsmouth, NH: Heinemann.

Heilman, A.W. (2002) *Phonics in Proper Perspective* (9th edn), Upper Saddle River, NJ: Merrill.

Honig, B. (2001) *Teaching Our Children to Read* (2nd edn), Thousand Oaks, CA: Corwin Press.

Jorgensen, K. (2001) *The Whole Story*, Portsmouth, NH: Heinemann.

Opitz, M.F. and Ford, M.P. (2001) *Reaching Readers: Flexible and Innovative Strategies for Guided Reading*, Portsmouth, NH: Heinemann.

Ruddell, R.B. (2002) *Teaching Children to Read and Write* (3rd edn), Boston, MA: Allyn and Bacon.

Savage, J.F. (2001) *Sound It Out: Phonics in a Balanced Reading Program*, New York: McGraw Hill.

Serafini, F. (2001) *The Reading Workshop*, Portsmouth, NH: Heinemann.

Chapter 8

Planning effective intervention for literacy problems

> Since you know through observation and testing your students' reading strengths and weaknesses, you work toward providing them with successful experiences to develop their independence and confidence in reading.
>
> (Crawley and Merritt 2000: ix)

The previous chapter described some effective methods for teaching basic reading skills to a wide ability range. In this chapter the focus shifts to students who despite exposure to good-quality teaching are still exhibiting difficulty in becoming proficient readers.

The needs of students with learning difficulties

The child who is experiencing difficulty learning to read needs special consideration in his or her literacy programme. In general these students benefit from a more direct teaching approach, tailored to their current ability levels and coupled with strategies designed to restore lost confidence and motivation. Programmes that focus on teaching word building and phonic skills, as well as reading for meaning, are considered to have most value for children with learning difficulties (e.g. Fawcett *et al.* 2001).

A student with reading difficulties requires:

- an enthusiastic teacher who can model effective reading strategies;
- a teacher who can provide effective guidance and support;
- abundant opportunity to read for pleasure and for information;
- successful practice, often using material that has become familiar to the student;
- a carefully graded program, with supplementary materials used for additional practice alongside the mainstream curriculum;
- for beginners, more time spent on early reading activities (phonemic-awareness training, flashcards, word-to-picture matching, sentence building, copying, writing);

- more time spent in overlearning and reviewing new material at each stage;
- systematic teaching of phonic knowledge and word-attack skills;
- daily expressive writing activities with guidance and feedback;
- handwriting skills taught alongside reading and writing activities;
- improved self-esteem through counselling, praise, encouragement, increased success, and recognition of personal progress.

In order to plan instruction to meet these needs it is necessary to tailor the programme to match the student's current strengths and weaknesses. It is therefore important to find out as much as possible about the student's existing attitude, knowledge, skills and strategies.

Planning intervention from assessment data

The starting point for any literacy intervention programme should be the results from an assessment of the child's current abilities, indicating the stage of reading development he or she has reached. The assessment need not involve the use of detailed or complicated tests, nor should it be a lengthy procedure. The teacher is basically seeking answers to the following five key questions:

- What can the student already do without help?
- What skills and strategies has the child developed?
- What can the child do if given a little prompting and guidance?
- What gaps exist in the child's previous learning?
- What does the child need to be taught next in order to make good progress?

Figure 1 summarises the key steps involved in implementing an informal assessment procedure leading to programme planning for an individual learner. The outcome of such a procedure may be the writing of an individual education plan (IEP); or the data may simply guide the teacher's daily planning without the need for an IEP. The procedure is described here in relation to reading difficulties, but the same steps, and the same five key questions, are applicable to informal assessment and planning for individual support in any area of the curriculum.

The nine stages in Figure 1 on p. 119 may be interpreted thus:

Stage 1 involves naturalistic observation of the student at work, together with possible use of relevant checklists or tests for particular skills (sight vocabulary, phonic knowledge, spelling). The most useful procedure is to listen to the student read from an appropriate text, noting the strategies used and the errors made. A running record of errors, self-corrections,

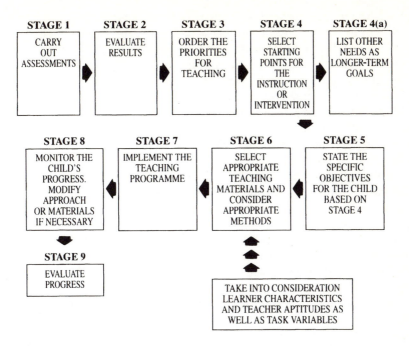

Figure 1 Assessment and planning model

and requests for help can be made if required. Other aspects of reading performance are also informally appraised such as motivation, interest, confidence, fluency, and dependency on adult assistance.

Stage 2 involves analysing the information obtained from Stage 1 and answering the first three diagnostic questions referred to above.

Stage 3 is the identification of the most serious gaps evident in the student's prior learning. Teaching to fill these gaps needs to be given high priority in any remedial intervention.

Stage 4 requires the teacher to decide the short-term goals for the intervention, based on data analysed at Stages 2 and 3. What will be the starting points for intervention? Where does the student require most help? Immediate goals would be written in the IEP. Longer-term goals would be recorded for attention at a later date.

Stage 5 involves the writing of some specific performance objectives to match the general aims and to permit accurate assessment of learning. The advantage of being precise with objectives is that assessment of learning can be more accurate and all persons involved in the child's programme are aware of exactly what is to be achieved.

Stage 6 requires the selection of appropriate teaching resources (books, kits, games, computer software, other print materials) to assist in working towards the stated objectives. Careful consideration needs to be given to the most appropriate method of working with this student, based on knowledge of his or her learning characteristics (motivation, interests, concentration span). A decision must be made concerning how the programme will be delivered (e.g. by the teacher; by classroom assistant; through peer tutoring; parent tutoring; computer-assisted learning).

Stage 7 involves implementation of the teaching programme with sufficient intensity and duration to have some impact on the student's learning. The programme should be operated within the whole-class setting if possible, rather than in isolation; and it should be geared as closely as possible to the mainstream curriculum. It may be necessary at times to provide individual or small-group tuition in a withdrawal situation, particularly in the case of students with learning disabilities. A combination of in-class and withdrawal may be required.

Stage 8 involves regular and frequent assessment of the student's responses to the programme while it is in operation. It is important to monitor the effectiveness of the teaching methods and materials. This is achieved through ongoing (formative) evaluation of the student's performance.

Stage 9 involves assessing how much improvement has occurred in the student's motivation, knowledge, skills, strategies and confidence on completion of the programme. This summative evaluation is carried out at the end of the teaching block and is linked directly with the stated objectives generated at Stage 5. If appropriate, the programme continues with new objectives and changes to materials.

General principles of assessment

Learning difficulties are rarely due only to factors within the student. Assessment must also involve consideration of the total situation in which the learner operates. It is important to consider the curriculum (level of difficulty, relevance to the child's age and interests). It is also necessary to consider the teaching methods being used, the physical environment in which the child is being taught, and the quality of the relationship between the child, the teacher (or tutor) and the peer group. Learning difficulty usually stems from a complex interaction among all these variables, and effective intervention may require the teacher to manipulate any or all of these variables. Brophy (2001: 2) states that '. . . good teaching will vary with the situation . . . the relevance of particular methods and activities will vary with the nature of the students, the instructional goals, and the curricular activities'.

When working with and assessing a student it is important to observe his or her manner of approach to the tasks as well as the responses being given. For example, has the child given a particular answer after careful thought or was it an impulsive guess? Is the child hesitant because he or she is wary of the adult and unwilling to take a risk? Does he or she show genuine interest in the tasks and activities you are presenting? Does he or she self-correct if an error is made?

Diagnostic assessment is referred to as either formal or informal. The 'formal' diagnosis usually implies that published tests (reading attainment tests or reading diagnostic tests) are used to obtain specific information about a learner's current skills or knowledge in certain selected areas, such as comprehension, word recognition, phonic knowledge and spelling. Sometimes particular sub-skills are assessed, such as phonemic awareness, visual discrimination or short-term auditory memory. Formal assessment may be carried out for a whole class simultaneously, for example, by the use of pencil-and-paper group testing. At other times formal assessment involves the careful and detailed testing of one child, using standardised or criterion referenced tests. Formal assessment can be useful in indicating quickly where current achievement stops and new learning needs begin. The results from formal assessment usually need to be supplemented with information from informal testing, such as observation, classroom records, discussions with parents.

Informal diagnosis involves procedures such as direct observation of learners in action and an examination of what they produce during a lesson. Informal assessment in reading includes, for example, listening to a child read aloud from a class book and detecting the presence or absence of particular strategies for word attack, use of context, prediction, and comprehension. General fluency and expression can also be appraised. The use of teacher-made informal reading inventories may be of value. The inventory comprises sample paragraphs, graded from very easy to more complex, taken from books available in the classroom. A child's level of success on the inventory will provide a good indication of the readability level of books he or she can cope with independently. For independent reading the passage should be read with 95 per cent accuracy. For material to be used within an instructional programme the success rate should be at least 90 per cent (Hoffman and Duffy 2001). Material with an error rate of 15 per cent or more is considered to be too difficult (frustration level). Performance on the reading inventory will also indicate the child's general approach (e.g. slow but accurate; hasty and careless; hesitant and unwilling to guess).

In the following sections additional suggestions are made for assessing students who are at various levels of reading proficiency. The lists are not prescriptive; it is not expected that a teacher would need to find answers to all the questions. Relevant items can be selected according to the student's characteristics.

Assessing a non-reader

If an individual, regardless of age or degree of disability, appears to be a non-reader it is worth considering some of the following issues:

- Can the student concentrate on a learning task and attend to the teacher for long enough to benefit from instruction; or is he or she too distractible or hyperactive?
- Is the student capable of carrying out visual discrimination and matching letters and words?
- Can the student identify speech sounds (phonemes) at the beginning, middle, and ends of spoken words (see also auditory discrimination below)?
- Has the student developed 'word concept' – an understanding that words in print are units separated by spaces?
- Does the student have concepts of 'a sound' and 'a letter'?
- Does the student have an awareness of the left-to-right direction in a printed sentence?
- Does the student recognise any words by sight (e.g. own name; environmental signs)?
- Can the student complete picture-to-word matching activities correctly after a brief period of instruction?
- Can the student succeed in a simple learning task involving sight recognition of three words taught from flashcards without picture clues (e.g. 'my', 'key' and 'book')?
- Does the student know the names or sounds associated with any letters?

If the student appears to have very poor phonic knowledge, it is necessary to check in more detail his or her level of phonological awareness. In particular consider:

Auditory discrimination

Can the child discriminate between similar but not identical words when these are presented orally in word-pairs (e.g. mouse–mouth; cat–cap; money–monkey)? Teachers can devise their own word lists for this purpose.

Auditory analysis

Can the child analyse and segment familiar words into their component sounds or syllables? This is a listening activity, not a reading test. If the child hears the word 'remember' can he or she break this into the units re-mem-ber? It may be necessary to give some practice first so that the child understands what is required.

Sound blending

Can the child blend or synthesise sounds in order to pronounce a given word (e.g. cr-isp, st-o-p, m-i-l-k)? Again, this is a listening activity, not a reading test. The child does not see the word in print. The following simple test is useful for assessment of this blending skill:

Say: 'I am going to say some words very slowly so that you can hear each sound. I want you to tell me what the word is. If I say "i-n" you say "in". If I say "d-o-g" you say . . .?' Sound the phonemes at the rate of about one each second. Discontinue after five consecutive failures.

i-f	g-o-t	sh-o-p	c-r-u-s-t
a-t	m-e-n	s-t-e-p	b-l-a-ck
u-p	b-e-d	l-o-s-t	f-l-a-sh
o-n	c-a-t	j-u-m-p	c-l-o-ck
a-m	d-i-g	t-r-u-ck	s-p-i-ll

Auditory discrimination, auditory analysis (segmentation) and phoneme blending are regarded as important aspects of a phonological awareness. It is claimed that phonological knowledge is essential for beginning readers if they are to learn the alphabetic principle easily, and that specific training in skills such as rhyming, alliteration, segmentation, blending, and isolation of sounds within words can result in improvement in early reading and spelling (Blachman *et al.* 2000; Torgesen and Mathes 2000).

Assessment for a student above beginner level

For the child who is not a non-reader and has a few functional skills the following areas may yield useful information to answer the diagnostic questions:

Basic sight vocabulary

What can the child already do in terms of recognising the most commonly occurring words in print? Many vocabulary lists exist for the assessment of sight vocabulary (e.g. Gunning, 2001). See also Chapter 9.

Phonic knowledge

The student's knowledge of letter-to-sound correspondences can be checked, either using a test sheet or by presenting each phonic unit on a separate card. Phonic knowledge can also be checked by dictating phonemes to the student and requiring the student to write the appropriate letter or letters to represent that sound. Single letters, digraphs and blends should be checked. Examples are provided in Chapter 9.

Word-attack skills

When reading aloud does the child attempt to sound out and build an unfamiliar word without being instructed to do so? If not, can the child do this when he or she is encouraged to try? Has the child developed any phonic skills? In particular, does the child know all the common single-letter sounds, digraphs, blends, prefixes and suffixes? Can the child divide a phonetically regular word into component syllables?

Miscues and use of context

When the child is reading aloud from age-appropriate material, what errors are made? Do the incorrect words conform to the meaning of the sentence or are they totally out of keeping with the message? Does the child make any use of cues such as initial letter sound? Does the child tend to self-correct when errors are made in order to restore meaning?

Comprehension

Informal questions can be asked after a student has read a passage silently or aloud. The questions should not be restricted to the factual level (literal comprehension) but should also probe for understanding at the higher levels of inference and critical interpretation: 'Why did the man in the story act in that way? When the lady suggested they look for the goods in another shop was she being helpful or rude? What do you think they should do next?'

Exercises using *cloze procedure* are useful in both testing and developing comprehension and contextual cueing. A passage of some 100 to 150 words is selected and approximately every fifth or sixth word is deleted leaving a gap. Can the child read the passage and provide a word in each case that conforms to the meaning of the passage and the grammatical structure of the sentence? Cloze materials used for teaching can be drawn from any subject area; and cloze exercises can be attempted by individuals or by groups of students (Eells 2000). An example of cloze is provided in Chapter 9.

A useful instrument for evaluating reading rate, accuracy and comprehension is the *Neale Analysis of Reading Ability* (1999). The test also allows for appraisal of the student's auditory skills in discrimination, blending and simple spelling. An analysis sheet is provided to facilitate the recording and classification of errors.

Assessing the student who has reached a reading plateau

Some children appear to reach a temporary plateau in reading development at or about a reading age of 8 to 9 years. Many of the assessment techniques covered in the previous section may help to uncover the possible areas of difficulty in these children. The following procedures are also helpful at this level.

Error analysis

It is with children who have reached a reading plateau that error analysis can be extremely valuable in pinpointing specific gaps in the child's current reading skills. Possibly the child has not yet mastered certain letter clusters as phonic units, and will either make random guesses at unfamiliar words or will refuse to attempt words containing these phonic units. The implication is that students who appear to have reached a temporary plateau may need to be taught to identify and use larger orthographic units for decoding, rather than single letters. For details of basic phonic units see Chapter 9. They may also need additional practice to build up a more extensive sight vocabulary. Inefficient phonic skills can result in a failure to add new words to sight vocabulary because of difficulty in decoding the words when first encountered. Poor progress can also be due to lack of regular reading practice.

When employing error analysis it is usual to listen to the student read aloud on several different occasions, using material that is reasonably challenging but not at frustration level. The performance can be recorded on audiotape for later analysis. Errors can be coded on a running record sheet, and classified as: self-correction (SC); appeal for help (A); teacher intervention (TTA if the child is told to 'try that again'; or T for 'told' if the word is supplied by the teacher); substitutions (S – the substituted word is written above the text word); omissions (line drawn above the word omitted); repetition (underline word each time the child repeats it). Attempts at decoding a word should also be recorded in terms of phonemes and syllables. The procedure also allows for quantitative evaluations to be made leading to the calculation of error rate, self-correction rate and dependency rate. These measures can be used to compare a student's performance before and after an intervention programme. Useful information on the use of running records can be found in Barr *et al.* (2002) and Mariotti and Homan (2001).

Affective factors

With a student who has reached a plateau it is vitally important to consider affective as well as cognitive factors. For example, has the student developed a negative couldn't-care-less attitude towards reading, avoiding the task whenever possible? Does the student experience any enjoyment in reading? Is the material in the book in keeping with the student's real interests? Is the working relationship between the student and the teacher (or tutor) a positive one? Does the student respond positively to extrinsic motivation (rewards)? Where difficulties are detected in these areas it is important to attempt to bring about change if possible. Merely concentrating on the skill aspect of reading will do little to modify the student's attitude or feeling of self-efficacy.

Additional factors to consider when students are not successful

Readability of the text

For the student who has reached a temporary plateau in reading it is important to consider the difficulty level of the material the child is attempting to read. Has he or she selected books that are at frustration level? Reading skills will not advance if the child is constantly faced with text that is too difficult, and lack of success can reduce motivation and confidence. Readability is influenced by much more than the number of difficult words. The ease with which a text is read is also related to the reader's familiarity with the topic, the complexity of the syntax used, sentence length, and even the size of the print and format of the pages. The most useful index of readability is a student's actual performance on the text. The simplest check for matching book to student is to apply the 'five finger test'. Select a passage of approximately 100 words from the book and ask the child to read aloud. Each time an error is made the teacher folds one finger into the palm of the hand. If the teacher runs out of fingers before the student reaches the end of the passage, the material is too difficult for independent reading (the error rate more than 5 per cent).

Selecting appropriate reading material

When selecting texts for students to read teachers should consider the following points:

- Is the topic within the experience of the students?
- Is it meaningful and relevant to the age and interest level of the students?
- Is the book itself attractive and appealing?
- Is the language used in the text natural and easy to predict?
- Are there many unfamiliar words?
- Are the sentences complex?
- Are there many useful contextual and pictorial clues?
- Will this type of text expand the student's experience of different genres?

Information collected from procedures described above can help a teacher select appropriate teaching strategies and materials to meet students' specific needs. Some aspects of the Literacy Hour represent application of effective teaching strategies. Literacy Hour enables teachers to make optimum use of available time to increase children's reading skills through intensive daily guidance and practice (Berger and Morris 2001). The basic principles of effective teaching are also embedded within early intervention programmes, such as Reading Recovery and Success for All. All intervention programmes are based on an underlying belief that reading failure is preventable for nearly all children (Slavin and Madden 2001).

Reading Recovery

Reading Recovery is an early intervention programme first developed in New Zealand (Clay 1985, 1993) and now used in many other parts of the world. Children identified as having reading difficulties after one year in school are placed in the programme and receive daily intensive individual tuition. They remain in the programme for approximately fifteen weeks, or until they have reached the average reading level of their class. The aim of Reading Recovery is to reduce substantially the number of children with on-going literacy problems. This is achieved through individually tailored instruction based on a combination of whole language and skills-based teaching principles.

Mainstream primary school teachers in New Zealand are trained mainly to use a whole language approach to reading, with reduced emphasis on teaching phonics in the mainstream classroom. It is pertinent to note that under this system up to 25 per cent of children have to enter Reading Recovery programmes (Tunmer *et al.* 2002). The 'successful' 75 per cent presumably did manage to acquire phonic skills and word identification for themselves – but a 25 per cent failure rate supports the view that a significant minority of children do not discover phonic principles without direct teaching.

Evidence has accumulated to indicate that Reading Recovery as an early intervention can be effective in raising young children's reading achievement and confidence (e.g. Slavin and Madden 2001). It is claimed that the programme can be so effective that only 1 per cent of children attending the individualised sessions require further, long-term assistance with reading and writing (Clay 1990). This 1 per cent may represent the students with specific learning disabilities. It should be noted, however, that some observers question this reported success rate and believe that gains made in the programme are not always maintained over time. Elbaum *et al.* (2000) indicate that up to 30 per cent of children enrolled in the intervention do not complete the programme and do not therefore improve. It has been observed that skills and motivation acquired in the Reading Recovery programme do not necessarily spill over into better classroom performance, possibly because the reading materials provided in the regular setting are not carefully matched to the child's ability level (Wheldall, Center and Freeman 1993). Other researchers have suggested that often Reading Recovery does not manage to raise a child's attainment level to the class average, although some improvements are made.

Despite the criticisms, Smith-Burke (2001: 229) in a review of research on the effects Reading Recovery concludes:

> A common pattern in several studies using both Reading Recovery and standardized measures is that Reading Recovery students who have successfully completed the program are just within the average band in second grade, but move to within the average band in third and fourth grades, continuing to progress and maintain their gains.

A typical Reading Recovery lesson includes seven activities:

- rereading of familiar books;
- independent reading of a book introduced the previous day;
- letter-identification activities with plastic letters;
- writing of a dictated or prepared story;
- sentence building and reconstruction from the story;
- introduction of a new book;
- guided reading of the new book.

The texts selected are designed to give the child a high success rate. Frequent rereading of the familiar stories boosts confidence and fluency. Optimum use is made of the available time and students are kept fully on-task. Teachers keep running records of children's oral reading performance and use these to target accurately the knowledge or strategies a child still needs to learn. Some attention is given to listening for sounds within words and practising phonic skills in context. It has also been recommended that attribution retraining be included within the lessons (Chapman, Tunmer and Prochnow 1999).

The obvious stumbling block with Reading Recovery is the need to find time in the school day and to provide appropriately trained personnel to give the daily tuition to the selected students. Cost effectiveness remains an unresolved issue. There is some indication that tutoring children in pairs or in small groups of up to four can be as effective as individual teaching (Tunmer et al. 2002). It is probable that volunteer helpers used within Learning Assistance Programmes (LAP) in schools would improve the quality and impact of their assistance to individual children if they utilised teaching strategies similar to those in Reading Recovery under the teacher's direction.

Details of the Reading Recovery programme, including instructional strategies, practical ideas and use of time, are given in Clay's (1985) book *The Early Detection of Reading Difficulties*. See also Clay (1993).

Success for All

Success for All, an early intervention programme designed in the US by Robert Slavin and his associates, has also being adopted for use in several other countries. It involves intensive one-to-one teaching using teachers or paraprofessionals to help improve the literacy learning rate for at-risk and socially disadvantaged children (Morrow and Woo 2001; Slavin and Madden 2001). Lessons operate daily for 20 minutes. One unique feature of Success for All is that junior classes throughout the school usually regroup for reading, with children going to different classrooms based on their own ability level. This arrangement necessitates block timetabling, an organisational pattern that some schools find difficult to adopt.

Chan and Dally (2000: 226) describe the intervention thus:

> The tutoring process in Success for All is similar to the Reading Recovery program in that its first emphasis is on reading meaningful texts. Initial reading experiences are followed by phonics instruction which provides systematic strategies for cracking the reading code. Emphasis is also given to strategies to assist and monitor comprehension, such as teaching students to stop at the end of a page and ask, 'Did I understand what I just read?'

In an attempt to overcome the reported lack of generalisation and transfer of skills, said to be found with Reading Recovery, the Success for All teacher also participates in the mainstream reading programme and assists with reading lessons in the regular classroom. This helps to ensure that the one-to-one tutoring later is closely linked to mainstream curriculum, not divorced from it. Slavin and Madden (2001: 9) state that:

> In general the tutors support students' success in the regular reading curriculum rather than teaching different objectives. For example, the tutor generally works with a student on the same story and concepts being read and taught in the regular reading class. However, tutors seek to identify learning problems and use different strategies to teach the same skills. They also teach metacognitive skills beyond those taught in the classroom program.

Research evidence in general has been very supportive of Success for All as an effective intervention model (Morrow and Woo 2001), but some observers question its longer-term benefits. McEwan (1998), for example, reports that Success for All is still not entirely successful in developing mastery of word identification skills in the weakest students. A few students with learning disabilities appear to require even more direct and intensive instruction. Allington (2001) remarks that even though students in Success for All schools do make progress, they still tend to be well behind national and state averages for reading achievement. For additional information on early intervention programmes see Brooks *et al.* (1999), Morrow and Woo (2001), and Slavin and Madden (2001).

Literacy Hour

In the UK the Literacy Hour emerged as a component of the *National Literacy Strategy* (DfEE 1998). It is believed that a dedicated hour per day for literacy work will help ensure that all children have adequate opportunities to learn. One hour devoted to literacy activities each day ensures that the teaching of reading and writing receives appropriate time and attention. Studies of teaching have proved a direct and positive relationship between the effectiveness of students' learning and the time spent in practice and application (Eggen and Kauchak 2001; Hoffman and Duffy 2001).

It should be noted that a similar literacy strategy has been introduced to schools by the commonwealth government in Australia (DETYA 1998); and several Australian states are also applying the notion of a daily literacy hour. In the US the Reading Excellence Act of 1998 is evidence of that country's attempt to reduce the prevalence of reading difficulties and raise reading standards by insisting on research-based teaching methods and appropriate allocations of time (Allington 2001).

Gross, Berger and Garnett (1999) comment that the Literacy Hour provides a vehicle for quality teaching of literacy, with high expectations of what children can achieve. They point out that, for students with learning difficulties, the Literacy Hour is particularly beneficial because of its structure, predictability, regular bursts of focused teaching, practice, reinforcement and a careful balance between whole-class, group and individual work. The time is not spent in boring drills and exercises but rather the children are exposed each day to a much wider range of opportunities to interact with interesting literature, and read and write for genuine purposes of communication. In particular, strategies such as shared-book experience, shared writing and guided reading are strongly recommended for use. The Literacy Hour is also an opportunity to provide specific encouragement, practice and support for any students with reading difficulties.

The suggested structure for the hour is:

- shared-text experience with whole class (approximately 15 minutes);
- activities involving differentiated reading and writing work at sentence and word level – organised as group work, or individualised assignments (approximately 35 minutes);
- plenary session with whole class (reporting and discussion) (approximately 10 minutes).

Excellent practical advice on implementing the Literacy Hour can be found in Berger and Morris (2001).

General principles for literacy intervention

In recent years educators have discovered much about the essential ingredients for successful intervention for learning difficulties in reading (Morrow and Woo 2001). It seems from firsthand observation and from research studies that the following general principles need to be incorporated in any form of early intervention:

- At-risk children will need to be *taught individually* for part of the time, graduating later to *small groups* and to in-class support, before independent progress in the regular class is viable.
- Children experiencing difficulties in learning must spend considerably more time receiving help and guidance from teachers and parents.
- *Frequent successful practice* is essential to build skills to a high level of automaticity.
- *Daily instruction* will achieve much more than twice-weekly intervention.
- The instruction provided in intervention programmes must be of a very high quality and delivered with *clarity and intensity*.
- As well as attempting to improve basic academic skills, early intervention must also focus on the *correction of any negative behaviours*, such as disruption, poor attention to task, or task avoidance that are impairing the student's progress.
- Although withdrawing a student for individual or group work can achieve a great deal, it is also essential that the *regular classroom programme be adjusted* to allow at-risk children a greater degree of success in that setting. Failure to adapt the regular class programme frequently results in loss of achievement gains when the student no longer receives assistance.
- Have a *genuine and realistic reason* for engaging in reading, writing and spelling activities. There is a danger that children with severe reading problems may receive a remedial programme containing too many decontextualised skill-building exercises.
- The *texts* used with at-risk children must be carefully selected to ensure a *very high success rate*. Repetitive and predictable texts are particularly helpful in the early stages.
- Repeated reading of the same text seems to increase *fluency and build confidence*.
- For students with reading disability, *training in phonemic awareness, letter knowledge and decoding* is almost always necessary.
- *Multisensory and multimedia* approaches often help children with learning disabilities assimilate and remember particular units such as letter–sound correspondences and sight words.
- Children should be *explicitly taught* the knowledge, skills and strategies necessary for identifying words, extracting meaning from text, spelling and writing.

- *Writing* should feature as much as reading in early literacy interventions. Concepts about print can be acquired through writing as well as reading; and a great deal of phonic knowledge can be developed through helping children work out the sounds they need to use when spelling words.
- The use of *other tutors* (aides, volunteers, peers, parents) can be very helpful. These individuals need to be taught how to function in the tutor-supporter role.
- Maximum progress occurs when parents or others can provide *additional support and practice* outside school hours.
- Children should be provided with *books they can read successfully at home*.

Teaching procedures in successful intervention programmes draw on what is known about effective teaching. As suggested in Chapter 1 effective teaching involves:

- creation of a friendly, supportive learning environment;
- presentation of the learning task in easy steps;
- resource materials provided at an appropriate readability level;
- direct teaching of task-approach strategies;
- clear modelling and demonstrations by the teacher or tutor;
- provision for much guided practice with feedback;
- efficient use of available time;
- close monitoring of the child's progress;
- reteaching particular skills where necessary;
- independent practice and application;
- very frequent revision of previously taught knowledge and skills.

Further reading

Adams, A. (1999) *Handbook for Literacy Tutors*, Springfield, IL: Thomas.

Fields, M.V. and Spangler, K.L. (2000) *Let's Begin Reading Right*, Upper Saddle River, NJ: Merrill.

Fisher, R. (2002) *Inside the Literacy Hour*, London: RoutledgeFalmer.

Glass, L., Peist, L. and Pike, B. (2000) *Read! Read! Read! Training Effective Reading Partners*, Thousand Oaks, CA: Corwin Press.

Mariotti, A.S. and Homan, S.P. (2001) *Linking Reading Assessment to Instruction* (3rd edn), Mahwah, NJ: Erlbaum.

Morrow, L.M. and Woo, D.G. (2001) *Tutoring Programs for Struggling Readers*, New York: Guilford Press.

Rubin, D. (2002) *Diagnosis and Correction in Reading Instruction* (4th edn), Boston, MA: Allyn and Bacon.

Schumm, J. and Schumm, G.E. (1999) *The Reading Tutor's Handbook*, Minneapolis, MN: Free Spirit Publishing.

Slavin, R.E. and Madden, N.A. (2001) *One Million Children: Success for All*, Thousand Oaks, CA: Corwin Press.

Strickland, D.S., Ganske, K. and Monroe, J.K. (2002) *Supporting Struggling Readers and Writers*, Portland, ME: Stenhouse.

Chapter 9

Strategies for overcoming or preventing reading difficulties

> In a viable diagnostic-reading and correction program teachers must be able to envision the totality of the reading program. They must have basic developmental reading skills at their fingertips, as well as various strategies to help their students become proficient readers.
>
> (Rubin 2002: xxi)

Following the assessment of a learner's abilities as suggested in the previous chapter, it should be possible to plan appropriate starting points for intervention. This chapter provides some additional strategies and techniques suitable for use at various stages of reading development from beginner to post-secondary school level and with students who may have disabilities. These additional strategies might be included within the general language and reading programme of the regular classroom, or used to match the specific needs of individual students engaged in individual tutoring sessions.

Pre-reading and early reading experiences

For most children a carefully structured pre-reading programme is unnecessary. Their previous experiences before school and in kindergarten have provided them with an understanding of what reading is all about. In many cases early childhood experiences will have equipped them with the required perceptual, linguistic, and cognitive skills ready to begin reading (Ruddell 2002). For a few children, particularly those with significant intellectual impairment or perceptual difficulties, the situation is rather different; for them it may be necessary to provide specific activities to facilitate their entry into reading. The readiness activities should be clearly and directly linked to the language programme of the classroom, not something that is done in isolation and out of context. For example, games and activities involving word matching, visual memory and visual discrimination should use words arising from stories the children have just heard, or should be words that are personally relevant and meaningful to the children.

For a very few children (particularly those with impaired vision or with neurological problems) visual discrimination may need to be the focus of some early reading activities. In order to begin to recognise words by sight a child needs to attend to key features of words, such as initial letters or sequences of letters (Heilman 2002). Undoubtedly, one of the most valuable activities at this level is sentence building. At any age level, a learner who is beginning to read should be given the opportunity to construct and reconstruct meaningful sentences from word cards. This sentence-building procedure is valuable for assessment and as a teaching technique. A child's ability to construct, reconstruct and transform sentences reveals much about his or her language competence and memory for words. Sentence building can be incorporated into the language-experience approach described in Chapter 7.

For students with intellectual disability, word-to-picture matching is a useful activity in the beginning stage of word recognition. Colourful pictures can be cut from magazines and catalogues, or the child's own drawings and paintings can be used. Words and captions suggested by the child are printed on slips of card. The child places a card on or next to the appropriate picture and reads the word. The activity can be used with groups of children, with the pictorial material and words displayed on an easel. This activity is valuable for holding children's attention, ensuring their active participation, and for establishing word concept and letter concept. It leads naturally and easily to both shared-book experience and language-experience approach.

If very young children or older children with disabilities such as cerebral palsy or traumatic brain injury are experiencing problems with visual perception it may be necessary to begin at an even simpler level. For example, activities can be used involving the fitting of regular and irregular shapes into form-boards, matching and sorting simple shapes, and feeling these shapes hidden within a puzzle box or bag where the child can handle but not see them. Later the activities can be reintroduced using small plastic letters of the alphabet and numerals.

If a child above the age of 7 years is still confusing the letters p, b, d, q, or u, n, it is essential that he or she be given a motor cue (kinaesthetic training) to establish the correct direction for forming these letters in writing. Finger-tracing one of the letters until it is mastered is probably the most positive way to overcome the problem. For example, the child should close eyes or wear a blindfold while the teacher guides the index finger of the child's preferred hand over the shape of the letter 'b' on the blackboard. The letter is simultaneously sounded or named as tracing is repeated several times. The teacher now takes the child's finger over a series of other letters and the child must indicate quickly and clearly (but still with eyes closed) each time a letter 'b' is traced. The aim here is to give a child a physical image against which to discriminate the letters d and b. It is also useful to provide the child with a self-help card showing that 'little b' is really only the bottom half of a capital B. This card can be left displayed in the classroom for some time after training. If children are given the correct motor cue for letter and numeral formation in the early stages of learning handwriting, many reversal problems will not persist.

Building sight vocabulary

Children need to acquire, as rapidly as possible, a bank of words they know instantly by sight. Much of a child's learning in this area arises naturally from daily reading and writing experiences. The more frequently a child encounters and uses a word the more likely it is that the word will be retained in the long-term memory. Some students, particularly those with reading difficulties, may need to have sight words practised more systematically. The use of flashcards can be of great value. Playing games or participating in other activities involving the reading of important words on flashcards can help provide the repetition necessary for children to read words with a high degree of automaticity. Immediate recognition of these words contributes significantly to fluent reading and comprehension of text.

Teachers often remark that children with learning difficulties can recognise a word one day but appear to have forgotten it completely by the next day. This problem can be explained in part by what learning theory tells us concerning the acquisition of new knowledge. New information is not necessarily fully assimilated on first exposure. Acquisition of a correct association, say, between the spoken word and the printed word-pattern on the page, involves two distinct stages. The first stage is that of *recognising* the printed word when someone else pronounces the word. For example, with word-cards spread on the table, the teacher might say, 'Kathryn, point to the word "London". Dennis, pick up the word "caravan". Show me the word "castle".' The second stage involves the child's *recall* of the word from long-term memory without prompting. The teacher shows the child a particular word on a card and asks, 'What is this word, Mary?' Children with learning problems usually need much more practice at the recognition stage before they can easily store and recall the word from memory.

Many writers have produced lists of words, arranged in frequency of usage, beginning with the most commonly used words (e.g. Gunning 2001; Leech, Rayson and Wilson 2001). The list below contains the first sixty most commonly occurring words derived from various lists:

> a I in is it of the to on and he she was are
> had him his her am but we not yes no all said
> my they with you for big if so did get boy look
> at an come do got girl go us from little when as
> that by have this but which or were would what

Some high-frequency sight words are often confused and misread by beginning readers and students with reading difficulties. Sight words often confused include:

were where when went with want which will what
here there their they them then than

Teachers of reading and others involved in preparing or assessing reading materials for children will find the book *Word Frequencies in Written and Spoken English* (Leech *et al.* 2001) a valuable reference.

Phonological awareness

Aural and oral language enrichment activities form the basis of beginning reading programmes. Encouraging a liking for stories, establishing familiarity with language patterns, training in listening skills, and discussions based on the stories are important features of approaches such as shared-book experience. For many children, these experiences, together with their daily exposure to language, will develop the necessary awareness that spoken words are made up from separate sounds (phonemes). Careful listening enables us to identify those sounds, and recognise that some words contain sound units that rhyme.

It has been shown conclusively that auditory skills play a major role in the process of learning to read (Blachman *et al.* 2000; Torgesen and Mathes 2000). Research in recent years has confirmed that difficulties in learning to read are more likely to be related to problems with phonological processing than to problems with visual perception. Students with hearing loss and those with a specific language disorder or dyslexia are most at risk.

Progress in reading beyond the initial stage of building up a basic sight vocabulary using whole-word recognition is totally dependent upon the development of phonic skills. Acquisition of phonic skills is in turn dependent upon a child's phonemic awareness. Understanding the alphabetic principle requires the child to appreciate that words are made from separate sounds. As Tompkins (2002: 148) notes, 'Phonemic awareness is the foundation for phonics.' Phonological processes are involved to a very significant extent also in spelling. The most important phonological skills appear to be auditory discrimination (including the detection of rhyme), auditory analysis and phoneme blending.

Auditory discrimination and rhyme

Auditory discrimination involves the ability to detect similarities and differences among speech sounds – for example, to know that /f/ sound and /th/ sound are different, as in 'finger' and 'thumb'; or that 'church' and 'children' both begin with the same /ch/ sound. To help children who seem to have difficulty with auditory discrimination, a teacher might find it useful to collect pictures of objects from catalogues and colour supplements to use in games requiring careful listening. The pictures may be set out in pairs and the child must quickly touch one picture when the word is called: for example, 'pear' (pictures show 'bear' and 'pear'), 'three' (pictures show '3' and 'tree'). Activities can also use pictures of objects to be identified by the initial sound (bride = /br/; bus = /b/; train = /tr/). It is important to check children's accurate pronunciation of words containing the target sounds.

The ability to detect rhyming words is also considered important for learning to read and spell. It may be that understanding rhyme makes it easier later to recognise and use the letter groups that represent those rhymes (for example, /ent/: bent, sent, tent, rent, went, lent, dent). 'Word families' are often constructed based on common letter groups representing the rhyming units. Attention to rhyme and the use of word families can be incorporated in all beginning reading approaches.

Glass, Peist and Pike (2000) recommend using onset-rime training activities to help children understand sounds within words: for example, the word *stick*: /st/ (onset) /ick/ (rime). Being able to break single-syllable words into onset and rime units is the starting point for more demanding word analysis and segmentation. Glass *et al.* (2000) identify the following 38 common rime units that can be used to build more than 650 one-syllable words:

-ay, -ill, -at, -am, -ag, -ack, -ank, -ick, -ell, -ot, -ing, -ap, -unk, -ail, -ain, -eed, -y, -out, -ug, -op, -in, -an, est, -ink, -ow, -ew, -ore, -ed, -ab, -ob, -ock, -ake, -ine, -ight, -im, -uck, -um, -ust

Students with severe reading difficulties appear to have great difficulty in mastering phonic units and in particular recognising pronounceable parts of words based on letter groups (sub-word orthographic units) (Compton 2002; Gang and Siegel 2002). Practice in onset and rime activities may help these students grasp the value of processing letter groups rather than single letters (Tunmer *et al.* 2002).

Auditory analysis (segmentation)

Auditory analysis can be taught by spending a little time taking words apart into their component sounds or syllables, making the learner concentrate and reflect upon the process. For example, 'What's this picture, Jackie? Yes. It's a frog. Let's listen to that word FROG. Let's say it very slowly. Let's stretch the word: FR-O-G. You try it.' The child could be asked to count the number of sounds in the word. Analysing a few target words each day can be used as one of many follow-up activities in shared-book, language-experience and guided reading.

Some of the activities listed above under auditory discrimination have already included a simple level of auditory analysis. Activities can be extended to listening for final sounds; for example, 'Put a line under the pictures that end like *snake*' (pictures show *rake*, bucket, *cake*, ball). Attention can then be given to middle sounds. Tunmer *et al.* (2002: 18) have observed, 'To discover mappings between spelling patterns and sound patterns children must be able to segment spoken words into subcomponents.' These researchers also report that students with reading disabilities tend to pay too much attention to initial letter and final letter when trying to identify the word; they need to be taught to analyse the whole word more effectively.

Phoneme blending

Phoneme blending is also referred to as 'sound blending' and is the reverse process to auditory analysis. Blending is one of the most important sub-skills required for effective phonic decoding. Teachers or tutors can encourage children to gain more experience in putting speech sounds together to build a word. For example, 'I spy with my little eye a picture of a /CL/ – /O/ – /CK/.' Blending can also be practised in context when the student is reading aloud.

Sound blending is essential even in the earliest stages of learning to decode words with simple consonant-vowel-consonant words (l-o-t; m-a-n). It is also important much later when dealing with multi-syllabic words (re-mem-ber; cal-cu-la-tor).

Phonological training: general principles

Young children should be exposed to activities that raise their awareness of speech sounds, rhymes and alliteration through daily activities in preschool settings. Listening games and puzzles may require the children to clap out the number of syllables in their names, the number of words in a phrase, and later the number of sounds within a familiar word. Activities can also be introduced which require children to blend sounds or syllables together to make words. Many commercially published phonological training programmes are available – for example, Blachman *et al.* (2000) and Goldsworthy (2001).

In most training programmes, six aspects of phonological awareness are specifically taught alongside reading of authentic texts for enjoyment and information. The six aspects are:

- *Rhyming*: listening to and saying nursery rhymes; finding words that rhyme; generating a new word to rhyme with a given word.
- *Alliteration*: 'the greedy green gremlins are grinning'; 'Hannah's house is high on the hill'.
- *Blending*: combining sounds into syllables and syllables into words.

- *Segmentation*: analysing sentences into words; words into syllables; syllables into separate sounds.
- *Isolation*: identifying the initial, final and medial sounds in a target word.
- *Exchanging*: substituting a new initial sound for another sound to produce a new word: 'met' becomes 'pet'; 'lost' becomes 'cost'.

The use of invented spelling by children almost certainly helps them develop phonemic awareness and an understanding of the alphabetic principle. It is often useful to inspect young children's spelling in their early attempts at writing as this can reveal the extent to which they have developed phonemic awareness. The same is true of older students with learning difficulties.

Children's use of word processors for story creation may also indirectly assist the development of phonic analysis and segmentation. Word processing requires students to pay attention to the phonological and orthographic bases of language in order to type correct sequences of letters to spell words correctly.

Teaching letter–sound correspondences

Tompkins (2002: 153) observes that; 'Phonics is the set of relationships between phonology (the sounds in speech) and orthography (the spelling patterns of written language).' Reading experts differ in their views on how much direct teaching of phonics should occur within the reading curriculum. Most, if not all, educators providing support to students at risk of developing learning difficulties believe that phonic skills should be clearly and directly taught.

As a general principle, phonic knowledge and decoding skills should not be practised totally out of context – but some students with learning disabilities may need specific time devoted to mastering phonic units or analysing word families through activities tailored to their needs. When work of this type is necessary, every effort must be made to ensure that knowledge and skills taught out of context are quickly applied to 'real' reading and writing in context.

The common associations between letters or letter groups (graphemes) and sounds (phonemes) may be introduced in any order; and in practice the order is often dictated by the nature of the reading materials the children are using and the writing they are doing each day. However, when working with students who have difficulties in mastering phonics, it is useful to consider how the task of learning letter–sound correspondences might be organised into a logical sequence. Holdaway (1990) recommends beginning by selecting highly contrastive sounds such as /m/, /k/, /v/, and avoiding confusable sounds such as /m/ and /n/, or /p/ and /b/. There is certainly some merit in applying this principle in the beginning stages. It is also helpful to teach first the most consistent letter–sound associations (Heilman 2002). The following consonants represent only one sound, regardless of the letter or letters coming after them in a word: j, k, l, m, n, p, b, h, r, v, w.

Identifying initial consonants can be made the focus within many of the general language activities in the classroom. For example, when children are consolidating their knowledge of single letter-to-sound links they can begin to make picture dictionaries. Each letter is allocated a separate page and the children paste or draw pictures of objects beginning with that letter on the appropriate page. The 'T' page might have pictures of a **T**able, **T**ie, **T**insel, and **T**adpole.

Wall-charts can also be made with pictured items grouped according to initial letter:

Children's names: **M**egan, **M**ichelle, **M**artin, **M**ark, **M**ary, **M**ichael
Animals and birds: **p**arrot, **p**enguin, **p**ig, **p**ython, **p**latypus

Vowel sounds are far less consistent than consonants in their letter-to-sound correspondences. After first establishing the most common vowel sound associations (/a/ as in apple, /e/ as in egg, /i/ as in ink, /o/ as in orange and /u/ as in up) variations are best learned later in combination with other letters when words containing these units are encountered (e.g. -ar-, -aw-, -ie-, -ee-, -ea-, -ai-, etc.).

With the least able children it is likely that even more attention will need to be devoted to mastery of letter–sound correspondences. This can be achieved through games, rhymes and songs rather than 'drills'. Stories can also be used to help establish links between letters and sounds. For example, the *Letterland* system developed in England uses alliteration in the names of the key characters (e.g. Munching Mike, Ticking Tom, Golden Girl, Robber Red) to help the children associate and remember a sound with a symbol and to create a story link in the child's mind (Wendon 2001). The pictograms used in *Letterland* are capital and lower-case letters with features superimposed. The h is presented as the Hairy Hatman who walks along in words whispering /hhh/. The /w/ sound is introduced as the Water Witch, with her two pools of water held within the shape of the letter. More complex combinations are also covered in the scheme. For example, when /a/ (for apple) is next to /w/ (for Water Witch) the witch casts a spell which makes the apple taste *awful*, thus introducing the tricky /aw/ phonic unit. Although it is a programme in its own right *Letterland* could easily be integrated into the shared-book programme. It is a comprehensive scheme covering phonological skills, reading, spelling and writing.

There are many other programmes designed to teach phonic knowledge in a very systematic way. For example, THRASS (*Teaching Handwriting, Reading and Spelling Skills*: Davies and Ritchie 1996) is designed to teach students how specific letters and letter groups represent the forty-four phonemes in the English language. Approaches such as THRASS, using direct teaching, are highly appropriate for students with learning difficulties who otherwise remain confused about the fact that the same sound units in English can be represented by different orthographic units (e.g. /-ight/ and /-ite/) and how the same orthographic pattern can represent different sounds (e.g. /ow/ as in flower or /ow/ as in snow).

Another example of a very successful programme is *Jolly Phonics* (Lloyd 1992). *Jolly Phonics* sets out to teach 42 basic sound-to-letter correspondences by using a multi-sensory approach involving finger-tracing.

For teachers wishing to have a well-argued rationale for constructing a phonic skills curriculum, this can be found in books such as *Phonics in Proper Perspective* (Heilman 2002) and *Rethinking Phonics* (Dahl *et al.* 2001).

Simple word-building experience

It is important that simple word-building and sound-blending activities are included as soon as the common vowel sounds and consonants have been taught. For example, adding the sound /a/ to the /m/ = am; adding /a/ to /t/ = at; adding /o/ to /n/ = on; adding /u/ to /p/ = up, etc. As well as reading these small units in print the children should also learn to write them unaided when the teacher dictates the sounds. As simple as this basic work may appear, for many students with learning problems it is often the first real link they make between spoken and written language. It is vital that children who have not recognised the connection between letters and sounds be given this direction early. The only prerequisite skills required are adequate visual discrimination of letter-shapes and adequate phonemic awareness.

Onset and rime practice: *Example*: 'Add the sound and say the word':

   t: -ag, -en, -ub, -op, -ip, -ap
   s: -ad, -ix, -un, -it, -ob, -et
   c: -up, -ot, -ap, -an, -ub -ent

Attention may also be given to final sounds: *Example:* 'Add the sound and say the word':

   d: da-, ha-, be-, fe-, ki-, ri-, ro-, po-
   g: sa-, be-, le-, pi-, di-, ho-, lo-, ru-, tu-, etc.

Experience in attending to the middle vowel in consonant-vowel-consonant (CVC) words should also be provided. Children with learning difficulties frequently pay inadequate attention to medial vowels when trying to identify words (Tunmer *et al.* 2002). *Example:* 'Add the sound and say the word':

a: r-g, b-t, t-p, b-d, c-n
e: t-n, p-g, n-t, f-d, g-m
i: p-n, b-t, b-d, r-g, etc.

Later these simple word-building activities will extend to the teaching of digraphs (two letters representing only one speech sound, as in sh, ch, th, wh, ph) and blends (two or three consonants forming a functional sound unit: br, cl, sw, st, str, scr, etc.).

Onset and rime practice: *Example*: 'Add the sound and say the word':

sw: -im, -ing, -ell, -eep
ch: -eer, -in, -op, -urch.
ck: ba-, de-, ro-, du-
str: -ong, -ing, -ike, -ap

These letter groups are among the important early orthographic units for children to master. As stated in Chapter 8 some students reach a reading progress plateau at around reading age 8 years because they have grasped the value of identifying a word from pronounceable groups of letters.

For the highest level of proficiency in recognising and spelling unfamiliar words, children need experience in working with longer and more complex letter-strings (orthographic units) such as: -eed, -ide, -ight, -ound, -own, -ous, -ough, -tion, etc. Gunning (1995) provides a useful core list of 101 of these most common phonograms.

It must be remembered that all word-building activities are used as a supplement to reading and writing for real purposes, not as a replacement for such authentic literacy experiences. For example, words used to generate lists containing important phonograms for children to learn can be taken from words encountered in their shared-book experience, language-experience books, guided reading activities, or from their daily writing. The aim of word study is to help students recognise important phonic units and to seek out these pronounceable parts of words (Gunning 1995, 2001). As Stahl (1992: 620) indicates, 'Good phonics instruction should help make sense of patterns noticed within words.'

Games and apparatus

The literature on remedial teaching encourages teachers to use games and word-building equipment as adjuncts to their literacy programmes. Games, it is argued, provide an opportunity for learners to practise and over-learn essential material that might otherwise become boring and dull. Such repetition is essential for children who learn at a slow rate or who are poorly motivated. Concrete and visual materials such as flashcards, plastic letters and magnet boards can be very effective in holding the student's attention and ensuring active involvement in the lesson. The use of games and equipment may also be seen as non-threatening, thus serving a therapeutic purpose within a group or individual teaching situation.

There can be little doubt that well-structured games and apparatus perform a very important teaching function. Games and apparatus should contribute to the objectives for the lesson, not detract from them. A game or piece of equipment must have a clearly defined purpose, matched to genuine learning needs in the children who are to use it.

Multi-sensory or multimodal approaches

For students with severe learning difficulties who cannot easily remember letters or words it is helpful to use methods that engage them more actively with material to be studied and remembered. The abbreviation VAKT is often used to indicate that multi-sensory methods are visual, auditory, kinaesthetic and tactile (Crawley and Merritt 2000). The typical VAKT approach involves the learner in finger-tracing over a letter or word, or tracing it in the air, while at the same time saying the word, hearing the word, and seeing the visual stimulus.

Fernald VAK approach

- First the learner selects a particular word that he or she wants to learn. The teacher writes the word in blackboard-size writing (cursive) on a card. The child finger-traces the word, saying each syllable as it is traced. This is repeated until the learner feels capable of writing the word from memory. As new words are mastered they are filed away in a card index for later revision. As soon as the learner knows a few words these are used for constructing simple sentences.
- The second stage involves elimination of direct finger-tracing and the child is encouraged to learn the words through studying their visual appearance and then writing them from memory. This stage helps to improve visual imagery and may be used for instruction in correct spelling of irregular words. Words are recorded on cards and stored for later revision.
- The third stage continues to develop visual recognition techniques and encourages more rapid memorisation of the words, followed by swift writing. Word-card drill is usually retained only for specific words that have caused unusual difficulty. At this stage the child is also beginning to read new material prepared by the teacher.
- The final stage involves the child becoming entirely independent in his or her reading and spelling skill, having generalised an understanding of word structure and having been helped to make use of contextual cues.

It can be argued that multi-sensory approaches using several channels of input help a child to integrate, at a neurological level, what is seen with what is heard, whether it be a letter or a word. On the other hand VAKT approaches may succeed where other methods have failed because they cause the learner to focus attention more intently on the learning task. Whatever the reason, this teaching approach, which brings vision, hearing, articulation and movement into play, does appear to result in improved assimilation and retention. It is obviously easier to apply this approach with younger children, but in a one-to-one remedial situation it is still a viable proposition with older students.

Cloze procedure

Cloze procedure was mentioned briefly in Chapter 8. It is a simple technique designed to help a reader become more aware of the value of using context cues and meaning as an aid to guessing unfamiliar words. The procedure merely requires that certain words in a sentence or paragraph be deleted and the reader asked to read the paragraph and supply possible words that might fill the gaps.

> It was Monday morning and Leanne should have been going to sch____.
> She was still in ____. She was hot and her throat was ____.
> 'I think I must take you to the d____,' said her ____. 'No school for you
> t____.'

Variations on the cloze technique involve leaving the initial letter of the deleted word to provide an additional clue; or at the other extreme, deleting several consecutive words, thus requiring the student to provide a phrase that might be appropriate. The use of the cloze procedure can be integrated into shared-book experience and guided reading activities already described.

Cloze activities can involve group work. The prepared paragraphs are duplicated on sheets for the children or displayed on the overhead projector. As a group the children discuss the best alternative and then present these to the teacher. Reading, vocabulary and comprehension are all being developed by a closer attention to logical sentence structure and meaning.

Repeated reading and the Impress method

Repeated reading is a procedure designed to increase fluency, accuracy and expression (Stahl and Kuhn 2002). It simply requires readers to practise reading a short passage aloud until success rate is above 95 per cent and the material can be read aloud fluently. Repeated reading has been found to build children's confidence. Samuels (1997) reports that there is a transfer of fluency in reading from familiar texts to unfamiliar texts.

The teacher first models the reading while the student follows in the text. The teacher spends a few minutes making sure that the student fully understands the material. The student then practises reading the material aloud with corrective feedback from the teacher. The student continues to practise until nearly perfect, and finally records the reading on tape. When the recording is played back the student hears a fluent performance, equal in standard to the reading of even the most competent student in class. This provides an important boost to the student's self-esteem.

Allington (2001) reviewed a number of studies evaluating the effectiveness of repeated reading and concludes:

> The evidence available provides reliable and replicated scientific evidence of the positive impact of repeated readings on a variety of reading tasks and outcome measures. These studies also indicate that engaging children in repeated readings of a text is particularly effective in fostering more fluent reading in children struggling to develop proficient reading strategies.
>
> (Allington 2001: 73)

The Impress method is a unison reading procedure in which the student and teacher read aloud together at a natural rate (Crawley and Merritt 2000). The student is permitted to use the index finger to keep place on the page. The Impress method is particularly useful when a child has developed a few word-recognition skills but is very lacking in fluency and expression. It is recommended that sessions should last no more than five to ten minutes, but be provided on a very regular basis for several months. It may be necessary to repeat the same sentence or paragraph several times until the student becomes fluent at reading the material with low error rate.

The Impress method is very appropriate for use in peer tutoring, where one child who is a better reader provides assistance for a less able friend. In such cases the peer tutor usually needs to be shown how to act effectively as a model reader, and how to be supportive and encouraging to the tutee.

Pause, Prompt, Praise (PPP)

A procedure known as Pause, Prompt, Praise was developed by Glynn at the University of Auckland. It has been applied very successfully in many reading-intervention contexts. The principles can easily be taught to parents, aides, peer-tutors and volunteer helpers in schools as a strategy to use with children they are assisting (Wheldall 1995).

The procedure involves the following simple steps:

- The child encounters an unfamiliar word.

- Instead of stepping in immediately and saying the word, the teacher/tutor waits a few seconds for the child to work it out.
- If the child is not successful the teacher/tutor prompts by suggesting perhaps guessing the word from the meaning of the passage, or attending to the initial letter, or reading to the end of the sentence.
- When the child succeeds in identifying the word he or she is praised briefly.
- If the child cannot get the word after brief prompting, the teacher/tutor quickly supplies the word.
- The child is also praised for self-correcting while reading.

Wheldall (1995) reports that low-progress readers make significantly more progress when tutored by volunteers trained in PPP than when tutored by untrained personnel. When combined with specific instruction in phonics and decoding, PPP resulted in an average increase in reading age of nearly 14 months from seven weeks of daily tutoring in Wheldall's study.

Sustained Silent Reading (SSR)

Sustained Silent Reading describes a specific period of classroom time set aside each day for students and teacher to read material of their own personal choice. Often ten to fifteen minutes of the afternoon session are devoted to SSR across the whole school. Fenwick (1988) reported that SSR – if well implemented – can result in students engaging in much more reading than previously. He states that in doing so the students develop their ability to concentrate on reading tasks for longer periods. In some cases the students are seen to become more discriminating readers, and the range and quality of what they read improves. Fenwick also reports the development of more positive attitudes towards reading.

If SSR is implemented inefficiently it can result in some students wasting time. A problem emerges when students with reading difficulties select books that are too difficult for them to read independently. Teachers need to guide the choice of books to ensure that all students can read the material successfully during these silent reading periods. Biemiller (1994: 206) warns that poor readers often spend substantial periods of SSR time 'covertly avoiding reading'.

Computers, ICT and reading

Word processors can be used most effectively to help students acquire confidence in creating their own reading material. It has been suggested that the use of word processors for desktop publishing adds a valuable new dimension to the literacy programme in any classroom. Creating and printing one's own stories can enhance a child's interest in books and at the same time develop skills in composing, editing, proofreading, spelling and design.

At the most basic level, computer programs exist that will help students to improve their word recognition, decoding, sentence-completion, cloze, and spelling skills (MacArthur *et al.* 2001). At beginner level useful programs exist to aid letter recognition and alphabet knowledge; Duffelmeyer (2002) provides information on a number of websites for this purpose. At higher levels, programs may focus more on word recognition and spelling. For example, a target word may be displayed on the screen and the student is required to copy (retype) the word using the keyboard. The word is then embedded in a sentence for the student to read and again copy. The word is presented again with the initial letter missing and the student is required to complete it. Gradually the cues are removed until the student is reading and writing the word correctly with a high degree of automaticity.

Meyerson and Kulesza (2002) describe how a student with learning difficulties would read carefully for detailed information in the book *My Side of the Mountain* to help him create a scene using 'My Own Story' software. These writers point out, however, that students with reading problems are often as limited in their ability to use computers as they are in other literacy activities, particularly when expected to use ICT to research information for classroom projects. Close monitoring by the teacher and judicious use of peer tutoring can help to reduce this problem and help the student to acquire computer skills.

Minton (2001) described two case studies of students with severe literacy problems who were taught for one hour each week, part of the time on the computer. The greatest value in the computer time was seen to lie in improving the students' self-esteem, giving them independence and control, and making learning enjoyable. The programs themselves provide scaffolding and feedback, while at the same time ensuring practice with high success rate. The students were described as 'enthusiastic' in their approach to the computer sessions.

Casimir and Alchin (2001: 371) have observed:

> A benefit of computer-based assistive technology is that it can be used to effectively implement several well-established and accepted principles of instruction. For example, computers perform direct instruction very well and can help students achieve mastery learning. More specifically, students can use computers to achieve over-learning or automaticity because of the opportunity to repeatedly practice specific skills through customised learning in different interest-maintaining contexts.

In general, word processors are valuable because they integrate reading with writing and require the student to interact with the text that is presented. Computers are infinitely patient, allow for self-pacing by the student, present material in carefully sequenced steps and provide immediate feedback. Students are required to be active throughout the learning session and are found to have higher levels of motivation when working at the keyboard. Van Kraayenoord (2002: 409) states, 'Research evidence shows that computers heighten motivation and lead to higher quality work. In turn, this increases the chance of literacy success.'

Whether used by one student alone, or by students working together, the computer is an excellent tool within the regular classroom. In the home situation the computer can aid literacy development. Children can work with a parent on early reading skills such as word recognition, simple spelling and following instructions. Parents can also help their children seek information through Internet.

Finally, Graham and Kelly (2000: 48) remind us that '. . . however enticing a video, CD-ROM or website may be, its use can only be as good as the considered learning intentions of the teacher for her class. ICT can enhance good teaching; it cannot replace it.'

Further reading

Anderson, R.S. and Speck, B.W. (2001) *Using Technology in K–8 Literacy Classrooms*, Upper Saddle River, NJ: Merrill-Prentice Hall.

Casey, J.M. (2000) *Creating Early Literacy Classrooms: Activities for Using Technology to Empower Elementary Students*, Englewood, CO: Libraries Unlimited.

Cunningham, P.M. (2000) *Phonics they Use* (3rd edn), New York: Longman.

Graham, J. and Kelly, A. (2000) *Reading Under Control* (2nd edn), London: Fulton.

Heilman, A.W. (2002) *Phonics in Proper Perspective* (9th edn), Upper Saddle River, NJ: Merrill-Prentice Hall.

Meyerson, M.J. and Kulesza, D.L. (2002) *Strategies for Struggling Readers: Step by Step*, Upper Saddle River, NJ: Merrill-Prentice Hall.

Opitz, M.F. (2000) *Rhymes and Reasons: Literature and Language Play for Phonological Awareness*, Portsmouth, NH: Heinemann.

Rasinski, T.V. and Zimmerman, B.S. (2001) *Phonics Poetry: Teaching Word Families*, Boston, MA: Allyn and Bacon.

Savage, J.F. (2001) *Sound It Out: Phonics in a Balanced Reading Program*, New York: McGraw Hill.

Topping, K.J. (2001) *Thinking, Reading and Writing: A Practical Guide to Paired Learning with Peers, Parents and Volunteers*, New York: Continuum.

Vukelich, C., Christie, J. and Enz, B. (2002) *Helping Young Children Learn Language and Literacy*, Boston, MA: Allyn and Bacon.

Chapter 10

Helping students improve their writing skills

> Writing competence is based on the successful orchestration of many abilities, including those needed for lower level transcription skills as well as those essential for higher level composing abilities . . . Students who struggle to develop written language often construct a negative perception of the writing process as well as a negative image of their own capabilities to communicate ideas through writing.
>
> (Gregg and Mather 2002: 7)

In order to help students improve their writing skills it is necessary first to consider the different stages of development reached by individuals in the class. In the same way that interventions for reading improvement need to be developmentally appropriate, so too do the teaching strategies used to improve children's writing. As Meier (2000: 16) points out, 'Good teaching matches or fits where children are both developmentally as a group – defined by age – and as individuals in their own right, defined by children's needs and interests.'

Sequential development of writing ability

The acquisition of skills in writing is generally believed to follow a predictable sequence, as evidenced in the many checklists and inventories available for teachers to use when determining a student's current stage of development (e.g. Griffin, Smith and Ridge 2001). Several researchers have described the different stages through which students pass as they move from the 'emergent writing' stage at approximately 5 to 6 years of age to the skilled writing stage in late adolescence and adulthood (e.g. Bissex 1980; Fitzgerald and Shanahan 2000). Although much of the work on developmental aspects of writing has focused on children's spelling (see Chapter 11) some indicators have also been suggested for observing increases in clarity, vocabulary, style and audience (Gregg and Mather 2002).

Morrow (2001) summarised the following stages or features in children's early writing development:

- *Writing as drawing*. The child uses a drawing to communicate information and will typically 'read' the drawing as if there is writing on it.
- *Writing as scribbling*. The child imitates the actions of writing, but with no awareness of letters and words. At this stage the child may even have grasped the left-to-right directionality of writing – but if not, this usually emerges during the next stage.
- *Writing via the use of letter-like forms*. The imitation gets closer to real writing, but the letters are invented shapes.
- *Writing as reproduced familiar letter strings*. The child writes strings of real letters already learned, for example, from his or her own name.
- *Writing with invented spelling*. This stage has many sub-stages within it, each one reflecting a growing awareness that letters can represent the speech sounds in words. Phonemic awareness influences competency at this stage. The messages written may contain simple sentence structures.
- *Conventional spelling*. The child can use accurate or reasonable attempts at spelling almost all the words he or she wants to use. Sentence patterns are established.

Fitzgerald and Shanahan (2000) also identified six stages of development in writing, closely linked to parallel developmental stages in reading acquisition and influenced to some degree by reading experience. While reading and writing are separate processes, and in some respects draw upon different areas of knowledge and skill, there is also considerable overlap between reading and writing. For example, automaticity in recognition of key words is fairly closely linked with automaticity in writing those words, knowledge of phonics helps both reading and spelling, knowledge of grammar and sentence structure is important in writing and is also one of the cueing systems used in fluent reading. Several authorities have discussed the reading–writing connection in great detail (e.g. Cramer 1998; Nelson and Calfee 1998) and teachers are referred to these sources for additional information.

It is generally agreed that reading and writing should be taught together from the earliest stages because, as Cox (1999: 340) states, '. . . the teaching of one can affect the learning of the other.'

Difficulties in writing

Written expression is often considered to be the most difficult of the language skills for children to acquire – its development involves much more than adding discrete skills in a linear sequence. Competence in writing relies heavily on competence in listening, speaking and reading, as well as on possession of necessary strategies for planning, encoding, reviewing, and revising written language. Perhaps more than any other area of the curriculum, writing can present major problems for students with learning difficulties. According to Hess and Wheldall (1999) these students often exhibit weaknesses in planning, sequencing ideas, editing and revising. Some students also have problems with mechanical aspects of the task, such as handwriting, spelling and punctuation.

In Isaacson's (1987) review of research in which unskilled writers are compared with skilled writers, unskilled writers tended to:

- spend very little time planning and thinking before starting to write;
- prepare no rough draft or notes before writing;
- compose ideas in no logical order;
- use very simple sentence structures; or produce long and rambling sentences with repetitive use of conjunctions;
- favour simple words over more interesting and expressive words;
- use certain words or phrases repetitiously (e.g. 'and then', 'nice', 'really big', 'really small', 'really fast');
- produce very little material in the available time;
- show reluctance when required to review and revise their work;
- make many spelling errors;
- omit punctuation, or use it idiosyncratically.

Topping *et al.* (2000: 79) remarked: 'In weak and novice writers, planning is often insufficient and there are likely to be difficulties with ideas generation, text organization and metacognitive knowledge of the writing process.' It is clear that these students need to be taught effective strategies for approaching writing tasks.

Losing confidence and motivation

Features typical of the 'failure cycle' apply particularly to difficulties in writing. The child who has problems writing will experience very little satisfaction in attempting the task and will try to avoid writing whenever possible. The avoidance leads to lack of practice, and lack of practice in turn results in no improvement. The student will lose confidence and self-esteem in relation to writing. The challenge for the teacher is to motivate such students to write and to provide them with enough support to ensure increased success.

It is fortunate that contemporary approaches to the teaching of writing have done much to alleviate the anxiety and frustration that many of the lower-ability students experienced in years gone by whenever 'composition' appeared on the timetable. To them it meant a silent period of sustained writing, with little or no opportunity to discuss work with others or ask for assistance. Great importance was placed on accuracy and neatness at the first attempt and many children felt extremely inhibited. Even when the teacher wasn't a severe judge of the product, the children themselves sometimes carried out self-assessment and decided that they couldn't write because their product was not perfect. An attitude quickly developed in the child, 'I can't write' or 'I hate writing', and a failure cycle was established. It is therefore important to consider approaches to teaching that may prevent loss of confidence and motivation, and instead make students feel successful as writers.

Teaching approaches

Pollington, Wilcox and Morrison (2001) suggest that there are two main approaches to teaching writing – the 'traditional approach' with a focus on instruction in basic skills of writing, and the 'process approach' (or writers' workshop). Van Kraayenoord (2002) and Chan and Dally (2000) also refer to the process approach as the dominant method, but indicate that 'strategy training' has also influenced instruction in writing in recent years. These approaches will be examined briefly as each has a contribution to make to the teaching of students with learning difficulties.

Skills-based, teacher-centred approach to writing

The skills-based or 'traditional approach' usually involves fairly tight control by the teacher, with writing skills being developed mainly through structured exercises, practice materials, and set topics. When more extensive writing is required the teacher usually selects the essay topic about which all students will write. The audience for the writing is usually the teacher. Pollington *et al.* (2001) point out that often the teacher simply sets a topic for the children but does not *teach* the children how to go about the writing task, or provide them with enough guidance – so the activity becomes an *assessment* procedure rather than a teaching and learning experience.

This traditional skills-based approach is often believed to be potentially less motivating for students than having them working collaboratively on topics and genres they have chosen for themselves. There is also some doubt that skills taught in routine exercises ever transfer to children's free writing, and it is argued that these component skills of writing and editing should be taught in an integrated way as part of the feedback given to children as they write on their own chosen topics. Tompkins (2002: 91) states, 'Rather than teaching isolated skills with fragmented bits of language, stripped of meaning, teachers [should] scaffold and support students' developing writing strategies and skills through interaction with authentic and meaningful texts.'

It should not be assumed, however, that all skills-based teaching of this type is intrinsically boring for the students. Some commercially published resource material is quite motivating, and students gain satisfaction in completing the required written assignments successfully. Imaginative teachers always have and always will create interesting and enjoyable themes to use within a skills-based approach. In general it appears that the most important variable in children's motivation and achievement in writing is the enthusiasm of the teacher, not the specific method of instruction (Pollington *et al.* 2001).

Chan and Dally (2000) summarised possible benefits of teacher-centred instruction in writing, including the fact that some students clearly require explicit instruction in basic skills and strategies for writing because they do not learn them effectively through exposure and immersion. There is some indication that certain students make better gains in writing through direct teaching, just as some students make optimum progress in reading if more time is spent in skill development through direct instruction and practice.

The process approach to writing

A change that occurred in the 1980s was a shift of emphasis from skills-based instruction to the actual processes of composing, editing and revising. The new method was termed a *process approach* to writing (Graves 1983). In recent years the approach has become extremely popular in primary and secondary schools around the world, and strategies for using process approach or its variants (for example, 'writing workshop', 'shared writing' and 'guided writing') have been published in many texts and journals. Detailed strategies for classroom application of process writing can be found in the books *Writing Through Childhood* (Harwayne 2001), *Interactive Writing* (McCarrier, Pinnell and Fountas 2000) and *Guiding Readers and Writers in Grades 3–6* (Fountas and Pinnell 2001).

The process approach helps young children understand that a first attempt at writing rarely constitutes a finished product. Writing usually has to pass through a number of separate stages, from the initial hazy formulation of ideas to the first written draft, through subsequent revisions and editing to a final product (although not *all* writing should be forced to pass through all stages).

Teachers themselves should write in the classroom and thus demonstrate the planning, composing, editing and publishing stages in action. Fisher and Williams (2000: 25) remark, 'Much research points to the value of teachers modelling the writing process with their children, a process often called "scribing", which includes not only writing children's ideas for them but talking through the process, discussing choice of words and phrases, cutting out unnecessary words, creating poetic effects and so on.'

Perhaps the process approach is illustrated best in *writing workshop* and *shared writing* (Cox 1999; Pollington *et al.* 2001).

Writing workshop

Writing workshop is a whole-class session where all children are engaged in various forms of writing activity, and are supported in their endeavours by classmates and teacher. Children in writing workshop are helped to go through the complete prewriting, drafting, revising and publishing cycle, and their products become part of the reading material available in the classroom.

The motivation for writing workshop comes mainly through the freedom of choice children are offered in terms of topics and genre. Choice of topic on which to write is usually made by the writer, rather than the teacher. Personal narrative is likely to result in the most lively and relevant communications. It is also believed that selecting a personal topic reduces the problem of generating ideas for a teacher-chosen topic because knowledge of a familiar topic is better organised in memory and this reduces the cognitive load in the initial planning and drafting stages.

Typically a writing workshop session begins with a teacher presentation or sharing time (5–10 minutes), followed by a mini-lesson on some aspect of writing (for example, the use of adjectives) (10 minutes). Students then work independently on their own writing or work in small groups with the teacher (30–40 minutes). During this time word processing and access to other forms of information technology may be appropriate and beneficial. Finally children share their writings with their peers (Morrow 2001).

The teaching of specific skills takes place in three ways:

- at the beginning of the lesson in the form of a mini-lesson;
- in writing conferences with individual children throughout the lesson;
- through whole class sharing time at the end of the lesson.

During the session the teacher should confer with almost every student about the writing being produced. This conference with the student involves far more than dispensation of general praise and encouragement. The conference between teacher and student should represent the 'scaffolding' principle in teaching and learning whereby the teacher supplies the necessary support, encouragement and specific guidance to help novice writers gain increasing control over their own writing strategies. Individual differences in abilities among the students will determine the amount of time the teacher spends with individuals.

Advice and feedback in writing workshops come not only from teacher but also from peers. A friend or partner can be used as a sounding board for ideas and can read, discuss and make suggestions for written drafts. Group sharing and peer editing are essential elements in the sessions. The underlying principle is 'writers working together', sharing and providing feedback, with peers acting as the audience for the children's writing.

Peer critiquing is often written about and talked about as if it is a simple strategy to employ in the classroom; but in reality it needs to be done with great sensitivity. Teachers may need to spend time in modelling the critiquing process before expecting students to implement it skilfully – how to give descriptive praise, how to highlight good points, how to detect what is not clear, how to help with the generation of new ideas, and how to assist with polishing the final product. It must be noted that children are not always skilled in the art of critiquing and providing comments to others, and they may need help with this aspect of process writing. Children with learning difficulties or with low social status within the class may not cope well with negative and critical feedback from their peers because it may seem to draw public attention to their weaknesses (Dahl and Farnan 1998).

Since the process approach depends so much upon the student-writers having someone with whom to confer, it is important to consider other possible sources of assistance in the classroom beyond the teacher and classmates. Teacher aides, older students (cross-age tutoring), college and university students on field placements, and parent volunteers can all provide help within the classroom programme. In all cases these helpers must understand their role and they require some informal training by the teacher if they are to adopt an approach that is supportive rather than didactic.

For children in lower primary school there is evidence that the writing-workshop approach has more positive effect on achievement than a traditional approach (Pollington *et al.* 2001). However, students in intermediate grades show little difference in achievement regardless of which approach to writing they experience.

Shared writing

Shared writing is a component within a process approach, and may be an aspect of any writing workshop stressing collaboration. At the simplest level, or in remedial situations, the teacher does the actual writing while incorporating students' ideas. Through questioning and discussion the teacher activates the students' prior knowledge, encourages critical thinking and reflection, and ensures student participation. Worthy, Broaddus and Ivey (2001: 227) state:

> Shared writing is an effective technique to guide a group of students through a new form of writing. It is also an excellent method to use to support an individual student who will not attempt an assignment. The teacher serves as the recorder, brainstorming with the student and taking a dictation to begin the piece of writing, then handing the paper over for the student to complete.

Guided writing

Guided writing is also an element within the process approach. Its value is greatest in the early years of literacy development (Riley and Reedy 2000) but it also has a place in one-to-one remedial support. Guided writing implies some degree of modelling by the teacher of specific strategies or genres, followed by guided application of the same principles and techniques by the students. Worthy *et al.* (2001) suggest that, using the overhead projector, a teacher might demonstrate how to choose a starting point to begin writing, show several different types of leads to students, and model the writing of a first paragraph. Later, students can take it in turns to present their own material to the group, and constructive suggestions and ideas can be shared in a type of reciprocal teaching situation.

Fountas and Pinnell (2001) recommend providing writers with guidelines or checklists to help with evaluating and revising their written work. For example, the checklist might ask:

- Did you begin with an interesting sentence?
- Are your ideas easy to understand?
- Are your ideas presented in the best sequence?
- Did you give examples to help readers understand your points?
- Is your writing interesting?
- Have you used paragraphs?
- Have you checked spelling and punctuation?

Strategy training

The weaknesses in writing skills described earlier indicate that students need to be taught effective plans of action for tackling writing tasks. In the same way that strategy training can be helpful in reading comprehension, it can also be effective in improving writing, particularly in the aspects of planning, drafting, revising and self-correcting.

The best starting point for strategy training is modelling by the teacher of an effective writing strategy suitable for the age and ability level of the students. The teacher uses 'thinking aloud' to reveal the way he or she goes about each step in planning, generating ideas, drafting, revising and polishing a piece of writing on the blackboard, overhead projector, or computer screen. Students then practise the application of the various steps within a strategy and receive feedback from the teacher.

During strategy training students are typically taught to use questioning or self-instruction to assist with the process of planning, writing and improving a written assignment (Van Kraayenoord 2002). Questions similar to those listed above under *Guided writing* can be used as prompts within the strategy. Emphasis is placed on metacognitive aspects of the writing process (self-checking for clarity in what is written, self-monitoring, self-correction). In the early stages the students may be required to verbalise aloud the steps or questions as they work through the plan of action; later verbalisation is faded as the student becomes more confident in using the strategy independently. The strategy may also embody the use of graphic organisers such as story planners or cues – described later in the chapter.

A simple example of a task-approach strategy for writing uses the mnemonic LESSER. The strategy helps some students to organise their thoughts for writing and then write a longer assignment than they would otherwise produce ('LESSER helps me write more').

L = List your ideas.
E = Examine your list.
S = Select your starting point.
S = Sentence one tells us about this first idea.
E = Expand on this first idea with another sentence.
R = Read what you have written. Revise if necessary. Repeat for the next paragraph.

Many of the lower-achieving students have, in the past, written very little during times set aside for writing. This is part of the vicious circle which might be described thus: 'I don't like writing so I don't write much, so I don't get much practice, so I don't improve . . .' Use of strategies such as LESSER can help to reduce this problem. A modified form of *precision teaching* can also be used to increase output of some students, with the number of words or sentences written in a set time counted and charted each day.

Intervention for individuals and groups

Students who exhibit difficulties in written expression fall into one of two groups. The groups are not mutually exclusive so there is overlap in terms of instructional needs. The first group comprises those students of any age level who have learning difficulties or who have a learning disability. For these students, the teacher needs to make any writing task very clear and structured enough to ensure their successful participation.

The second group comprises those students of any age who can write but don't like to do so – the reluctant and unmotivated students. These students appear not to see the relevance of writing, or have not experienced the excitement of written communication and get no satisfaction from it. Some of these students may have encountered negative or unrewarding experiences during the early stages of becoming writers. They may have acquired what has been termed 'writing apprehension' which now causes them to avoid the task whenever possible. Their problem is one of poor motivation leading to habitually low levels of productivity. Here the teacher must try to regain lost interest and build confidence.

Ideally, a student receiving extra assistance will choose his or her own topics for writing; if not, it is essential to give the student an appropriately stimulating subject. The topic must be interesting and relevant, and the student must see a purpose in transferring ideas to paper. Regardless of whether the activity involves writing a letter to a friend or composing a science-fiction fantasy story, the student should perceive the task as enjoyable and worthwhile.

The first important step in improving a student's writing skills is to allocate sufficient time for writing within the school day. It seems that writing is often treated as an adjunct to other subjects rather than something needing to have specific time allocated to it. If writing occurs daily there is much greater likelihood that motivation, confidence and writing skills will improve.

In general, students with difficulties need help in two basic stages of the writing process, namely planning to write, and later revising or polishing the final product. The teaching of each of these stages of writing should embody the basic principles of effective instruction, namely modelling by the teacher, guided practice with feedback (mainly via the conference process between teacher and student) and independent practice through application.

Paving the way to success

Students with writing difficulties need to be given a framework they can use whenever they write (see *Strategy training* and *Guided writing* above). In particular, novice writers appear to benefit most if they are taught a plan of action for generating ideas, composing and editing (Wong *et al.* 1996). They need to be given guidance in how to begin, how to continue and how to complete the writing task. In this context, students could be taught a set of questions to ask themselves which will facilitate the generation of ideas for writing and will assist with the organisation and presentation of the material across different writing genres.

A classroom atmosphere that encourages students to experiment with their writing without fear of criticism or ridicule is a very necessary condition for the least able students. In many cases, particularly with the upper primary or secondary student with a history of bad experiences in writing, simply creating the atmosphere is not enough. Much more than the ordinary amount of guidance and encouragement from the teacher will also be needed. Graves (1983) describes some such children in his chapters titled 'How to help children catch up' and 'How to help children with special problems of potential'. His studies of the ways in which very young children begin to write and compose throw some light on the performance and needs of older children with difficulties in writing. In particular these studies indicate how important it is to view a child's writing attempts *diagnostically*, to determine how much a child can achieve unaided, and to observe the strategies he or she brings to the planning, composing, spelling and revising stages.

Graves (1983) suggested the following possible sequence in assisting young children with difficulties to produce something satisfying:

- initial 'warm up' – perhaps a few minutes spent with handwriting patterns or letter formation, or copying of something previously written;
- discussion of new topic for writing;
- drawing a picture for the new topic;
- further discussion with teacher;
- composing one or two sentences;
- feedback from the teacher.

In addition Graves says that such students need to be helped *daily*, particularly during the first ten minutes of the lesson. With low-achieving students or those lacking in confidence, the teacher may have to structure the task very carefully at each stage, for example, writing down key vocabulary and possible sentence beginnings for the student to use, then reading these together twice before the child begins to work unaided. Graves advises teachers not to be afraid of saying, at times, 'Try doing it this way.' During the discussion and feedback stages the teacher should not over correct, but rather encourage the student to talk and to think. The main aim is to help the student generate ideas and then to sort these into a logical sequence.

In the early stages it is important not to place undue stress upon accuracy of spelling since this can stifle the student's attempts at communicating ideas freely. Invented spelling gives students the freedom to write with attention to content and sequence. As the student becomes more confident and productive, the teacher, while still remaining supportive, will make the conferring stage rather less structured. Open-ended questions are still used to extend the student's thinking and to build upon the writing so far produced.

Paired writing

In the same way that working with a partner can improve reading skills, having a partner for writing is also beneficial. The system can be used with cross-age tutoring, peer tutoring, parent–child tutorial groupings, and in adult literacy classes (Topping *et al.* 2000). The pairing comprises a helper and a writer. The helper's role is to stimulate ideas from the writer that the helper notes down on a pad. In Topping's method there are set questions for the helper to ask (e.g. Who? Do what? Where? When? What next? etc.). When sufficient ideas have been suggested the helper and writer review the notes on the pad and discuss the best sequence for presenting these. A story planner format could be used (see below). The writer then begins first draft writing, based mainly on the notes. In the case of students with severe learning difficulties the helper may act as scribe as the 'writer' dictates. The helper then reads aloud the draft that has been written. The writer then reads the draft. Working together the pair edit the draft for clarity, meaning, sequence, spelling and punctuation – with the writer taking the lead if possible. The writer then revises the material by writing or word processing a 'best copy'. Helper and writer discuss and evaluate the finished product.

Suggestions for reluctant writers

Small booklets are usually better than exercise books for students who are unskilled and reluctant writers. The opportunity to make a fresh start almost every week is far better than being faced with the accumulation of evidence of past failures which accrue in an exercise book. For students of all ages a loose-leaf folder may be a useful replacement for the traditional exercise book. There is a place for the daily diary, journal or news book, but teachers should avoid such writing becoming merely habitual and trite. There is a danger of this being the case, even with students who can write well.

The skeleton story

Getting started is the first obstacle faced by many students who find writing difficult. One simple way of helping them complete a story is by giving them the framework first, with sentence beginnings to be completed using their own ideas. Example:

> Something woke me in the middle of the night.
> I heard . . . .
> I climbed out of the bed quietly and . . . .
> To my surprise I saw . . . .
> At first I . . . .
> I was lucky because . . . .
> In the end. . . . .

With groups of low-achieving students it is useful, through collaborative effort, to complete one version of the skeleton story on the blackboard. This completed story is read to the group. Each student is then given a sheet with the same sentence beginnings, but he or she must write a different story from the one on the blackboard. The stories are later shared in the group. Students of limited ability find it very much easier to complete a story when the demands for writing are reduced in this way, and when a beginning has been provided.

Cues and prompts

Cues and prompts are similar to the questions posed by the helper in *paired writing* (see above). Martin and Manno (1995) suggest that students be taught a framework of questions which they can ask themselves during the initial stages of planning – e.g. 'What happened first?' 'Where did it happen?' 'To whom did it happen?' 'What happened next?' Questions may also help students become more descriptive in their writing – e.g 'What does it look like (size, colour, shape, etc.)' 'What does it feel like?' 'How fast would you be travelling?' Some generic questions can be recorded on a wall-chart and displayed in the classroom. These temporary props are useful for students who have difficulty at the planning stage of writing; but the students must not become too dependent upon such starting points. After a suitable period of time cues and prompts should be withdrawn.

Story planner

A story planner is a form of graphic organiser that provides students with learning difficulties with a starting point for generating ideas for writing (Riley and Reedy 2000; Silver and Hagin 2002). A 'story web' is created by writing the main idea in the centre of a sheet of paper, then branching off from the main idea into different categories of information. These ideas and categories might include: the setting for the story, the type of action to take place, the characters involved, the outcome, etc.

Prompts and cues could be used to stimulate the students' thinking as the web is constructed. Students brainstorm for ideas that might go into the story. In random order, each idea is briefly noted against a spoke in the wheel. The class then reviews the ideas and decides upon an appropriate starting point for the story. Number '1' is written against that idea. How will the story develop? The children determine the order in which the other ideas will be used, and the appropriate numbers are written against each spoke. Some of the ideas may not be used at all and can be erased. Other ideas may need to be added at this stage, and numbered accordingly. The students now use the bank of ideas recorded on the story planner to start writing their own stories. The brief notes can be elaborated into sentences and the sentences gradually extended into paragraphs.

By preparing the draft ideas and then discussing the best order in which to write them, the students have tackled two of the most difficult problems they face when composing, namely planning and sequencing.

Expanding an idea

Begin by writing a short, declarative sentence that makes one statement.

> *We have too many cars coming into our school parking area.*

Next, write two or three sentences that add information to, or are connected with, the first sentence. Leave two lines below each new sentence.

> *We have too many cars coming into our school parking area.*
>
> *The noise they make often disturbs our lessons.*
>
> *The cars travel fast and could knock someone down.*
>
> *What can we do about this problem?*

Now write two more sentences in each space.

> *We have too many cars coming into our school parking area.*

The noise they make often disturbs our lessons. The drivers sound their horns and rev the engines. Sometimes I can't even hear the teacher speak. The cars travel fast and could knock someone down. I saw a girl step out behind one yesterday. She screamed when it reversed suddenly.
What can we do about this problem? Perhaps there should be a sign saying 'NO CARS ALLOWED'. They might build some speed humps or set a speed limit.

Edit the sentences into appropriate paragraphs. Combine some short statements into longer, complex sentences. Edit for style. Use of a word processor makes each of these steps much faster and makes the process of editing and checking spelling easier. The teacher demonstrates this procedure, incorporating ideas from the class. Students are then given guided practice and further modelling over a series of lessons, each time using a different theme.

Shuffling ideas

This strategy helps to establish the value of planning and sequencing points before writing. As ideas for writing are generated, each is written on a separate card. Finally, the cards are reordered until the most suitable and appealing sequence is obtained. The sequence can become the focal point for discussion between teacher and student or between two students. The procedure avoids the problem of reluctance that sometimes occurs when a student is asked to revise and rewrite a draft.

'You write the rest' stories

A story is told or read to the class for enjoyment – but just when it gets to a cliffhanger climax, the story stops. What happens next? Individuals can write their own ending or can brainstorm ideas in a group.

For students of very limited ability a simplified version of the story can be pre-printed in a small booklet, with a frame for an illustration above each simple passage of text. The students who are not proficient readers can usually cope with the simplified material since it repeats a story just read to them. The second half of the booklet is blank to allow the children to write their own endings and provide illustrations.

This example is from a *Doctor Who* story. The teacher's story ends with this paragraph:

He was in for a shock when he switched on the televiewer. The giant spiders were spinning a web over the Tardis. The strands looked as strong as rope. Suddenly the lights went out. He dashed to the controls and frantically flicked the switches. Nothing happened. The Tardis refused to move. They were trapped!!!

Patricia (a special class student) continues:

> Dr Who was cross. The spiders sat on the Tardis and sang a jungle song. Dr Who took the plants he had collected and did an experiment on them. The plants turned into little people. The doctor put the little people outside and they began to chew through the web. Soon the wind came and the web blew away. The Tardis was free again.

All the suggestions above are designed to simplify the task demands for writing, and at the same time motivate the reluctant student to complete the work successfully. In most cases the use of a word processor will also add interest and an important element of control by the learner.

Word processors

Undoubtedly, the arrival of word processors in the classroom heralded a new opportunity for students of all levels of ability to enter the realm of writing and composing with enthusiasm and enjoyment. In particular, students with learning difficulties can gain confidence in creating, editing, erasing and publishing their own unique material through a medium that holds attention and is infinitely patient. Dahl and Farnan (1998) cite research showing that students work harder and produce longer essays, of better quality, when using word processors for writing. The effects are evident at all ages and stages of development. For students with learning difficulties word processing de-emphasises the mechanical aspects, such as handwriting and letter formation, and allows more mental effort to be devoted to generating ideas and vocabulary.

In a tutorial situation the use of a computer allows the tutor to observe the writing process more directly and gain better insights into the student's existing strategies for composing, editing and proofreading. Support can then be given to the student with greater precision.

Students with learning difficulties need first to develop some basic keyboard skills if the word processing is to be achieved without frustration. It is usually necessary to teach only the most essential skills to enable the student to access the program, type the work and save the material at regular intervals. Even this simple level of operation can give some students a tremendous boost to confidence and can encourage risk-taking in writing and composing. Van der Kaay, Wilton and Townsend (2000) used a word processor with students aged nine to eleven who were mildly intellectually disabled. They found that the students' written work improved significantly in terms of organisation and control over the writing process.

By combining the conference approach to writing with the use of a word processor, the student's story in draft form can be printed, first without using the spell-checker. Student and partner, or student and teacher, can then check the printout and discuss good features of the story, and identify sentences or phrases or particular words that might be improved. It is useful for the teacher to note the words the student can self-correct and which spelling errors are not detected without assistance. A second draft of the story can then be made after the student does the necessary revisions and uses the spell-checker.

Research evidence supporting the benefits of using word processors with learning-disabled students is growing all the time. Word processing seems to be of great benefit to students who don't usually write very much, and to those with the most severe spelling problems (Silver and Hagin 2002).

Ryba, Curzon and Selby (2002) provide a useful overview of IT resources available for literacy and other skill development for students with learning difficulties or disabilities.

Further reading

Burgstahler, S. and Utterback, L. (2000) *New Kids on the Net: Internet Activities in Elementary Language Arts*, Boston, MA: Allyn and Bacon.

Cunningham, P.M., Moore, S.A., Cunningham, J.W. and Moore, D.W. (2000) *Teachers in Action: Reading and Writing in Elementary Classrooms*, New York: Longman.

Fountas, I.C. and Pinnell, G.S. (2001) *Guiding Readers and Writers in Grades 3–6*, Portsmouth, NH: Heinemann.

Gunning, T.G. (2002) *Assessing and Correcting Reading and Writing Difficulties* (2nd edn), Boston, MA: Allyn and Bacon.

Harwayne, S. (2001) *Writing Through Childhood*, Portsmouth, NH: Heinemann.

McCarrier, A., Pinnell, G.S. and Fountas, I.C. (2000) *Interactive Writing*, Portsmouth, NH: Heinemann.

Meier, D.R. (2000) *Scribble Scrabble: Learning to Read and Write*, New York: Teachers College Press.

Vukelich, C., Christie, J. and Enz, B. (2002) *Helping Young Children Learn Language and Literature*, Boston, MA: Allyn and Bacon.

Worthy, J., Broaddus, K. and Ivey, G. (2001) *Pathways to Independence: Reading, Writing and Learning in Grades 3–8*, New York: Guilford Press.

Chapter 11

Developing spelling skills

> Poor spellers are not very adept at picking up the spelling of uninstructed words or acquiring new spellings through reading. Transfer effects from reading instruction to spelling are also quite limited for poor readers, and the spelling progress of students with special needs in whole language or process writing classes (programs compatible with the natural learning approach) is relatively limited.
>
> (Graham 2000: 244)

For many low-achieving students, spelling continues to present a problem long after reading skills have improved. This is sometimes due to the fact that too little attention is given to the explicit teaching of spelling skills and strategies. Instruction in spelling no longer features as prominently now in the primary school curriculum as it did some years ago, due mainly to the influence of whole-language philosophy.

Whole-language perspectives on spelling

The advent of whole-language philosophy saw the teaching of spelling become fully integrated into children's daily writing activities, rather than being treated as a subject in its own right. It was argued that spelling instruction must be kept within a meaningful context at all times, and students can be helped individually and incidentally to learn to spell the words they need to use as they write. This integrated approach is deemed to be the 'natural' way of acquiring spelling skill (Graham 2000) and is therefore regarded by whole-language exponents as preferable to any form of direct teaching based on the content of a predetermined word list (Worthy, Broaddus and Ivey 2001). Instead, children are taught the precise information they need at the exact moment they need it. For example, a student may want to write the word 'please' but is unsure of the /ea/ sound within it. The teacher spells the word, and takes a moment to explain that often the letters 'ea' together make the long /e/ sound, as in *sea, feast, deal, leap, seat, read*.

Used alone the integrated approach to spelling seems to be inadequate for students with learning difficulties. In classrooms containing 28 or more students it is virtually impossible to find the necessary time to devote to such a personalised approach. Even if a few moments can be devoted to each student within the writing lesson, helping the student with a spelling difficulty for a very brief period of time inevitably results in very superficial coverage of the specific spelling principle and letter pattern. Simply because the teacher has explained a particular rule on one day there is no reason to suppose that the student will remember this information the next day, unless it is reviewed and practised.

Dealing with words and spelling principles only as they are needed can also result in undesirable fragmentation of experience. For example, a child taught to spell the word 'fight' may not recognise that it belongs to the word family comprising *right, sight, might, tight, light, bright, flight*, etc. An essential part of understanding how words are constructed involves students in recognising that many words share predictable letter patterns. It does not make sense to leave students to acquire this important knowledge through incidental learning. As Templeton (1992: 455) has observed, 'Spelling knowledge grows out of, and supports reading, writing and vocabulary study. *It also grows out of examining words in and of themselves*' (emphasis added).

Rubin (2000: 309) advises:

> There is a definite place for spelling in any and all language arts programs. The emphasis on meaning-based language and literacy instruction is no reason to ignore spelling. Helping students gain spelling ability enhances their literacy rather than retards it [and] spelling is closely related to the other language arts areas and, in order to grow, it needs nurturing. This nurturing comes from students' continuous exposure to reading and writing and from both incidental and direct instruction.

Developmental stages in spelling acquisition

It is important for teachers to be aware of the normal stages of development through which children pass on their way to becoming proficient spellers (Riley and Reedy 2000). Students pass through these stages at different rates, and it is unrealistic to expect a student to achieve a level of independence or accuracy in spelling that is beyond his or her current developmental level. The stages have been described in the following way – although the exact title for each stage has differed among the various researchers (Bissex 1980; Moats 1995):

Stage 1: Prephonetic

At this stage the child 'plays' at writing (often using capital letters) in imitation of the writing of others. There is no connection between these scribbles and speech sounds or real words.

Stage 2: Phonetic

At this stage the child relies mainly upon auditory perception and phonemic awareness. In the child's spelling there is evidence of an emerging knowledge of letter–sound correspondences, picked up through incidental learning. The invented words are quite recognisable as children begin to apply basic phonic principles as they write. Sometimes the phoneme they identify is equated with the letter name rather than the sound, as for example in 'rsk' (ask), 'yl' (while), 'lefnt' (elephant).

Towards the end of the phonetic stage, approximations move much nearer to regular letter–sound correspondences, as in 'sed' (said) or 'becos' (because). Even at this stage some children have difficulty in identifying the second or third consonant in a letter-string and may write 'stong' (strong) or 'bow' (blow). Or they may fail to identify correctly a sound within the word and may write the incorrect letters, as in 'druck' (truck), 'jriv' (drive), 'sboon' (spoon), 'dewis' (juice).

It should be noted that the majority of individuals with poor spelling have reached this phonetic stage in their development but have not progressed beyond it. They now need to be taught to use strategies such as visual checking of words and spelling by analogy in order to move to the next stage. Activities involving word analysis are also useful in helping the student to recognise letter patterns within words (orthographic units) (Cox 1999).

Stage 3: Transitional

At this stage there is clear evidence of a more sophisticated understanding of word structure. The child has become aware of within-word letter strings and syllable junctures. Common letter sequences, such as -ough, -ious, -ea-, -ai-, -aw-, -ing, etc., are used much more reliably. The children who are gaining real mastery over spelling at this stage also begin to spell by analogy, using words they know already in order to spell words they have never written before (Dahl and Farnan 1998).

Stage 4: Independence

At this stage the child has mastery of quite complex graphophonic principles, and also uses visual imagery more effectively when writing and checking familiar words. Flexible use is made of a wide range of spelling, proofreading, self-help and self-correcting strategies.

Do we spell by eye, by ear or by hand?

The answer to the question do we spell by eye, by ear or by hand is almost certainly that we use all three modalities on the way to becoming proficient spellers. However, for many years teachers have regarded the encoding of words as predominantly a *visual* processing skill. For this reason, if students were fortunate enough to receive guidance in spelling the strategies they were taught have been mainly concerned with improving visual memory for word forms, for example, the 'look-cover-write-check' strategy. Much less importance has been attached to *auditory* processing strategies due to the erroneous belief that 'sounding out' words will lead to too many errors due to the irregularity of English spelling. Indeed, some authorities actively dissuade students from attending closely to the sound values heard within spoken words since the individual letters used to represent these sounds may not be entirely predictable. It is argued that because up to three words in every ten are not written precisely as they sound, with perfect letter-to-sound translations, it is not beneficial to teach children to utilise phonic information when spelling. Counter to this argument is evidence to suggest that learning to read and learning to spell, particularly in the beginning stages, are far more closely related to auditory-processing abilities than we previously believed (Treiman 1993).

Let us consider the general contributions made to spelling by visual perception, auditory perception and hand movements.

Visual perception: spelling by eye

Very proficient spellers appear to make great use of visual information when writing words. It is obvious that visual clues are extremely important for accurate spelling. The most common way of checking one's own spelling and detecting errors is to look carefully at the written word and ask oneself 'Does this word look right?' Strategies that involve the deliberate use of visual imagery, such as look-say-cover-write-check, are very effective for the learning of what are termed 'irregular' words, those with unpredictable letter-to-sound correspondences. To this extent we certainly do learn to spell by eye. The effective use of visual perception in learning to spell causes the student to build up a memory bank of visual images of words and of letter strings within words. The knowledge in this store can be called upon whenever the student attempts to write an unfamiliar word.

Learning to spell by eye does not mean, however, that learners simply acquire incidentally the ability to spell by seeing words as they read – just 'looking' at words does not seem to be enough for most learners (Graham 2000). It is necessary for them to examine a word very carefully, with every intention of trying to commit its internal structure and configuration to memory. As this behaviour does not come naturally to every learner, it is important that any student who lacks this experience be given the necessary instruction and practice. By implication, this may mean devoting specific time and attention to word study, over and above any help given to individual students as they write. It is most unlikely that such an important skill as word analysis could be adequately developed through incidental learning alone (Bear *et al.* 2000; Gunning 2001).

It must be noted that there is some indication that even good spellers may not really spell using visual imagery alone to the extent we once imagined. They may use visual memory effectively only to check the final appearance of a word written mainly by using other cues (Adams 1990). The current viewpoint is that spelling actually involves the coordinated use of several different complementary processes and strategies, including listening carefully to the component sounds and syllables within the word and by developing kinaesthetic images of the most commonly written words.

Auditory perception: spelling by ear

Research has indicated that in the early stages of learning to read and spell it is important that a child can identify the different sound units within spoken words (phonemic awareness) (Blachman *et al.* 2000; Torgesen and Mathes 2000). The basic knowledge upon which successful reading and spelling develop seems to depend upon the child's awareness that spoken words can be broken down into smaller units and that these units can be represented by letters. In order to spell, young children in the first years of schooling may use auditory perception to a much greater extent than older children, simply because they have not yet had as much exposure to letter patterns within words through daily reading and writing experiences. Building a memory bank of visual images of words and letter strings takes time and experience. The extent to which early attempts at spelling do rely upon attention to sounds in words and to letter–sound correspondences is evident in children's early attempts at inventing spelling.

Those who doubt the importance of auditory perception in spelling might ponder the fact that the spelling of many dyslexic individuals is frequently described as 'bizarre' in the sense that the letters written down often have no logical connection with the speech sounds they represent in the word. It is also clear that one of the most common problems exhibited by many dyslexic students is an inability to analyse words they hear in terms of syllable units and separate phonemes (Torgesen 1999) (see Chapter 1). It is likely that the bizarre spelling is a reflection of this auditory-processing problem.

When spelling a word there is actually a complementary association between auditory perception and visual perception. The process of writing an unfamiliar word requires the child first to identify the sound units within the word and to match these sound units with appropriate letter clusters stored as visual images in what is termed 'orthographic memory'. Having identified the sound values in the word, and having represented these units on paper by writing the specific letters in sequence, visual perception is then used to check that what the student writes on paper also 'looks right' – for example, *brek-first* should be recognised visually as an incorrect letter pattern for the word *breakfast*.

Motor memory: spelling by hand

Since the spelling of a word is typically produced by the physical action of writing, it is fair to assume that kinaesthetic memory may also be involved in learning to spell. Indeed, the rapid speed and high degree of automaticity with which a competent speller encodes a very familiar word directly from meaning to its graphic representation, supports the view that motor memory is involved. Nichols (1985: 3) has written, 'Spelling is remembered best in your hand. It is the memory of your fingers moving the pencil to make a word that makes for accurate spelling.' The frequent action of writing may be one of the ways of establishing in orthographic memory the stock of images of words and letter strings. The process of building up orthographic images in memory is also facilitated by the study of word families with common letter sequences, for example, 'gate, date, late, fate, mate, etc.' (Worthy *et al.* 2001).

It is often recommended that we should not think of spelling words letter-by-letter but rather by concentrating upon the groups of letters that form common units in many words. This has some implications for the way in which we teach handwriting in the early years of schooling. Some evidence exists to support the notion that it is beneficial to teach young children to join letters together almost from the beginning of their instruction in handwriting, rather than teaching print script first and linked script much later. It is believed that joining the letters together in one smooth action helps children to develop an awareness of common letter strings (Cripps 1990).

The relative contributions of vision, audition and hand movement

The extent to which visual perception, auditory perception and kinaesthetics contribute to the act of spelling a particular word seems to depend upon how familiar the word is to the writer. Unfamiliar words appear to require an analysis into their component sounds before an attempt can be made to write them. What has been written can then be checked for accuracy in terms of visual appearance. For example, when trying to spell the word 'work', the /w/ and the /rk/ can probably be encoded from their sound values, but the writer's orthographic visual memory has to be checked for the information that the vowel is o and not e in work. Very familiar, high-frequency words, such as 'and', 'the' and 'are', are probably written mainly from kinaesthetic memory and checked simultaneously for visual appearance.

Individual differences among spellers

Four types of imagery appear to be used in spelling a word:

- visual – the way the word looks;
- auditory – the way the word sounds;
- kinaesthetic – the way the word feels when written;
- speech-motor – the way the word articulates when spoken.

It seems that some students rely much more heavily on one type of imagery than on another and may need to be taught to use other types of imagery if possible. For example, dyslexic students are often found to be particularly weak in phonological skills and may rely too heavily on faulty visual memory for recall of letter patterns. Training them in phonemic awareness and the application of basic phonic knowledge appears to have a positive effect on spelling ability.

Examination of the written work produced by students with learning difficulties can reveal a great deal about their current skills and specific needs in spelling. One of the most common problems is the tendency of the student to be over-dependent on phonic knowledge and therefore to write irregular words as if they are regular. They appear to have remained at the phonetic stage of development for too long. Close examination of a student's exercise books, or the use of dictated word lists, will quickly reveal the extent to which the individual has this problem. The students producing these errors seem to lack the necessary strategies for carefully checking the visual appearance of a word, and will fail to identify the errors even when encouraged to proofread their material.

Teaching spelling by visual-emphasis approach

The visual approach to spelling requires the student to memorise the overall appearance of words. Rather than attending to sounds and syllables within the word, the student attempts to store a visual image of the word or key parts of the word in long-term memory. Research has suggested that children can be trained to focus more attentively on words and to improve their visual imagery for letter sequences. Writing a word many times may also help the learner to store the correct image of that word, as suggested previously.

To improve visual processing of words one of the simplest aids to make and use is the flashcard. These cards are particularly useful for teaching irregular words and for students who need to be weaned away from a predominantly phonetic approach to spelling – for example, students who have reached a plateau at the phonetic stage. The words are introduced to the student on cards about 30cm × 10cm. The word is pronounced clearly and attention is drawn to any particular features in the printed word that may be difficult to recall later. The child is encouraged to make a 'mental picture' of the word, and examine it. Some teachers say, 'Use your eyes like a camera. Take a picture of the word. Close your eyes and imagine you can still see the word.' With the eyes closed the child is then told to trace the word in the air. After a few seconds the student writes the word from memory, articulating it clearly as he or she writes. The word is then checked against the flashcard. The writing of the whole word avoids the inefficient letter-by-letter copying habit that some students have developed.

The general look-cover-write-check approach is based on the principle of learning words by giving attention to their visible sequences of letters, rather than using letter-to-sound correspondences. Some teachers add the word 'say' to the strategy, making it 'look-say-cover-write-check' to accommodate the importance of clear articulation for accurate spelling. The visual strategy in action involves the following steps:

- Look very carefully at the word in the list.
- Say the word clearly. Try to remember every detail.
- For some students, finger tracing over the word may help with assimilation and retention of the letter sequence.
- Cover the word so that it cannot be seen.
- Write the word from memory, pronouncing it quietly as you write.
- Check your version of the word with the original. If it is not correct go back through the steps again until you can produce the word accurately.
- Teachers should check for recall several days and weeks later.

The look-say-cover-write-check approach is far better than any rote learning and recitation procedure for learning to spell. It gives the student an independent system that can be applied to the study of any irregular words set for homework or to corrections or omissions from free writing. Students can work in pairs where appropriate, to check that the procedure is being followed correctly by the partner. It is claimed that children as young as five years old can be taught this visual strategy for spelling. Rosencrans (1998) describes a similar strategy that she calls 'looking good'. Her strategy is designed to help students become so familiar with commonly occurring letter groups that they can recognise immediately when a word or part of a word does not look right.

The look-say-cover-write-check strategy, although claiming to be a visual learning method, almost certainly is effective because students are identifying groups of letters that represent pronounceable parts of words (orthographic units). From the earlier chapter on reading skills we know that this is precisely the type of information that is also essential for swift and efficient reading.

Several computer programs designed to develop spelling skills have come on to the market. Teachers should ensure that the way in which the words are presented on the screen causes the students to attend carefully to the sequence and clusters of letters, and requires the student to type the complete word from memory each time. Programs that focus too much attention on spelling letter-by-letter or inserting missing letters into spaces are far less effective.

Applying phonic principles

It is unnecessary and inappropriate to use the look-cover-write-check strategy if the target word could be written correctly as it sounds. The phonemic approach encourages students to attend carefully to sounds and syllables within words and to write the letters most likely to represent these sounds. While it is true that some 30 per cent of English words are not phonemically regular, some 70 per cent of words do correspond reasonably well with their letter-to-sound translations.

The phonic knowledge necessary for this effective spelling goes well beyond knowing the common sound associated with each single letter. It is necessary to draw on knowledge of letter groups that represent pronounceable units within words – for example, to know that /ite/ and /ight/ are letter strings representing alternative spellings for the same sound unit. When students have acquired this level of proficiency the percentage of words that can be spelled as they sound increases very significantly.

The morphemic approach

This approach to spelling teaches students to apply knowledge of the small units of meaning within a word. The smallest unit of meaning is termed a morpheme. For example, the word 'throw' contains only one morpheme, but 'throwing' contains two. The word 'recovered' comprises three morphemes (re-cover-ed), as does 'unhappiness' (un-happ[y]-ness). The latter example also illustrates the use of a rule (changing y to i) when combining certain morphemes. When using a morphemic approach, teachers need to teach these rules.

Perhaps the best-known programme using a morphemic approach is *Morphographic Spelling* (Dixon and Englemann 1996). The materials are appropriate for students from Year 4 upwards and can be used with adults. In 140 lessons the students learn all the key morphographs and the basic rules of the spelling system. Whole-language enthusiasts would reject such an approach, but *Morphographic Spelling* has proved valuable for students with learning difficulties.

Spelling from meaning

Cramer (1998: 148) describes an approach to spelling that also stresses a link between meaning and spelling. He states:

The spelling–meaning connection is not complex. It consists of the fact that words that are related in meaning are often closely related in the way they are spelled. Thus if you know the meaning and spelling of *heal* you have a good shot at spelling *health*. Notice that the sound of *heal* by itself and the sound of *heal* in *health* are quite different. *Heal* has a long /e/ sound; *heal* in *health* has the short /e/ sound. So why are they spelled the same? Because spelling them the same way preserves the spelling–meaning connection between the two words. If this were not so, the English spelling system would be more arbitrary and more complex.

To facilitate the study of words related by meaning, students can be helped to compile word families sharing a common root or base. Dictionary skills can be used to identify such words. Rosencrans (1998) and Worthy *et al.* (2001) suggest that this type of activity is valuable because it makes spelling more predictable and reliable through relating it to meaning.

Spelling rules

Some experts advocate teaching spelling rules to students; but students with learning difficulties find most rules too obscure to be of help when they are faced with a particular word to spell. Worthy *et al.* (2001) indicate that teaching of rules and generalisations rarely works. In many cases rather than drilling complex rules it is easier to help the students spell the specific words they need for their writing and to teach them strategies to use when learning any new words.

There are some educators working with students with learning disabilities who suggest that rules may be of some value for older students of at least average intelligence. They can often understand the rule or principle and can appreciate when it might be applied. Even in these cases the rules should be simple and have few exceptions (e.g. 'i' before 'e' except after 'c'– *receive*; words ending with 'e', drop the 'e' when adding an ending that begins with a vowel – *hope, hoping*; words ending in a single vowel, double the consonant before adding an ending that begins with a vowel – *stop, stopped, stopping*).

Fountas and Pinnell (2001) suggest that students will learn rules more effectively if they have the chance to derive the rules themselves through exploring numerous examples. Rote learning of rules is counterproductive.

Dictation

It is sometimes suggested that dictation develops listening skills and concentration, and at the same time gives students experience of spelling words in context. It is recommended under this system that the material be presented in written form for the children to study *before* it is dictated. In this way there is an opportunity to point out any particularly difficult words.

Another approach encourages proofreading and self-correction. An unseen passage at an appropriate level of difficulty is dictated for students to write. They are then given a period of time to check and alter any words that they think are incorrect, perhaps using a different coloured pen. The teacher then checks the work and can observe two aspects of the student's performance. First, it is useful to look at the words the child has been able to correct (or at least knows to be wrong). Second, the teacher can record words that were in fact wrong but were not noticed by the student. If, based on their level of difficulty, these words should be known by the student, the teacher must make every effort to teach their correct spelling since they have become firmly set as incorrect responses.

The use of 'phonic dictation', where the teacher deliberately stresses the sequence of sounds in a tricky word or breaks a word into syllables, can be helpful in developing a student's sensitivity to the phonemic characteristics of words (Savage 2001). Such work at a very simple level can be incorporated into phonological training activities described in earlier chapters.

Should spelling lists be used?

The notion that lists can be compiled that contain words that all students should know and use at a particular year or grade level has, to some extent, been abandoned. However, spelling lists continue to form the core of many spelling programmes. The limitation of formal lists is that they usually fail to supply a particular word just when the student needs to use it for writing or proofreading.

The question most often asked by teachers is, 'Do students learn to spell best from lists?' If the question refers to lists of words that students actually use and need in their writing, the answer is certainly 'yes'. If the lists are based on other criteria – for example, words grouped according to visual or phonemic similarity – the decision to use such a list with a particular student or group of students must be made in the light of their specific learning needs. The most useful list from the point of view of the weakest spellers will be one compiled according to personal writing needs and common errors. A copy of this list can be kept in the back of the student's exercise book and used when he or she is writing a rough draft or proofreading a final draft of a piece of work.

The value of lists or word groups is that they may be yet another way of helping students establish an awareness of orthographic units. This awareness will help a student take a more rational approach to tackling an unfamiliar word.

Developing strategic spellers

Students have become truly independent in their spelling when they can look at an unfamiliar word and select the most appropriate strategy to use for learning that word. For example, they need to be able to look at a word and decide for themselves whether it is phonemically irregular or regular. For an irregular word they may need to apply the look-cover-write-check strategy, coupled perhaps with repeated writing of the word. For some irregular words they may also need to call upon knowledge of the simple principle about doubling letters, or dropping or changing a letter. If the word is regular they need to recognise that they can spell it easily from its component sounds. When students can operate at this level of judgement the shift is from rote learning to an emphasis on studying words rationally.

This level of independence does not come easily to all students. Many individuals need to be taught how to learn new material. Some students, left to their own devices, fail to develop any systematic approach. They may just look at the word. They may recite the spelling alphabetically. They may copy letter-by-letter rather than writing the whole word. They may use no particular strategy at all, believing that learning to spell the word is beyond them. Any serious attempt to help children with spelling difficulties will involve determining *how* they set about learning a word or group of words. Where a student has no systematic approach it is essential that he or she be taught one.

In cognitive and metacognitive approaches to spelling instruction students are taught specific self-regulatory strategies to use when learning new words or checking the accuracy of spelling at the proofreading stage of writing. For example, they are taught to ask themselves:

- How many syllables do I hear in this word?
- Do I have the right number of syllables in what I have written?
- Do I know any other words that sound like this word?
- Does this word look correct? I'll try it again.
- Does this look better?

As with all other examples of strategy training described in this book, the teacher's key role is to model effective strategies, to 'think aloud' and demonstrate ways of going about the task of spelling, checking and self-correcting.

Simultaneous oral spelling (SOS)

This approach was first developed by Gillingham and Stillman in 1960. It has been applied very successfully for remediation of spelling problems in individual tutorial settings and is appropriate for any age level beyond beginner. The approach involves five steps:

- select the word you wish to learn, and have the teacher pronounce it clearly;
- pronounce the word clearly yourself while looking carefully at the word;
- say each syllable in the word (or break a single-syllable word into onset and rime);
- name the letters in the word twice;
- write the word, naming each letter as you write it.

Repeated writing

The practice of having a student correct an error by writing the correct version of the word several times is believed by some teachers to serve no useful purpose. They consider that it is a form of rote learning that can be carried out without conscious effort on the part of the learner, and that words practised in this way are not remembered later. It is true that if the student is thinking of other things or is distracted by noise or activity while carrying out the repeated writing, the procedure is of little value. However, repeated writing of a target word can be very helpful if the learner has every intention of trying to remedy an error and is attending fully to the task. It is one way in which kinaesthetic images of words can be more firmly established. Only a few words (usually no more than three) should be practised in any one session.

Old Way:New Way method

Lyndon (1989) identified the psychological construct of 'proactive inhibition' as a possible reason for the failure of many conventional remedial methods to help a student 'unlearn' incorrect responses, such as habitual errors in spelling. Proactive inhibition (or proactive interference) is the term used to describe the situation where previously learned information interferes with one's ability to remember new information or to acquire a new response. What the individual already knows is protected from change.

Lyndon's approach, called 'old way:new way', uses the student's error as the starting point for change. A memory of the old way of spelling of the word is used to activate later an awareness of the new (correct) way of spelling the word. The following steps and procedures are used in 'old way:new way':

- Student writes the word in the usual (incorrect) form.
- Teacher and student agree to call this the 'old way' of spelling that word.
- Teacher shows student a 'new way' (correct way) of spelling the word.
- Attention is drawn to the similarities and differences between the old and the new forms.
- Student writes word again in the old way.

- Student writes word in the new way, and states clearly the differences.
- Repeat five such writings of old way, new way and statement of differences.
- Write the word the new way six times, using different colour pens or in different styles. Older students may be asked to write six different sentences using the word in its 'new' form.
- Revise the word or words taught after a two-week interval.
- If necessary, repeat this procedure every two weeks until the new response is firmly established.

The Directed Spelling Thinking Activity (DSTA)

Graham, Harris and Loynachan (1996) advocate this approach for use with learning-disabled students. It is basically a word-study activity in which a group of students are helped to compare, contrast and categorise two or more words based on discovery of points of similarity and difference. The goal is to raise the students' awareness of spelling patterns and the more complex grapho-phonic principles. For example, students may explore words with the long /a/ sound, as in *pay*, *pail*, *male*. They discover that the long /a/ is represented not only by 'ay', but also by 'ai' (*nail*) and by the letter 'a' in several words with the final 'silent e' (as in *lake*, *mate*, *made*, *late*). The students then classify other similar words into these groups, or decide that a particular word is an exception to the principle. Follow-up activities might include looking for words conforming to the rule in reading material, scanning their own writing for such words, adding similar words to a class list over a period of time.

Word sorts

Word sorts are similar to the DSTA approach. Students are provided with word cards containing the words to be studied and compared. The words might be: *sock*, *black*, *truck*, *lock*, *rack*, *trick*, *track*, *block*, *lick*, *sack*, *stick*, *flock*, *flick*, *suck*. The students are asked, 'What is the same about these words?' The response might be that the words all end with /ck/. The words might now be categorised in other ways by sorting the cards into groups (for example, words ending in /ock/; words ending in /ack/).

Zutell (1998) strongly supports the use of word sorts as a valuable method of helping children recognise important orthographic units in and across words. Zutell reports that primary students showed positive improvement in their spelling as a result of regular participation in word-sort activities.

At a more advanced level, word sorts could involve words that are grouped according to the meaning–spelling connection, as discussed above – for example, *played*, *playfully*, *replay*, *player*, *playground*, *horseplay*.

Programming for individual students

When planning an individualised programme in spelling the following points should be kept in mind.

- Apply the basic diagnostic questions and procedures described in Chapter 8.
- Daily attention will be needed for the least able spellers, with weekly revision and regular testing for mastery.
- Collect a list of words frequently needed by students to whom you are giving special help. Use this list for regular review and assessment. See also Cramer (1998) for lists of words most commonly misspelled at various ages.
- Try to obtain from teachers in secondary schools important vocabulary lists from specific subject areas: e.g. *ingredients, temperature, chisel, theory, science, equation*, etc. These can be a useful focus of study for older students.
- Within each tutorial session students should always work on specific words misspelled in free writing lessons as well as on more general word lists or word families. Studying word families is in order to develop insight into word structure. Tiedt, Tiedt and Tiedt (2001) recommend that a spelling programme should include at least three categories of words: high-frequency core words, personal words, and 'pattern' words that illustrate a specific phonological or morphological principle.
- When making a correction to a word, a student should rewrite the whole word not merely erase the incorrect letters.
- Repetition and overlearning are important, so it is useful to have a range of games, word puzzles and computer tasks available to reinforce the spelling of important words. The games and activities must be closely matched to the objectives of the intervention programme.
- A visual record of improvement, such as an individual progress chart or graph, can help to indicate the number of new words mastered each week.
- The value of having students spell words aloud without seeing them or writing them is very questionable because spelling is a visual, auditory and motor activity. The visual appearance of the word as it is being written provides important clues to the speller. These clues are absent when the word is spelled aloud unseen.
- A neat, careful style of handwriting that can be executed swiftly and easily by the student is an important factor associated with good spelling. It cannot be inferred that good handwriting *per se* causes good spelling, but laboured handwriting and uncertain letter formation almost certainly inhibit the easy development of spelling habits at an automatic response level.

Additional practical advice on activities to improve spelling skills can be found in the books listed under Further reading and in Tiedt *et al.* (2001) or Cunningham *et al.* (2000).

Further reading

Bear, D.R., Invernizzi, M., Templeton, S. and Johnson, F. (2000) *Words their Way* (2nd edn), Upper Saddle River, NJ: Merrill.

Gunning, T.G. (2001) *Building Words: A Resource Manual for Teaching Word Analysis and Spelling Strategies*, Boston, MA: Allyn and Bacon.

Henry, M.K. and Redding, N.C. (1998) *Patterns for Success in Reading and Spelling*, Austin, TX: ProEd.

Kress, G. (2000) *Early Spelling: Between Convention and Creativity*, London: Routledge.

Rasinski, T.V. (2000) *Teaching Word Recognition, Spelling and Vocabulary*, Newark, DE: International Reading Association.

Reason, R. and Boote, R. (1994) *Helping Children with Reading and Spelling*, London: Routledge.

Rosencrans, G. (1998) *The Spelling Book: Teaching Children How to Spell, not What to Spell*, Newark, DE: International Reading Association.

Topping, K. (1995) *Paired Reading, Spelling and Writing*, London: Cassell.

Westwood, P.S. (1999) *Spelling: Approaches to Teaching and Assessment*, Melbourne: Australian Council for Educational Research.

Chapter 12

Developing numeracy and math problem-solving skills

> In striving for educational excellence and higher standards we must provide students with disabilities with instruction to help them become problem-solvers and move beyond rote application of basic skills.
>
> (Parmar, Cawley and Frazita 1996: 427)

Many children with disabilities and learning problems experience difficulty in acquiring number concepts and coping with the demands of calculation and problem solving. In this chapter some of the reasons for their difficulties will be discussed. Suggestions will be made for assessing students' abilities in basic mathematical skills and teaching methods will be examined.

Contemporary perspectives on mathematics teaching

In most schools today mathematics teaching utilises a *constructivist* approach, often referred to as 'process maths' or activity-based mathematics. Rather than using direct instructional methods the teacher's role now is to create learning situations that provide opportunities for children to discover mathematical relationships, solve real problems and construct meaning for themselves (Battista 1999; Lampert 2001). It is believed that these constructivist methods have most to offer for the development of higher-order cognitive skills and strategies. Orange (2002: 113) writes:

> Constructivism is the most current learning theory. Educators are encouraged to release the grip the behaviorists have had on instruction and learning over the past several decades. Teachers are encouraged to allow students time to reflect and think about information rather than give them the answers right away. Teachers should view mistakes as an opportunity to learn and a natural part of the learning process ... If children are to learn to construct knowledge, the teacher must be willing

to assume the role of facilitator and resist the urge to make their instruction teacher-centred.

Constructivist approaches are not without their critics, and in the mathematics domain the 'maths wars' have developed in much the same way that 'reading wars' developed in the literacy domain. The notion that mathematics can be taught successfully by the same type of student-centred, immersion approach as advocated for language arts learning has been challenged by Hunting (1996). He suggests that there is so much content for students to learn in the mathematics domain that skilled teaching and the efficient use of time are essential for an effective classroom programme.

In countries where the highest achievement levels in mathematics occur (Japan, Korea, Singapore and Hong Kong) teachers have not moved whole-heartedly into student-centred activity methods. Typically the mathematics lessons in such countries reveal that teachers maintain fairly close control over the learning process, but ensure that all students participate collaboratively in interactive whole-class lessons to solve problems and apply new skills (Sawada 1999). The emphasis is certainly upon making meaning, but not through the medium of unstructured activities. It has been remarked already in this book that unstructured approaches appear to be relatively unsuccessful with some children and may even be a primary cause of their learning difficulties. Some students appear to make better progress when directly taught (Mastropieri, Scruggs and Butcher 1997).

The goals of mathematics education

According to Harniss *et al.* (2002: 123) the goals of instruction in mathematics, as stated by the National Council of Teachers of Mathematics in America, are not controversial. The goals indicate that students should:

- learn to value mathematics;
- become confident in their ability to do mathematics;
- become mathematical problem solvers;
- learn to communicate mathematically;
- learn to reason mathematically.

Almost identical goals can be found in curriculum guidelines in Australia and Britain. It is the basic right of all students to receive an education in mathematics that helps them achieve these goals to the best of their capabilities.

Contemporary views on what constitutes proficiency in mathematics suggests that students need to acquire five competencies (Kilpatrick, Swafford and Findell 2001):

- conceptual understanding: the ability to comprehend relations, operations and concepts;
- procedural fluency: skill, speed and accuracy in carrying out procedures;
- strategic competence: the ability to devise appropriate plans for solving problems or recording experiences;
- adaptive reasoning: flexibility in thinking, and the capacity to view problems from different perspectives;
- productive disposition: an inclination to enjoy mathematics and appreciate its relevance, together with a personal desire to master mathematical skills.

To achieve these competencies exposure to a wide variety of quantitative experiences and teaching methods is almost certainly necessary; it is unlikely that a single approach could ever ensure development in all five areas. The conclusion to be reached is that a balanced approach to the teaching of mathematics should include a significant measure of explicit teaching, as well as the valuable hands-on activities and exploration that typify constructivist programmes (Burns 1998; Fleischner and Manheimer 1997). The amount of explicit instruction required varies from student to student, with direct teaching often being of most benefit for students with learning difficulties and disabilities. The perspective presented in this chapter reflects this conclusion.

In general, research on teacher effectiveness in the area of mathematics supports the use of a structured approach within a carefully sequenced programme. Evidence seems to prove that effective teachers can provide systematic instruction in mathematics in such a way that understanding can accompany the mastery of number skills and problem-solving strategies with a minimum of confusion. Within such an approach, the use of practical work, collaborative group activities and open discussion will also have a vital role in developing understanding and positive attitudes in the learners.

Effective teachers of mathematics are good at constructing series of lessons that engage their students actively in the curriculum content (Chen, Lee and Stevenson 1993; Stigler, Fernandez and Yoshida 1996). Their lessons are typically clear, accurate and rich in examples and demonstrations of a particular concept, process or strategy. The teacher takes an active role in stimulating students' interest, imparting relevant information and teaching specific skills, while still providing abundant opportunities for active participation by students.

Whole-class teaching and group work

Although there is increasing support for interactive whole-class teaching in mathematics (e.g. Reynolds and Farrell 1996) the use of a direct teaching approach does not mean that teachers should make no use of group work or collaborative learning in the classroom. Lessons with well-planned group work included do facilitate student achievement and increase motivation. Group activities that involve students in discussion and sharing of ideas appear to help individuals negotiate a better understanding of key concepts and processes. It should be noted however that certain students don't seem to gain as much as others from small group processes, particularly those students who remain passive and allow others to make decisions and do most of the work. Students with learning difficulties appear often to receive too much help from their partners in typical group activities in mathematics (Bottge *et al*. 2002). Teachers need to recognise this potential problem and attempt to structure group work in such a way that all students can usefully participate (see Chapter 6).

Another difficulty associated with group work in mathematics is the paucity of curriculum materials specifically designed for collaborative learning. It is usually left to the teacher to develop appropriate resources; and the additional work involved may result in some teachers opting out of this pattern of organisation. It is not uncommon in primary schools to find classes physically arranged for group work, with four or five students seated together, but students actually working on *individual* mathematics assignments (Hastings and Schwieso 1995). This distracting arrangement results in poorer achievement, probably due to students' difficulties in maintaining attention to task.

Mathematics and special educational needs

It is suggested that approximately 6 per cent of students have significant difficulties in learning basic mathematical concepts and skills (Fleischner and Manheimer 1997). A much higher percentage of students are observed to be low achievers in mathematics, displaying a poor attitude towards the subject and having no confidence in their own ability to improve. Some students exhibit anxiety in situations where they are expected to demonstrate competence in applying mathematical skills (Battista 1999). While a very small number of these students may have a specific learning disability related to mathematics (*dyscalculia*), most have simply encountered difficulties with mathematics learning for a variety of different reasons, including the following obstacles:

- Insufficient or inappropriate instruction (Elliott and Garnett 1994).
- Pacing of the curriculum has outstripped the students' ability to assimilate new concepts and skills, and they have fallen behind and become discouraged (Harniss *et al*. 2002).
- Too little structuring of discovery learning or process maths situations, so they failed to abstract or remember anything from them. For many students the value of experiential learning is lost unless follow-up work is carefully structured and consolidated (Fleischner and Manheimer 1997).

- The teacher's use of language in explaining mathematical relationships or in posing questions may not have matched the students' level of comprehension (Cawley *et al*. 2001; Lever 1999).
- Abstract symbols may have been introduced too early in the absence of concrete materials or real-life examples. Concrete or visual aids may have been removed too soon for some students; or materials may have been used inappropriately and created confusion rather than clarity (Threlfall 1996).
- Students with reading difficulties may have been condemned to a diet of 'pure arithmetic' because they could not read the word problems in the textbook (Gucker 1999). Teaching only computational tricks does not amount to efficient teaching; such tricks are usually rapidly forgotten since they do not constitute meaningful learning.
- The students' grasp of simple relationships in numbers to ten or twenty may not have been fully developed before larger numbers involving complications of place-value were introduced (Ross 2002).
- The curriculum may have been presented in a linear sequence, with only a few lessons devoted to each topic before moving on to the next topic. The mathematics programme should be planned as a spiral, with key concepts and processes revisited at regular intervals in order to revise them and apply them to new situations. Regular revision is crucial for long-term retention and mastery of knowledge and skills (Dempster 1991). Less effective teaching of mathematics is characterised by infrequent review and revision, demonstrations that are too brief or unclear, insufficient guided practice, and too little corrective feedback.

What should be taught?

In the same way that views have changed in recent years on how best to teach mathematics to students with special needs, views are changing too on *what* should be taught to these students. Traditionally, students with learning problems were usually placed in the lowest-ability group and given a watered-down version of the mainstream curriculum. Sometimes (particularly in secondary school classes) a 'functional' curriculum would be developed with a title such as 'social maths' or, 'real life maths'. The belief was that students with special needs required an alternative to the mainstream programme, with the content significantly reduced in both depth and quantity, and focused clearly on numeracy skills required in adult life. However, it is argued now that students with special needs, like all other students, are entitled to engage in an interesting, challenging, relevant and inclusive mathematics curriculum (Cawley *et al*. 2001; Harniss *et al*. 2002). The suggestion now is that the content of the mathematics course should be reduced as little as possible for lower-ability students in order to maintain sufficient interest and challenge. This is an admirable notion, but is far from simple to put into practice. The dilemma concerning what should and should not be included in the curriculum for students with significant learning problems remains unresolved.

It has been said that:

> Although existing research does not provide clear guidelines for teaching mathematics to children with severe learning difficulties, existing evidence and experience suggest that the same teaching and learning principles apply to all children, including special-needs children . . . Common mistakes in their instruction include (a) not assessing, fostering and building on their informal knowledge, (b) overly abstract instruction that proceeds too quickly; and (c) instruction that relies on memorizing mathematics by rote. In other words, the learning difficulties of special-needs children and children in general are the same.
>
> (Kilpatrick, Swafford and Findell. 2001: 341)

A similar perspective is reflected in the *National Numeracy Strategy Framework* in Britain (DfEE 1999: 21). There it is stated:

> The needs of pupils regarded as 'special' are not essentially different from those of other children. Instead of focusing on differences, you might emphasise the links with the needs of all learners, and use them productively to improve learning opportunities for all children.

To help make mathematics more interesting and relevant to a wide and diverse range of students it has been suggested that it should also be integrated into other school subjects, particularly into literacy learning, social studies, environmental education and the sciences. For example, the value of using mathematical concepts and skills within the context of reading and writing has been stressed very strongly (Burns 2001; Martinez and Martinez 2001). An integrated approach appears to enhance student motivation and involvement, and also increases the likelihood that mathematical concepts and skills will transfer and generalise to other situations and uses. However, an integrated approach does not imply that basic skills of numeracy are devalued or left to incidental learning. It is clear that mastery of basic number skills must be given high priority in any mathematics programme (Aubrey 2001; OFSTED 1993).

A diagnostic approach

There are many reasons why some students experience difficulty in mastering the facts, concepts and operations in arithmetic and applying these successfully to problem solving. As with reading, writing and spelling, the first step toward, intervention should be to ascertain what the student can already do in this area of the curriculum, to locate any specific gaps which may exist, and to determine what he or she needs to be taught next (Silver and Hagin 2002). In other words, the diagnostic model presented in Chapter 8 can be applied to the assessment of skills in arithmetic, and can guide programme planning in mathematics interventions.

The first step in the diagnostic evaluation of mathematical skills might involve formal testing of the student to determine the level at which he or she is functioning. A comprehensive picture of a student's range of knowledge and skills can be obtained from teacher-made tests. These tests reflect the content of the curriculum being taught within the programme. Curriculum-based assessment is now widely acknowledged as a helpful approach for teachers to use when linking assessment to instructional design.

Teacher-made tests can be supplemented with information gleaned from teachers' anecdotal records and from examination of the student's exercise books, worksheets or portfolio. The nature of a student's errors over a period of time can be appraised and follow-up diagnostic tests assessing proficiency in particular processes could be used.

Teachers can construct their own 'informal mathematical skills inventory' containing test items covering key concepts, knowledge and skills presented in earlier years together with essential material from the current year. Such an inventory can indicate precisely what the student can and cannot do, and will assist with the ordering of priorities for teaching.

Concrete to abstract

There are various levels of abstraction involved in diagnostic work in mathematics. Identification of these levels will help a teacher to answer the question 'What can the student do in mathematics if given a little help and guidance?' The levels are concrete, semi-concrete and abstract. At the *concrete level* the student may be able to solve a problem or complete a process correctly if permitted to manipulate real objects. At the *semi-concrete level* pictorial representations of the objects, together with the symbols, will be sufficient visual information to ensure success. At the *abstract level* the student can work with symbols only. During the diagnostic work with the student, the teacher may move up or down within this hierarchy from concrete to abstract in an attempt to discover the level at which the child can succeed.

Informal diagnostic interviews

The main goal in teaching mathematics to *all* students is the development of everyday problem-solving skills, and therefore diagnosis of a student's current ability in this domain should have high priority. Close investigation of strategies used by a student in carrying out a computation or solving a problem can be achieved in an informal *diagnostic interview* (Buschman 2001).

Using appropriate calculations or problems as a focus, discussion between teacher and student can reveal much about the student's level of confidence, flexibility of thinking and underlying knowledge. Teachers should probe for understanding in the following areas when appraising a student's problem-solving abilities:

- detecting what is called for in a problem;
- identifying relevant information;
- selecting correct procedure;
- estimating an approximate answer;
- computing the answer;
- checking the answer.

It may be helpful to keep the following thoughts in mind when attempting to discover the student's functional level. Referring to any items the student fails to solve in a test or during deskwork, ask these questions:

- *Why* did the student get this item wrong?
- Can he or she carry out the process if allowed to use concrete aids, count on fingers, use a number line or calculator?
- Can he or she explain to me what to do? Ask the student to work through the example step by step. At what point does the student misunderstand?

The value of this procedure cannot be over-stressed. If a student explains how he or she tackles the problem the teacher can pick up at once the exact point of confusion, and can teach from there. Too often in remedial intervention situations teachers quickly reteach the whole process, but still fail to help the student recognise and overcome the precise point of difficulty

In many ways, assessing problem-solving skills and strategies in mathematics has much in common with assessing comprehension in reading. Additional information on teaching problem-solving strategies is provided later in the chapter.

Three levels of assessment

The following three levels of assessment may help a teacher design appropriate assessment materials. It is likely that the first two levels will be the most applicable for students with learning difficulties, including students with intellectual disability.

Level 1

If the student's performance in basic number is very poor consider the following points. At this stage almost all the assessments will need to be made at an individual level, using appropriate concrete materials such as toys, blocks, pictures, number cards.

- Check the student's grasp of *vocabulary* associated with number relation-ships (e.g. 'bigger than', 'altogether', 'less', 'share', etc.).
- Check the student's *conservation of number*.

Then check the following knowledge and skills in the following order.
    Can the student:

- sort objects given one attribute (colour, size, shape, etc.)?
- sort objects given two attributes?
- produce equal sets of objects by one-to-one matching?
- count correctly objects to ten? twenty?
- recognise numerals to ten? twenty?
- place number symbols in correct sequence to ten? twenty?
- write numerals correctly from dictation to ten? twenty?
- understand ordinal values (fifth, tenth, second, etc.)?
- perform simple addition with numbers below ten (e.g. 3 + 5 =). With counters? In written form?
- perform subtraction with numbers below ten (e.g. 8 − 5 =). With counters? In written form?
- count-on in a simple addition problem?
- answer simple oral problems involving addition or subtraction with numbers below ten?
- recognise coins and paper money (lp 2p 5p 10p 50p £1 or 5¢ 10¢ 20¢ 50¢ $1.00 $2.00)?

Level 2

If the student's performance in number is slightly better than Level 1 consider the following areas. Harniss *et al.* (2002) refer to some of the basic principles listed below as 'big ideas' – they underpin much of the understanding at the next level.
    Can the student:

- carry out simple mental addition with numbers below twenty?
- carry out simple mental problem-solving without use of finger-counting or tally marks?
- carry out simple subtraction mentally as above? Is there a marked difference between performance in addition and subtraction?
- perform both vertical and horizontal written forms of simple addition?
- understand the *commutative law* in addition (i.e. that the order of items to be totalled does not matter)? Does the child see for example that 5 + 3

and 3 + 5 are bound to give the same total? When counting-on to obtain a total in such problems does the child always count the smaller number on to the larger; or are these problems always solved from left to right $(2 + 8 = 12 + 5 =$)?

- understand *additive composition* (i.e. all the possible ways of producing a given set or total)? For example, 5 is 4 + 1, 3 + 2, 2 + 3, 1 + 4, 5 + 0.
- understand the complementary or reversible character of addition and subtraction $(7 + 3 = 10, 10 - 7 = 3, 10 - 3 = 7)$?
- watch an operation demonstrated using concrete material and then record this in written form?
- translate a written equation into a practical demonstration (e.g. using Unifix cubes to demonstrate $12 - 4 = 8$)?
- listen to a simple real-life situation described in words and then work the problem in written form? (Seven people were waiting at the bus stop. When the bus came only three could get on. How many were left to wait for the next bus?) Use numbers below 20. Can the child work problems at this level mentally?
- recognise and write numerals to fifty?
- tell the time: read a digital clock correctly? Read an analogue clock to the nearest hour and half-hour?
- recite the days of the week?
- recite the months of the year?

Level 3

If students are able to succeed with most of the items in the previous levels, or if they seem reasonably competent in most areas of basic number work, consider these questions.

Can the student:

- read and write numbers to 100? To 1000? Can he or she read and write sums of money correctly?
- halve or double numbers mentally?
- add money mentally? Give change by the counting-on method?
- recite the multiplication tables correctly and answer random facts from these tables?
- perform the correct procedures for addition of hundreds, tens, units (HTU) and thousands, hundreds, tens and units (ThHTU). Without carrying? With carrying in any column?
- understand place value with T U? With H T U? With Th H T U?
- perform the subtraction algorithm, without exchanging in any column? With exchanging? It is important to note the actual method used by the child to carry out subtraction. Is it 'decomposition' using only the top

line of figures; or the 'equal addition' method using top and bottom lines? Perform the correct steps in the multiplication algorithm? To what level of difficulty?

- perform the correct steps in the division algorithm? To what level of difficulty?
- recognise fractions: ½, ¼, 3½, 7¼, ⅒, 5³⁄₁₀, 0.8, 5.9, etc.?
- read and interpret correctly simple word problems?

The following sections present some teaching points for the most basic levels of number work. Children with learning difficulties, including those with intellectual disability, may benefit from application of the following principles within their programmes.

Teaching and learning at the concrete and semi-concrete levels

The use of structural equipment such as Dienes MAB, Cuisenaire Rods and Unifix is strongly advocated in the early stages of any student's mathematics programme (Tucker, Singleton and Weaver 2002). In theory, using such material provides a bridge between concrete experience and abstract reasoning by taking learners through experiences at the intermediate levels of semi-concrete (not the real object but another object or picture used to represent it) to the semi-abstract (the use of the first stages of symbolic representation such as tally marks).

Reys *et al.* (1998: 45) conclude that:

> . . . research indicates that lessons using manipulative materials have a higher probability of producing greater mathematical achievement than do lessons without such materials . . . Handling the materials appears to help children construct mathematical ideas and retain them.

Structural material is particularly important for students with learning difficulties and learning disabilities as it helps them to perceive and retain visual representations of number relationships. The use of apparatus is also helpful for making word problems more visual and concrete, and for establishing an understanding of place value. However, it must be recognised that manipulatives have to be used effectively if students are to form the necessary connections between the materials and the underlying concepts and processes they are designed to illustrate. Problems arise if students come to rely too much on apparatus and do not progress to the pencil and paper or mental level of processing number relationships (Threlfall 1996).

Counting

Counting is perhaps the most fundamental of all early number skills (Staves 1999). Counting can assist with the development of conservation of number because it facilitates comparing of groups. If a child has not acquired accurate counting of objects the skill must be taught by direct instruction. The problem is often that the student fails to make a correct one-to-one correspondence between the word spoken in the 'number rhyme' and the objects touched in order. If the physical act of counting a set of objects appears to be difficult for the student with a disability, manual guidance of his or her hands may be needed. For young children the use of 'finger plays' and 'number rhymes and songs' may assist with the mastery of counting.

Counting of actual objects will eventually be extended to encompass 'counting-on' strategy for addition, and the 'counting-back' strategy for subtraction, in the absence of real objects. These strategies may have to be taught directly to certain students.

Recognition of numerals

The cardinal value of number symbols should be related to a wide variety of sets of objects. Teachers can make numeral-to-group matching games (the numeral 11 on a card to be matched with eleven birds, eleven kites, eleven cars, eleven dots, eleven tally marks, etc.). Also useful are teacher-made lotto cards containing a selection of the number symbols being taught or over-learned (one to ten, or one to twenty, or twenty-five to fifty, etc.). When the teacher holds up a flashcard and says the number the student covers the numeral on the lotto card. At the end of the game the student must say each number aloud as it is uncovered on the card. Later these same lotto cards can be used for basic addition and subtraction facts, the numerals on the cards now representing correct answers to some simple question from the teacher (5 add 4 makes . . .? The number 1 less than 8 is . . .?).

Activities with number cards can also be devised to help students sort and arrange the numerals in correct sequence from one to ten, one to twenty, etc. The early items in the Unifix mathematics apparatus can be useful at this stage (e.g. the inset pattern boards, number indicators, number line to twenty).

The writing of numerals should be taught in parallel to the above activities. Correct formation of numerals should be established as thoroughly as correct letter formation in handwriting: this will reduce the incidence of reversals of figures in written recording.

Written recording

There is a danger that some very young students or those with moderate learning difficulties will be expected to deal with symbolic number recording too early. Pictorial recording, tally marks and dot patterns are all very acceptable forms of representation for the young or developmentally delayed child. Gradually, the writing of number symbols will accompany picture-type recording and then finally replace it, by which time the cardinal values of the numerals are understood. It is important that written recording should evolve naturally from concrete experiences. In the same way that 'emergent writing' occurs in the literacy domain so too 'emergent number skills' are evident in the numeracy domain.

Number facts

Many students with learning disabilities have problems in learning and recalling number facts and tables (Ostad 1999) and require extra attention devoted to this key area. Number facts (e.g. $5 + 4 = 9$) are involved in all steps of the sub-routines carried out in complex computations, so they need to be recalled with a high degree of automaticity. Functional knowledge in arithmetic involves two major components: mastery of number facts that can easily be retrieved from memory (to $9 + 9$ and 9×9), and a body of knowledge about computational procedures. Both components are needed in typical arithmetic problem-solving situations.

It is essential that students be helped to develop automatic recall of the basic number facts rather than having to calculate with fingers each time they are needed. Being able to recall number facts easily is important for two main reasons: it makes calculation easier and it allows time for the deepening of understanding (Isaacs and Carroll 1999). Knowing number facts is partly a matter of learning through repetition (remembered through constant exposure and practice) and partly a matter of grasping a rule (e.g. that zero added to any number doesn't change it: $3 + 0 = 3$, $13 + 0 = 13$, etc.; or if $7 + 3 = 10$ then $7 + 4$ must be 'one more than ten', etc.).

Speed and accuracy

For students with difficulties, something as simple as a daily worksheet to practise number facts and the four processes can be of tremendous value – although frowned upon in some constructivist classrooms. Students should aim to increase their personal score each day in a three-minute session, competing against themselves, not the class average.

Mathematics educators sometimes complain that drilling basic arithmetic skills in this decontextualised way is boring and contrary to constructivist principles of learning (Tucker *et al.* 2002). However, if a student encounters basic computation only in the context of problem solving he or she is unlikely to acquire the necessary facility in rapid calculation. Regular practice will help to develop the necessary automaticity. For this purpose daily speed and accuracy sheets can be useful; but of course they must not be allowed to become ends in themselves; a student must have the opportunity also to *apply* arithmetic skills to problem solving (Robert 2002).

Number games

Almost any simple game involving a scoring system can be used to practise recall of number facts or simple addition or subtraction. For example, a skittle game can be played using empty bleach or cordial containers with a value (score) painted on each. The student has to add the value for any knocked down with each roll of the ball. Card games can be designed that involve adding and subtracting scores at each turn.

Tucker *et al.* (2002) have recommended that teachers devise or select games carefully in order to complement the objectives of the lesson rather than provide amusement. Students must be taught the appropriate way to play a game, and they should be made aware of what the game is teaching them.

Computer programs have proved useful in providing the necessary amount of drill and practice without boredom (Flores 2002). Drill sessions on a computer can develop automaticity in recall of facts for students with learning difficulties.

Pocket calculators

The pocket calculator provides a means of bypassing the computational difficulties of some students. There is a valid argument that time spent on mechanical arithmetic is largely wasted on a student who cannot seem to retain the steps involved in a particular procedure when working through a calculation with pencil and paper. The use of the calculator as a permanent alternative is totally defensible in such cases (Huinker 2002). Use of the calculator removes a major obstacle for students with poor computational skills, and they can all calculate with speed and accuracy. The instructional time saved can then be devoted to helping the students select the correct type of operation needed to solve particular problems; the result is more time on problem solving, not less.

It is likely that in the foreseeable future many teachers will still wish to teach computational procedures in traditional written forms, as well as permitting students to use a calculator (Fleischner and Manheimer 1997). It is to these teachers that the following paragraphs are directed.

Computation and algorithms

Once young students have evolved their own meaningful forms of recording in the early stages one must move on carefully to the introduction of conventional forms of vertical and horizontal computation. A student should be able to watch as a bundle of ten rods and two extra ones are added to a set already containing a bundle of ten rods and three extra ones and then write the operation as

12 + 13 = 25 or

$$\begin{array}{r} 12 \\ + \ 13 \\ \hline 25 \end{array}$$

The reverse of this procedure is to show the student a 'number sentence' (20 − 13 = 7) and ask him or her to demonstrate what this means using some form of concrete material. Dienes' MAB blocks are particularly useful for this purpose. Stern's equipment and Unifix blocks, being larger in size, are more appropriate for children with poor manipulative skills.

This stage of development is likely to require careful structuring over a long period of time if the student with learning difficulties is not to become confused. The careful grading of the examples, and the amount of practice provided at each stage, are crucial for long-term mastery. Once the students reach this stage of applying the basic algorithms for addition (with and without carrying), subtraction (with and without exchanging), multiplication and division, the demands on their thinking and reasoning increase rapidly.

It is, of course, valuable to teach students verbal self-instructions when carrying out the steps in a particular calculation. For example, using the decomposition method for this subtraction problem the student would be taught to verbalise the steps in some way similar to the wording below.

$$\begin{array}{r} 5_7 8^1 1 \\ - 1 \ 3 \ 9 \\ \hline 4 \ 4 \ 2 \end{array}$$ The child says: 'Start with the units. I can't take 9 from 1 so I must borrow a ten and write it next to the 1. Cross out the 8 tens and write 7. Now I can take 9 from 11 and write 2 in the answer box. 7 take 3 leaves 4 in the tens column. 5 take 1 leaves 4. Write 4 in the answer space. My answer is 442.'

A support teacher or parent who attempts to help a student in this area of school work must liaise closely with the class teacher in order to find out the precise verbal cues ('scripts') that are used in teaching the four processes so that the same words and directions are used in the remedial programme to avoid confusion.

Learning these scripts has fallen somewhat into disrepute in recent years. It is felt by some experts that these directed methods inhibit the more able students' thinking, and may prevent them from devising insightful and rapid methods of completing a calculation. Slavishly following an algorithm may represent purely mechanical performance based on rote learning. Neverthe-less, for students with poor aptitude for arithmetic, it is essential that the teacher does teach these paper-and-pencil skills thoroughly to the point of mastery. Without the verbal and mechanical procedures for working through a calculation the lower-ability students are likely to remain totally confused and utterly frustrated. It is often the absence of these basic skills that causes students with learning difficulties to become frustrated and disheartened in process-type mathematical activities and in problem-based learning.

It is important that students also be taught other strategies for solving addition and subtraction problems, preferably those which will help to develop insight into the structure and composition of the numbers involved. For example, if the student is faced with $47 + 17 = ?$, he or she is encouraged to think of this regrouped as a set of $(40 + 7)$ added to a set of $(10 + 7)$. The tens are quickly combined to make 50, and the two 7's make 14. Finally 14 combined with 50 is obviously 64. Fewer errors seem to occur with this method than with the 'carry ten under the line' type of vertical addition. This is almost certainly because the approach is meaningful and does help to develop insight into the structure of number. It can also be easily demonstrated using MAB blocks or similar concrete materials.

With subtraction the procedure may be illustrated thus:

    $(53 - 27 = \ )$ 53 can be regrouped as $40 + 13$
                     27 can be regrouped as $20 + 7$
                     Deal with the tens first: $40 - 20 = 20$
                     Now the second step: $13 - 7 = 6$
                     We are left with 26.

Once this method is established with understanding it appears to result in few errors than either 'decomposition' or 'equal addition' methods for subtraction. Equal addition method has fallen out of favour in recent years. It was once considered the best method to use for students with learning difficulties because it led to fewer errors when tackling difficult subtraction problems involving zeros in the top line.

In surveys carried out to determine adult needs in arithmetic (e.g. Knight *et al.* 1995), multiplication and division do not appear to be greatly used in everyday life. Certainly it is useful to be able to multiply, say, twenty-three lengths of wallpaper by 3m to find out how much to order to paper a room, but the adult who has difficulty with multiplication will usually solve the problem correctly as an addition process (setting down twenty-three three times and adding). It seems that if teachers are to identify the priorities for curriculum content in mathematics, addition and subtraction should be given high ranking, multiplication moderate ranking, and division lower ranking. For students of limited ability, a pocket calculator may well be the most obvious answer for multiplication and division.

The paper-and-pencil performance of students with perceptual difficulties or coordination problems is often a source of frustration. For some students it is necessary to rule up the pages of their exercise books in ways that will make it easier for them to write the digits in correct spatial positions (Lever 1999). Heavy vertical lines will assist with the correct placement of H, T and U, and thus maintain place values. Squared paper will usually assist with the general arrangement of figures on the page. Teachers may need to anticipate the difficulties some students will have in reversing not only single digits but tens and units (e.g. 61 written as 16). Much specific teaching, with cues and prompts such as small arrows or dots on the page, will be needed to overcome this tendency.

Developing problem-solving skills and strategies

Lampert (2001: 3) observes: 'Teaching with problems is an approach to instruction that has gone in and out of favour with education reformers.' Currently, the emphasis in mathematics teaching from the earliest years is to use a problem-based approach. According to Enright and Choate (1997: 280):

> Problem solving is the primary function of mathematics education. Students must learn how and when to use the computational and fact skills they develop, or these skills will be of no use at all. Solving problems involves the application of reading, computation, and a host of other skills specific to the process.

Students with learning difficulties frequently exhibit confusion when faced with a math problem to solve (Xin and Jitendra 1999). They may have difficulty in reading the words in the problem, or with comprehending the meaning of specific terms. Some students do not automatically apply the strategy of visualising the problem (Wiest 2001). They may also be uncertain of which process or processes to use. They may fail to generalise from one form of successful problem solution to another. Most students with these difficulties need to be taught a range of effective strategies to use. The aim is to teach students how to approach a problem without a feeling of panic or hopelessness. They need to be able to sift the relevant from the irrelevant information and impose some degree of structure on the problem.

Strategy training, including the use of mnemonics, has proved to be a promising approach to improving problem-solving ability in students with learning difficulties (Greene 1999; Harniss et al. 2002). Some examples of procedural and strategic methods for problem solving will be discussed.

How do we solve problems?

Although described differently by different writers it is generally accepted that there are recognisable and teachable stages through which an individual passes when solving math problems. These stages can be summarised as:

- interpretation of the problem to be solved;
- identification of processes and steps needed;
- translation of the information into an appropriate algorithm (or algorithms);
- calculation;
- evaluation of the result.

It is also recognised that in addition to the cognitive skills involved in the above five stages there are also significant metacognitive components. These components include the self-monitoring and self-correcting questions the learner needs to use when approaching a problem. For example:

- 'What needs to be worked out in this problem?' (identify the problem).
- 'How will I try to do this?' (select or create a strategy).
- 'Can I picture this problem in my mind?' (visualise).
- 'Is this working out OK?' (self-monitoring).
- 'How will I check if my solution is correct?' (evaluation).
- 'I need to correct this error and then try again' (self-correction).

Solving a problem is not always as easy as simply applying a pre-taught algorithm. Non-routine problems need to be analysed, explored for possible procedures to use, and then the result checked.

Most students with learning difficulties need to be taught how to approach a problem in mathematics without a feeling of panic or hopelessness. They need to be taught effective cognitive strategies for approaching any problem. A cognitive strategy can be thought of as a mental plan of action that enables an individual to approach a task in a reasonably systematic manner, and at the same time monitor the effectiveness of that strategy in operation (see Chapter 4). Students must be taught how to sift the relevant from the irrelevant information, how to identify exactly what the problem requires, and how to determine the best way of obtaining and checking their result. In other words they need to be taught the very things that other students who are efficient and confident problem-solvers already know and do. To achieve this outcome direct teaching in the early stage is a necessary step towards greater independence later.

Much of what we already know about effective teaching has an important place here. In particular, when teaching a problem-solving strategy, the teacher needs to:

- model and demonstrate effective use of the strategy for solving routine and non-routine problems;
- 'think aloud' as various aspects of the problem are analysed and possible procedures for solution identified;
- reflect upon the effectiveness of the procedure used and the result obtained.

A problem-solving strategy might, for example, use a particular mnemonic to aid recall of the procedure. For example, in 'RAVE CCC' the word RAVE can be used to identify the first four possible steps to take:

- R = Read the problem carefully.
- A = Attend to key words that may suggest the process to use (for example, *share*, *altogether*, *less than*).
- V = Visualise the problem, and perhaps make a sketch or diagram.
- E = Estimate the possible answer.

Then the letters CCC suggest what to do next:

- C = Choose the numbers to use.
- C = Calculate the answer.
- C = Check the answer against your estimate.

Once students have been exposed to an effective strategy they must have an opportunity to apply the strategy themselves under teacher guidance and feedback. Finally they must be able to use the strategy independently and to generalise its use to other problem contexts. The sequence for teaching problem-solving to students with learning difficulties therefore follows a typical sequence beginning with direct teaching and guided practice and ending with student-centred control and independent use.

Since there is evidence that students can be helped to become more proficient at solving problems, teachers of students with learning difficulties should devote more time to this area of work. As mentioned earlier, perhaps the students' use of pocket calculators will enable teachers to spend more time on this rather than restricting the students to a diet of mechanical arithmetic. Calculators do not inhibit the development of students' computational skills; and children who are permitted to use calculators often develop a better attitude towards mathematics.

Additional teaching points to consider when improving the problem-solving abilities of students with learning difficulties include:

- pre-teaching any difficult vocabulary associated with specific word problems so that comprehension is enhanced;
- providing cues (such as directional arrows) to indicate where to begin calculations and in which direction to proceed;
- linking problems to the students' own life experiences;
- giving children experience in setting their own problems for others to solve;
- stressing self-checking and praising self-correction.

In a review of interventions reported by Xin and Jitendra (1999) the following approaches all proved to be effective in improving students' ability to solve problems:

- computer-aided instruction (CAI);
- training in visualisation;
- metacognitive training;
- use of diagramming;
- use of manipulatives;
- estimating;
- use of calculator;
- attending to key words.

The results from their review suggested that CAI, the use of visual representations (e.g. draw a picture or diagram), explicit strategy training and metacognitive training (e.g. teaching the students to self-question and self-instruct using previously taught steps) all proved to be helpful in advancing students' problem-solving skills. Xin and Jitendra (1999) also point out that different students respond differently to the same intervention, suggesting that prior knowledge and existing skill level influences response. For interventions to be truly effective they need to be based on a careful appraisal of the students' existing knowledge and skills.

The text by Booker *et al.* (1997) is particularly useful in helping teachers to understand more about the processes involved in solving problems, with some excellent examples provided.

Further reading

Berger, A., Morris, D. and Portman, J. (2000) *Implementing the National Numeracy Strategy for Pupils with Learning Difficulties*, London: Fulton.

Fox, B., Montague-Smith, A. and Wilkes, S. (2000) *Using ICT in Primary Mathematics*, London: Fulton.

Harries, T. (2000) *Mental Mathematics for the Numeracy Hour*, London: Fulton.

Hughes, M., Desforges, C. and Mitchell, C. (2000) *Numeracy and Beyond*, Buckingham: Open University Press.

Kamii, C. (2000) *Young Children Reinvent Arithmetic* (2nd edn), New York: Teachers College Press.

Kilpatrick, J., Swafford, J. and Findell, B. (eds) (2001) *Adding It Up: Helping Children Learn Mathematics*, Washington, DC: National Academy Press.

Pound, L. (1999) *Supporting Mathematical Development in the Early Years*, Buckingham: Open University Press.

Thornton, C.A. and Bleys, N.S. (1994) *Windows on Opportunity: Mathematics for Students with Special Needs*, Reston, VA: National Council of Teachers of Mathematics.

Westwood, P.S. (2000) *Numeracy and Learning Difficulties*, Melbourne: Australian Council for Educational Research.

Chapter 13

Adapting curriculum and instruction

> Adaptive teaching is an educational approach that clearly recognizes differences between learners – especially cognitive differences or other specific characteristics. Teachers accept that their students differ in capabilities and take these differences as the starting point for teaching and learning.
>
> (Van den Berg, Sleegers and Geijsel 2001: 246)

In the previous six chapters attention has been given to the teaching and learning of what are known as the 'basic academic skills' – reading, writing, spelling and using numbers. Strategies have been presented for adapting methods and curriculum content in these areas to meet the special requirements of some students. The basic academic skills are obviously not the only areas of the curriculum where adaptation may be necessary when teaching students with special needs. In this chapter some generic principles for developing inclusive practice through differentiation across the curriculum will be discussed, together with specific suggestions for adapting curriculum content and resources, or modifying teaching approaches.

Differentiation

In the simplest of terms, differentiation can be defined as '. . . teaching things differently according to observed differences among learners' (Westwood 2001: 5). Differentiation strategies can be applied to:

- teaching approach;
- content of the curriculum;
- assessment methods;
- classroom organisation;
- student grouping;
- teachers' interactions with individual students.

Differentiation is attempted mainly as a response to diversity among students, but it is also a strategy for accommodating students with disabilities by removing some of the barriers to learning (Byrnes 2000). It should be noted that differentiation within the classroom addresses not only the needs of students with disabilities or learning problems but also the needs of the most able or gifted students (Kerry and Kerry 1997).

It must be acknowledged from the start that differentiation is never a simple matter in practice. Teachers may believe that their teaching should address students' individual needs and differences in principle, but in reality they have great difficulty in translating this belief into action. Effective differentiation invariably places very heavy demands on teachers' time, knowledge and organising skills (Babbage, Byers and Redding 1999; Peetsma *et al.* 2001; Pettig 2000). Webster (1995: 47) has observed:

> . . . whilst most teachers see the value in planning their teaching to enable all pupils to participate effectively at one level or another, classroom realities sometimes constrain good intentions. Differentiation is probably best viewed as an aspiration, and whatever steps teachers make towards achieving the kind of flexibility described here, will certainly benefit all pupils, not just those with special needs.

Differentiation first involves recognising that children differ one from another in many ways, and then planning and teaching lessons so that any educationally significant differences are taken into account. It is argued that when differentiation occurs all students can make optimum progress. The main advocate for differentiated instruction in the US, Carol Tomlinson (1996, 1999, 2001), refers to *personalising* instruction to take account of students' current levels of ability, prior knowledge, strengths, weaknesses, learning preferences and interests in order to maximise their opportunities to learn.

To achieve a personalised approach it is necessary to respond to individual differences among students by (for example):

- setting individualised objectives for learning;
- modifying curriculum content to match more closely the cognitive level of the students;
- providing different paths to learning to suit differing learning styles and preferences;
- varying time allocation for classroom tasks to take account of students' differing rates of learning;
- adapting instructional resource materials;
- encouraging students to produce their work in different forms or through different media;
- using flexible groupings of students;
- varying the amount of guidance and assistance given to individual students.

Most advocates of an adaptive approach to teaching consider the above eight areas to be the major focus for differentiated practice (e.g. Dettmer, Thurston and Dyck 2002). Each area will be discussed more fully, but first it is important to stress the *simplicity principle*.

Keep it simple

The whole process of applying differentiation in the classroom can sound very daunting for teachers because so many different ways of adapting instruction and modifying curricula have been described in the literature. Although in theory there are many potential strategies for meeting students' different needs in practice, it is not always feasible or desirable to apply more than one or two such strategies at any one time, particularly in large classes. The following advice from Deschenes, Ebeling and Sprague (1999: 13) is well worth noting:

> Adaptations are most effective when they are simple, easy to develop and implement, and based on typical assignments and activities. Adapting in this way is feasible for the classroom teacher because it is relatively unobtrusive, requiring little extra time for special planning, materials development, and/or instruction.

Applying the simplicity principle, Falvey, Givner and Kimm (1996) have recommended that adaptations and modifications should not be used unless absolutely necessary, and should be faded as soon as possible in order to liberate, not limit, a student's possibilities. It is important to ensure that a differentiated curriculum does not become an *impoverished* curriculum, with the lower-ability students always receiving less demanding work than the more able students.

Specific examples of differentiation

The mnemonic CARPET PATCH can be used to summarise the main ways in which teachers might adapt their approach in order to establish more inclusive classroom practice and meet their students' individual needs.

C = *Curriculum content:* The curriculum to be studied may be increased or decreased in terms of depth and complexity. Aspects of the curriculum may be sequenced into smaller units and presented in smaller steps. Lesson content may draw more on students' own interests.

A = *Activities:* Teachers can vary the difficulty level of the tasks and activities the students are required to undertake in the lesson.

R = *Resource materials:* Teachers could select or create a variety of different texts and instructional materials for students to use (e.g. some requiring less reading or writing).

P = *Products from the lessons:* Teachers might plan for students to produce different outputs from a lesson, according to their abilities, interests and aptitudes.

E = *Environment:* The classroom might be set up to support more individualised or group work. Use may be made of learning centres, computer-assisted learning, or resource-based learning.

T = *Teaching strategies:* Teachers might adopt particular ways of teaching designed to stimulate the poorly motivated students; or they may use more explicit and direct forms of instruction for certain groups in the classroom. Teachers may use tactics such as differentiated questioning, more frequent revising, practising, prompting, cueing, according to individual needs and responses from students. They may also set individual learning contracts for students.

P = *Pace:* Teachers may vary the rate at which teaching takes place, or the rate at which students are required to work and produce outputs.

A = *Amount of assistance:* Teachers could vary the amount of help given to individuals during a lesson. They may encourage peer assistance and collaboration among students.

T = *Testing and grading:* Teachers may vary the ways of assessing students' learning and may modify grading to reflect effort and originality as well as the standard achieved.

C = *Classroom grouping:* Teachers can use various ways of grouping students within the class to allow for different activities to take place, under differing amounts of teacher direction.

H = *Homework assignments:* Teachers may give some students homework that involves additional practice at the same level of difficulty, while others have more demanding homework involving application and extension exercises.

Much longer lists of specific differentiation strategies exist – for example, Falvey *et al.* (1996) identify over 120 different ways of organising and delivering what they term 'multi-level instruction' in inclusive mixed-ability classrooms. Other practical ideas are contained in James and Brown (1998), Janney and Snell (2000) and Udvari-Solner (1998).

Starting points

Kameenui and Simmons (1999) recommend that teachers begin to plan for differentiated instruction by focusing on essential core content they would hope *all* students will learn from the lesson or series of lessons (information, concepts, rules, skills, strategies). They refer to this as identifying the 'big ideas'. Planning and differentiating the topic then becomes a process of creating many different ways the students can encounter these big ideas through a variety of coherent experiences matched to their abilities. For example, some students may encounter new ideas through reading about them in books; some may understand them only if they encounter them visually through direct experience or via video; others may gain most from talking with peers about the issues or problems; some will understand new ideas best by creating their own pictures or models; and some will acquire the concepts most easily through direct teaching. As a general rule, all students in the group will learn best if provided with a variety of activities and paths to learning. To avoid fragmentation of the total learning experience the teacher must not lose sight of the big ideas for the topic, regardless of the many and varied activities and tasks set for students.

Several writers have described appropriate procedures for adapting curriculum and instruction (e.g. Deschenes *et al.* 1999; Dettmer *et al.* 2002; Hoover and Patton 1997). The steps they identify can be summarised as:

- selecting the subject or topic to be taught;
- identifying the specific content to be included;
- prescribing the learning goals and objectives for the majority of students in the class;
- deciding on the way the lesson will be organised and conducted for most students;
- identifying any students who will need modifications to the general lesson format;
- modifying the objectives for these students, if necessary;
- preparing any necessary adaptations (e.g. shorter assignments, easier textbook, extra use of concrete materials);
- teaching the lesson, and making any necessary additional changes while teaching;
- providing extra assistance to certain students while the lesson is in progress;
- planning appropriate methods for assessing students' learning, based on the goals and objectives.

When planning the differentiated objectives for the lesson it is usually helpful to have in mind the three sentence starters:

- All students will . . . .
- Some students will . . .
- A few students might . . .

These subheadings help teachers to identify the essential core of knowledge and skills that *all* students will be expected to master, possibly through different activities and varied pathways. Some students will achieve more than this core; and a few may achieve one or two higher-order objectives through the medium of extension activities (Kenward 1997).

In terms of organisation for the lesson, it is important to consider how students will be grouped and how the available time will be used most effectively. Planning needs to include consideration of strategies for facilitating the delivery of additional help to certain students during the lesson (e.g. via peer assistance, a learning support assistant, or from the teacher).

The following questions may need to be answered concerning any student requiring adaptations:

- Does the student have the prerequisite skills for this work (e.g. adequate reading ability)?
- Can the student work without constant supervision?
- Can the student work cooperatively with others?
- What is the attention span of the student?
- Does the student have any behaviour problems?
- What will represent appropriate work output from this student?
- What feasible modifications to the activities or resources will need to be made?
- Will the assessment procedure have to be modified for this student?

Modifying curriculum content

Modifying curriculum content usually implies that:

- students with learning difficulties are required to cover less material in the lesson;
- the tasks or activities they attempt are usually easier to accomplish;
- in the case of gifted or more able students, the reverse would be true; they might cover more content and in greater depth;
- for certain students in the class the objectives set for the lesson might involve mastery of fewer concepts and the application of easier skills;
- the nature of the learning tasks set for the students will be matched to their learning rate and abilities; some tasks may take longer time to complete than others;
- differentiated content for homework assignments could be used as one way of meeting the needs of gifted and able students, as well as those of students with difficulties.

Some definitions of differentiation refer specifically to 'matching' the level of curriculum content to the differing capabilities of the students in the class (e.g. Carpenter and Ashdown 1996). Other writers argue that differentiation should be less about changing the level or type of work set by the teacher but much more about providing alternative paths and giving as much assistance as is necessary to enable all students to study the same curriculum content and achieve satisfactory outcomes (e.g. Dettmer *et al.* 2002; McNamara and Moreton 1997).

Potential problems with modified curriculum

Reducing the complexity and demands of the curriculum and setting easier objectives may sound like very good advice; but watering down the curriculum in this way can have the long-term effect of increasing the achievement gap between the students with learning difficulties and other students. By lowering the demands placed on students of lower ability we may be exaggerating the effect of individual differences and perpetuating inequalities among students. It can be argued, particularly in countries with national curricula, that rather than reducing our expectations for what students can achieve we should be finding ways of providing students with sufficient assistance to ensure that they can achieve the same core objectives applicable to the majority of the school population. The problem is one of giving additional support (scaffolding) rather than the provision of alternative curricula. Obviously this argument cannot easily be extended to cover students with moderate to severe disabilities integrated in inclusive classrooms. In such cases it will be necessary to modify significantly the demands of the mainstream curriculum to match more closely the students' cognitive level. In many countries this is achieved through the medium of an individual education plan (IEP) and the provision of additional services.

Adapting resources

One of the main areas where modifications are recommended to improve access to the curriculum is that of instructional resources. The resource materials used within a lesson (texts, worksheets, exercises, blackboard notes, computer software) may need to be modified, and apparatus or equipment may need to be provided for some students (e.g. blocks for counting or grouping in mathematics; pages taped to the desktop for a student with gross motor difficulties; a 'talking' calculator for a student with impaired vision; a pencil with a thick grip for a student with poor hand coordination).

When preparing print materials for students with learning difficulties the following strategies may be helpful (adapted from James and Brown 1998; Squires 2001):

* simplify the language (use short sentences, substitute simple words for difficult terms);
* pre-teach any new vocabulary (if a difficult word cannot be simplified, ensure that it is looked at and discussed before students are expected to read it unaided);

- provide clear illustrations or diagrams;
- improve legibility of print and layout;
- remove unnecessary detail;
- present information in small blocks of text, rather than dense paragraphs;
- use bullet points and lists, rather than paragraphs where possible;
- make printed instructions or questions clear and simple;
- use cues or prompts where responses are required from the students (e.g. provide the initial letter of the answer, or use dashes to show the number of words required in the answer);
- highlight important terms or information (e.g. use underlining, or print the words in bold type or colour);
- consider sentence construction to facilitate comprehension. (Active voice is easier to process than passive voice: e.g. 'The teacher draws a line' rather than 'A line is drawn by the teacher'.)

Applying some of the strategies listed above will often be sufficient to allow a student with a mild disability or with a literacy problem to access text elements of the curriculum without the need for further adaptation. Evidence indicates, however, that in general teachers do not engage in much modification of resource materials, possibly through lack of time or lack of knowledge and skills (Chan *et al.* 2002).

Potential problems with modified resource materials

Bearne (1996) warns against the tendency to provide differentiation merely by using graded worksheets. While there may be occasions where the use of graded worksheets is appropriate and helpful, their frequent use can label the students as belonging to particular ability groups. It is also relevant to heed the warning from Robbins (1996: 33) that differentiation should not lead to 'death by a thousand worksheets'!

Use of too many worksheet assignments in class can produce poorer outcomes than the use of direct teaching. Based on classroom evidence from research into mathematics teaching in British primary schools, Reynolds and Muijs (1999: 21) report that:

> . . . there was often an over-reliance on worksheets and published [texts]. While these were not necessarily poor in themselves, they simply isolated pupils in ways that made it difficult for them to receive any sustained, direct teaching at all. In other words, more often than not complex arrangements for individual work were self-defeating; they dissipated rather than intensified the quality of the teaching and reduced the opportunities for children to learn.

On the issue of using simplified resources with some students there has been an interesting finding – in general, students *don't like* to use modified materials or to be given easier tasks (Hall 1997; Klinger and Vaughn 1999). Students with special needs, particularly those in the secondary and upper primary age range, want to have the same activities, books, homework, grading criteria, and grouping practices as their classmates – but they appreciate any extra help the teacher may give them while attempting that work. Students do not like to be given simplified tasks, materials or tests because these practices mark them out as 'different' and undermine their status in the peer group. Adolescents in particular are acutely sensitive to peer-group reactions, and they may deeply resent being treated as if they are lacking in ability. There is also some evidence that parents don't like their children to be given what they perceive to be easier work in the class.

Adapting instruction

Adapting instruction covers all the major and minor changes that may be made to the way teaching occurs in the classroom. It includes the method of instruction, how students are grouped, the nature of their participation in the lesson, and the interactions between teacher and students, and among the students themselves.

When teaching and learning processes are modified some of the following strategies may be used:

- The teacher may give more assistance or less assistance to individual students according to their needs.
- The teacher may reteach some concepts or information to some students, using simpler language and more examples.
- Questions asked during the lesson may be pitched at different levels of difficulty for different individuals.
- Closer monitoring of the work of some students may take place throughout the lesson.
- The teacher may use particular tactics to gain and maintain the interest of poorly motivated students.
- Feedback may be given in more detail or less detail, according to the students' needs.
- The rate at which the students are expected to work may be varied, with extra time allowed for some students to complete tasks.
- Extra practice may be provided for students who need it, often via differentiated homework assignments.
- Extension work may be set for the most able students, requiring mainly independent study, investigation, and application.
- The ways in which students are grouped for specific purposes (e.g. by ability, interest, friendships) may also be part of differentiation within the teaching process. The aim may be to encourage cooperation and peer

assistance; or grouping may facilitate the matching of learning tasks to students' ability levels; or grouping may help the teacher to give more assistance to certain students.

- Classroom learning centres may be set up, individual contract systems established, and computer-assisted-instruction (CAI) may be used.

Difficulties in adapting teaching process

There is evidence to suggest that teachers are much better at using the modifications to teaching process described above than they are at modifying the curriculum – there are fewer difficulties (Chan *et al.* 2002; Leyser and Ben-Yehuda 1999). They appear to find teaching process modifications more natural and much easier to accomplish within their personal teaching style. For example, skilled teachers do tend to provide additional help to students when necessary, they do use differentiated questioning, and they do make greater use of descriptive praise, encouragement and rewards during lessons. These are all strategies that can be applied while the teacher is still following a common curriculum with the whole class – and for this reason they are regarded as the most feasible adaptations for teachers to make. They certainly provide a very sound starting point for any teacher moving from a formal, whole-class method of instruction to a more personalised approach. What we know about the dynamics of change processes in education suggests that change is most likely to occur when teachers are required to take small steps in a new direction rather than giant leaps, and when they can build on their current practices.

Differentiating student output

The term 'student output' refers here to the products from the learning process. Often these will be tangible products such as written work, graphics, or models; but sometimes the 'product' refers to other forms of evidence of learning such as an oral report, a performance, a presentation to the group, participation in discussion, or the answering of oral questions.

Differentiating the products of learning may mean that:

- Each student is not expected to produce exactly the same amount or quality of work as every other student.
- A student may be asked to produce work in a different format; for example, an audio recording, a drawing or poster, rather than an essay.
- The student may complete a multiple-choice exercise rather than prepare a project involving extensive writing.
- Individual students might negotiate what they will produce, and how they will produce it, in order to provide evidence of their learning in a particular topic.

Potential problems with differentiating output

Whether or not teachers expect students to produce different amounts and varying qualities of work, they will of course do so – and have always done so. The potential danger in setting out from the start to accept less work from some students or a poorer quality of work, is that this strategy represents a lowering of expectations that can result in a self-fulfilling prophecy. The students produce less and less, and we in turn expect less and less of them. A different perspective suggests that teachers need to help students achieve more, not less in terms of work output, than they would have achieved without support.

The second suggestion of encouraging quite different products can be applied more easily in some subject areas rather than in others. For example, in social studies, language arts, expressive arts, and environmental education it is quite feasible and desirable to differentiate the product and encourage diversity in what the students produce. On the other hand, in mathematics for example, it is more difficult to find acceptable variations in the way that students can demonstrate their mastery of key understandings and skills.

Differentiation of product should never be seen as offering a 'soft option'. It should never lead to a student consistently managing to avoid tasks he or she does not like to complete.

Differentiation of assessment and grading

'Assessment' refers to any process used to determine how much learning, and what quality of learning, has occurred for each student in the class. Assessment provides an indication of how effective a particular episode of teaching and learning has been. The process of assessment also highlights anything that may need to be taught again, revised, or practised further by some students.

'Grading' refers to the fairly common practice of indicating the quality of the work a student has produced for assessment purposes. Often a letter grade (e.g. A, B, C, D) is used, or the work may be given a mark out of 10 or 100. In some countries there has been a trend away from this form of grading in favour of more descriptive comments and written feedback.

Modifications to assessment processes include such options as:

- simplifying the assessment task for some students;
- shortening the task;
- allowing longer time for some students to complete the task or test;
- allowing a student with special needs to have some assistance in performing the task (e.g. dictating answers to a scribe);
- enabling the student to present the work in a different format (e.g. scrapbook rather than essay).

Classroom tests are one of the ways in which some teachers assess the progress of their students. Students with special needs may require modification to the test format, or additional time allowed to complete the test. Some may need a variation in the mode of responding.

Standard adaptations for test formats include:

- enlarging the print;
- leaving more space for the student to write the answer;
- using more variety in question type (e.g. short answer, multiple-choice, sentence completion, gapped paragraphs, matching formats);
- rewriting the instructions in simple language, and highlighting key points;
- keeping directions brief and simple;
- providing prompts such as: *Begin the problem here* ⇒.

Modifications to test administration procedures include:

- using oral questioning and answering;
- using a scribe (someone else to write down what the student says);
- allowing the student to dictate the answers on to audiotape;
- giving short rest breaks during the test without penalty;
- allowing extra time to complete the test;
- avoiding any penalty for poor spelling or handwriting;
- allowing the student to use a laptop computer to complete the test;
- giving credit for drawings or diagrams if these help to indicate that the student knows the concept or information;
- spending adequate time making sure that *all* students understand the requirements before the test begins;
- reducing the anxiety that some students have in test situations;
- for some students, testing in an environment other than the classroom (e.g. social worker's office, withdrawal room) may help the student to relax and do his or her best.

Some ways of modifying grading to take account of learning difficulties, adapted from Wood (1998), include:

- using 'Satisfactory/Unsatisfactory' as the yardstick for grading a subject;
- reporting achievement not as a grade but as the number of specific objectives achieved in the course. This becomes a more *descriptive* report and can include indications of areas still needing to be improved as well as what was achieved;
- providing two grades for every subject. One grade represents 'effort' while the other grade represents 'achievement' (e.g. D for achievement; A for effort);

- recording results in numerical form (e.g. achievement: 66%; effort: 90%). Achievement is calculated from test scores or marks obtained for assignments. Effort is estimated rather more subjectively, but might also have specific criteria made known to the students before the course begins (e.g. 'You will receive 25 per cent if all classroom assignments are completed; 20 per cent for neatness and presentation; 30 per cent for participation during lessons; 25 per cent for all homework completed').

Potential problems in differentiating assessment and grading

Differentiation of grading procedures for students' work in inclusive classrooms is particularly problematic. The main debate concerning modifications to grading systems for students with special needs tends to focus on 'fairness'. For example:

- Is it fair to judge the standard of work produced by a student with mild intellectual disability, or a student who is deaf, against the standard applying to students of average or good ability in the class?
- Is it fair to give a student of very limited ability a report card showing Ds and Fails when he or she has worked extremely hard: doesn't this lower motivation and self-esteem?
- Is it fair to students who do not have learning difficulties or disabilities if we give 'good' grades to lower achievers simply based on the fact that they 'tried hard' and to encourage them?
- Is it fair to parents and employers to misrepresent a student's actual abilities and achievements on school reports by giving grades to encourage the student rather than to represent actual attainment? Shouldn't a grading system be the same for all students if it is to be fair and accurate?

For these and other similar questions there are no easy answers. Those who provide simplistic advice on adapting assessment procedures and grading criteria seem, at times, to be unaware of the complexity of some of the underlying dilemmas.

Accommodations for students with disabilities

The term 'accommodation' usually conveys the notion of making sure that students with disabilities can participate fully or partially in a particular lesson by varying the type of activities or the method of instruction, providing additional human and technical resources, giving extra support, modifying the ways in which the student will respond, or changing the classroom environment. Janney and Snell (2000: 16) suggest: 'Accommodations are changes that others make to assist the student. They are provided to enable the student to gain access to the classroom or the curriculum.'

Many of the modifications and adaptations already described above are equally appropriate for students with disabilities. For example, simplifying objectives and tasks, frequently reteaching important concepts and skills, allowing more time for students to complete work, encouraging different outputs from students, and facilitating peer assistance are all strategies that reduce or remove barriers to learning. Some students will also need additional support and modified equipment.

Technological accommodations often involve the use of assistive devices to help a student to communicate or to produce work output (e.g. modified keyboard, a computer with a visual display and touch screen or with voice synthesiser, braillers for blind students, greatly enlarged text on a computer screen for a student with partial sight, radio-frequency hearing aids for students with impaired hearing). Less sophisticated aids might include school-made communication boards for students without speech, or using symbol or picture-card systems for communicating. Technology has also increased the mobility and independence of many students with severe physical disabilities. It is beyond the scope of this book to discuss assistive technology in detail. Appropriate texts have been listed under Further reading.

The specific needs of students with disabilities are usually identified in their individual education plans (IEPs). The IEP should be seen as the main source of advice of the types of differentiation needed by the students.

Differentiation is not easy

It is important to state again that many teachers experience significant difficulty in implementing and *sustaining* a differentiated approach (Babbage *et al*. 1999; Pettig 2000; Scott, Vitale and Masten 1998). When advising teachers to become more responsive to individual differences among their students it is important not to overlook the real difficulties in practical implementation. As Rose (2001: 147) has remarked, 'The teaching methods and practices required for the provision of effective inclusion are easier to identify than they are to implement.' The problems, as well as the practices, have been addressed in this chapter.

Davies (2000) suggests that differentiation might prove to be impracticable for three main reasons:

- Teachers' inability to judge accurately the different ability and performance levels in their students.
- Teachers' inability to change their teaching to match observed differences among students.
- Unintended effects of differentiation that negate any benefits (e.g. students' negative reactions to being treated differently; failure to cover

the work required within a prescribed curriculum or for public examinations).

The following five barriers have been identified as preventing teachers from engaging in adaptive teaching (Schumm and Vaughn 1995):

- Planning for differentiated lessons is extremely time consuming.
- It is difficult to implement different procedures and tasks while managing the whole class.
- To simplify the curriculum or slow the pace of instruction may compromise the progress of the higher-achieving students.
- Using different tasks and resources may draw more attention to the students with difficulties.
- Simplifying everything (and making success easy) does not reflect the real world in which the students will need to function.

Prerequisites for using a differentiated approach

Based on information from international literature, it seems that the following five conditions need to be satisfied if teachers are to introduce differentiation in their classrooms and sustain the practice over time:

- Teachers have to *believe* that the investment in time and effort will produce significantly better results in terms of students' learning and motivation (Weston *et al.* 1998).
- Teachers have to have adequate *time to plan lessons* much more carefully if tasks are to be set for different levels of ability and if different resources are to be designed (Dettmer *et al.* 2002).
- Teachers need to *know the individuals in their classes extremely well* in order to match class work to students' differing abilities (Pettig 2000; Udvari-Solner 1998). It should be noted that teaching large classes militates against getting to know students well; and being a subject specialist who teaches many different classes also militates against knowledge of individual students.
- Teachers need to have access to a *varied range of resource materials* in their subject area, rather than being confined to a single standard textbook (James and Brown 1998).
- There needs to be *general support* for a differentiated approach to teaching within the school (Weston *et al.* 1998). It is even suggested that there must be an explicit commitment in the school's written policy to indicate that students' individual needs will be met through differentiated practices.

Given that differentiation as a strategy within classroom teaching has the potential to increase success rates for all students and remove some of the barriers to learning for students with disabilities it is hoped that teachers will continue to become more adaptive in their approach. Despite the difficulties mentioned in this chapter, many teachers already do a great deal to respond to their students' unique needs; given appropriate motivation, they will continue to increase their expertise. Advisers, inspectors, and support teachers need to be aware of the ways in which classroom instruction can be adapted so that the advice they give to teachers is of practical value. They also need to be fully aware that teachers will not necessarily find it easy to implement such advice and will require much support in moving in that direction.

Further reading

Deschenes, C., Ebeling, D. and Sprague, J. (1999) *Adapting the Curriculum in Inclusive Classrooms*, New York: National Professional Resources.

Fisher, D. and Frey, N. (2001) *Responsive Curriculum Design in Secondary Schools: Meeting the Diverse Needs of Students*, Lanham, MD: Scarecrow Press.

Flippo, K.F. (1995) *Assistive Technology: A Resource for School, Work and Community*, Baltimore, MD: Brookes.

Gregory, G.H. and Chapman, C. (2002) *Differentiated Instructional Strategies: One Size Doesn't Fit All*, Thousand Oaks, CA: Corwin Press.

Hart, S. (1996) *Differentiation and the Secondary Curriculum*, London: Routledge.

James, F. and Brown, K. (1998) *Effective Differentiation*, London: Collins.

Janney, R. and Snell, M.E. (2000) *Modifying Schoolwork*, Baltimore, MD: Brookes.

McNamara, S. and Moreton, G. (1997) *Understanding Differentiation: A Teacher's Guide*, London: Fulton.

Schumm, J. (1999) *Adapting Reading and Math Materials for Inclusive Classrooms*, Reston, VA: Council for Exceptional Children.

Stakes, R. and Hornby, G. (2000) *Meeting Special Needs in Mainstream Schools* (2nd edn), London: Fulton.

Tomlinson, C.A. (1999) *The Differentiated Classroom: Responding to the Needs of All Learners*, Alexandria, VA: Association for Supervision and Curriculum Development.

References

Adams, M.J. (1990) *Beginning to Read: Thinking and Learning about Print*, Cambridge, MA: MIT Press.

Agran, M. (1997) *Student Directed Learning: Teaching Self-determination Skills*, Pacific Grove, CA: Brooks-Cole.

Agran, M., Blanchard, C., Wehmeyer, M. and Hughes, C. (2001) 'Teaching students to self-regulate their behavior: the differential effects of student-vs-teacher-delivered reinforcement', *Research in Developmental Disabilities* 22: 319–32.

Alban-Metcalfe, J. and Alban-Metcalfe, J. (2001) *Managing Attention Deficit-hyperactivity Disorder in the Inclusive Classroom*, London: Fulton.

Alberto, P.A. and Troutman, A.C. (1999) *Applied Behavior Analysis for Teachers* (5th edn), Upper Saddle River, NJ: Merrill.

Alderman, M.K. (1999) *Motivation for Achievement: Possibilities for Teaching and Learning*, Mahwah, NJ: Erlbaum.

Algozzine, B. and Kay, P. (eds) (2002) *Preventing Problem Behaviors*, Thousand Oaks, CA: Corwin Press.

Allington, R.L. (2001) *What Really Matters for Struggling Readers?* New York: Longman.

Allington, R.L. and Baker, K. (1999) 'Best practices in literacy instruction for children with special needs'. In L.B. Gambrell, L.M. Morrow, S.B. Neuman and M.Pressley (eds) *Best Practices in Literacy Instruction*, New York: Guilford Press.

Alvermann, D.E. and Hruby, G.G. (2001) 'Content area reading and literature studies'. In J. Brophy (ed.) *Subject-specific Instructional Methods and Activities*, Amsterdam: JAI Elsevier Science.

American Psychiatric Association (APA) (1994) *Diagnostic and Statistical Manual of Mental Disorders* (4th edn), Washington, DC: APA.

Arter, C., Mason, H.L., McCall, S., McLinden, M. and Stone, J. (1999) *Children with Visual Impairment in Mainstream Settings*, London: Fulton.

Ashman, A. (1998) 'Students with intellectual disabilities'. In A. Ashman and J. Elkins (eds) *Educating Children with Special Needs* (3rd edn), Sydney: Prentice Hall.

Attwood, T. (1998) *Asperger's Syndrome: A Guide for Parents and Professionals*, London: Jessica Kingsley.

Aubrey, C. (2001) 'Early mathematics'. In T. David (ed.) *Promoting Evidence-based Practice in Early Childhood Education: Research and its Implications*, v.1, Oxford: Elsevier Science Press.

Babbage, R., Byers, R. and Redding, H. (1999) *Approaches to Teaching and Learning: Including Pupils with Learning Difficulties*, London: Fulton.

Badian, N.A. (1996) 'Dyslexia: A validation of the concept at two age levels', *Journal of Learning Disabilities* 29, 1: 102–12.

Barnes, W. (2001) 'Deaf children can'. *Special Children* 134: 24–7.

Barr, R., Blachowicz, C., Katz, C. and Kaufman, B. (2002) *Reading Diagnosis for Teachers* (4th edn), Boston, MA: Allyn and Bacon.

Bartlett, L.D., Weisenstein, G.R. and Etscheidt, S. (2002) *Successful Inclusion for Educational Leaders*, Upper Saddle River, NJ: Merrill-Prentice Hall.

Batshaw, M.L. (1997) *Children with Disabilities* (4th edn), Sydney: Maclennan and Petty.

Battista, M.T. (1999) 'The mathematical miseducation of America's youth: ignoring research and scientific study in education', *Phi Delta Kappan* 80, 6: 425–33.

Bauer, A.M. and Shea, T.M. (1999) *Inclusion 101: How to Teach all Learners*, Baltimore, MD: Brookes.

Bauer, A.M., Keefe, C.H. and Shea, T.M. (2001) *Students with Learning Disabilities or Emotional and Behavioral Disorders*, Upper Saddle River, NJ: Merrill.

Bear, D.R., Invernizzi, M., Templeton, S. and Johnson, F. (2000) *Words their Way* (2nd edn), Upper Saddle River, NJ: Merrill.

Bearne, E. (1996) *Differentiation and Diversity in the Primary School*, London: Routledge.

Beattie, R.G. (ed.) (2001) *Ethics in Deaf Education*, San Diego, CA: Academic Press.

Begun, R.W. (1996) *Ready-to-use Social Skills Lessons and Activities for Grades 4–6*, New York: Center for Applied Research in Education.

Beirne-Smith, M., Ittenbach, R.F. and Patton, J.R. (1998) *Mental Retardation* (5th edn), Upper Saddle River, NJ: Merrill.

Bender, W.N. (2001) *Learning Disabilities: Characteristics, Identification and Teaching Strategies* (4th edn), Boston, MA: Allyn and Bacon.

Berger, A. and Morris, D. (2001) *Implementing the Literacy Hour for Pupils with Learning Difficulties* (2nd edn), London: Fulton.

Best, A.B. (1992) *Teaching Children with Visual Impairments*, Milton Keynes: Open University Press.

Bibby, P., Eikeseth, S., Martin, N.T., Mudford, O.C. and Reeves, D. (2001) 'Progress and outcomes for children with autism receiving parent-managed intensive interventions', *Research in Developmental Disabilities* 22: 425–47.

Biddle, B.J. and Berliner, D.C. (2002) 'Small class size and its effects', *Educational Leadership* 59, 5: 12–23.

Biemiller, A. (1994) 'Some observations on beginning reading instruction', *Educational Psychologist* 29, 4: 203–9.

Bigge, J.L., Best, S.J. and Heller, K.W. (2001) *Teaching Individuals with Physical, Health, or Multiple Disabilities* (4th edn), Upper Saddle River, NJ: Merrill-Prentice Hall.

Biggs, J. (1995) 'Motivating learning'. In J. Biggs and D. Watkins (eds) *Classroom Learning*, Singapore: Prentice Hall.

Birsh, J.R. (1999) *Multisensory Teaching of Basic Language Skills*, Baltimore, MD: Brookes.

Bissex, G. (1980) *GYNS AT WRK: A Child Learns to Write and Read*, Cambridge, MA: Harvard University Press.

Blachman, B.A., Ball, E.W., Black, R. and Tangel, D.M. (2000) *Road to the Code: A Phonological Awareness Program for Young Children*, Baltimore, MD: Brookes.

Blair-Larsen, S.M. and Williams, K.A. (1999) *The Balanced Reading Program: Helping all Students Achieve Success*, Newark, DE: International Reading Association.

Blum, P. (2001) *A Teacher's Guide to Anger Management*, London: RoutledgeFalmer.

Booker, G., Bond, D., Briggs, J. and Davey, G. (1997) *Teaching Primary Mathematics* (2nd edn), Melbourne: Addison-Wesley Longman.

Bottge, B.A., Heinrichs, M., Mehta, Z.D. and Hung, Y.H. (2002) 'Weighing the benefits of anchored math instruction for students with disabilities in general education classrooms', *Journal of Special Education* 35, 4: 186–200.

Bradshaw, K. (1995) 'Learning disabilities: a cautionary tale', *Australian Journal of Remedial Education* 27, 4: 15–17.

Brennan, W. (1985) *Curriculum for Special Needs*, Milton Keynes: Open University Press.

Brooks, G., Flanagan, N., Henkhuzens, Z. and Hutchinson, D. (1999) *What Works for Slow Readers?* Slough: NFER.

Brophy, J. (1998) *Motivating Students to Learn*, Boston, MA: McGraw Hill.

Brophy, J. (2001) 'Introduction'. In J. Brophy (ed.) *Subject-specific Instructional Methods and Activities*, Amsterdam: JAI Elsevier Science.

Browder, D.M., Wood, W., Test, D.W., Karvonen, M. and Algozzine, B. (2001) 'Reviewing resources on self-determination', *Remedial and Special Education* 22, 4: 233–44.

Bullis, M., Walker, H.M. and Sprague, J.R. (2001) 'A promise unfulfilled: social skills training with at-risk and antisocial children and youth', *Exceptionality* 9 (1–2): 67–90.

Burns, M. (1998) 'Can I balance arithmetic instruction with real-life math?' *Instructor* 107, 7: 55–8.

Burns, M. (2001) *Writing in Math Class*, Sausalito, CA: Math Solutions Publications.

Buschman, L. (2001) 'Using student interviews to guide classroom instruction', *Teaching Children Mathematics* 8, 4: 222–7.

Butler, K.G. and Silliman, E.R. (eds) (2002) *Speaking, Reading and Writing in Children with Language Learning Disabilities*, Mahwah, NJ: Erlbaum.

Byrnes, M. (2000) 'Accommodations for students with disabilities: removing the barriers to learning', *NASSP Bulletin* 84, 613: 21–7.

Caldarella, P. and Merrell, K.W. (1997) 'Common dimensions of social skills of children and adolescents: a taxonomy of positive behaviours', *School Psychology Review* 26 (2): 264–78.

Capute, A.J. and Accardo, P.J. (1996) 'Cerebral palsy: the spectrum of motor dysfunction'. In A.J. Capute and P.J. Accardo (eds) *Developmental Disabilities in Infancy and Childhood*, v. 2, Baltimore, MD: Brookes.

Carpenter, B. and Ashdown, R. (1996) 'Enabling access'. In B. Carpenter, R. Ashdown and K. Bovair (eds) *Enabling Access: Effective Teaching and Learning for Pupils with Learning Difficulties*, London: Fulton.

Carter, C.J. (2001) *Reciprocal Teaching: The Application of a Reading Improvement Strategy on Urban Students in Highland Park*, Geneva: International Bureau of Education.

Carver, C.S. and Scheier, M.F. (1999) 'Themes and issues in the self-regulation of behavior'. In R.S. Wyer (ed.) *Perspectives on Behavioral Self-regulation*, Mahwah, NJ: Erlbaum.

Carver, R.P. (2000) *The Causes of High and Low Reading Achievement*, Mahwah, NJ: Erlbaum.

Casimir, G. and Alchin, G. (2001) 'Enhancing learning with assistive technology'. In P. Foreman (ed.) *Integration and Inclusion in Action* (2nd edn), Melbourne: Nelson-Thomson.

Cawley, J., Parmar, R., Foley, T., Salmon, S. and Roy, S. (2001) 'Arithmetic performance of students: implications for standards and programming', *Exceptional Children* 67, 3: 311–28.

Chan, C., Chang, M.L., Westwood, P.S. and Yuen, M.T. (2002) 'Teaching adaptively: How easy is "differentiation" in practice? A perspective from Hong Kong', *Asian-Pacific Educational Researcher* (in press).

Chan, L. and Dally, K. (in press, 2002) 'Review of literature'. In W. Louden, L. Chan, J. Elkins, D. Greaves, H. House, M. Milton, S. Nichols, M. Rohl, J. Rivalland and C. van Kraayenoord (eds) *Mapping the Territory: Primary Students with Learning Difficulties in Literacy and Numeracy*, Canberra: Department of Education, Training and Youth Affairs.

Chang, C.C. and Westwood, P.S. (2001) 'The effects of ability grouping on low-achievers' motivation and teachers' expectations: a perspective from Hong Kong', *Hong Kong Special Education Forum* 4, 1: 27–48.

Chapman, J.W., Tunmer, W.E. and Prochnow, J.E. (1999) *Success in Reading Recovery Depends on the Development of Phonological Processing Skills*, Wellington: NZ Ministry of Education.

Charles, C.M. and Senter, G.W. (2002) *Elementary Classroom Management* (3rd edn), Boston, MA: Allyn and Bacon.

Chen, C., Lee, S.Y. and Stevenson, H.W. (1993) 'Students' achievement and mathematics instruction in Chinese and Japanses classrooms'. In G. Bell (ed.) *Asian Perspectives on Mathematics Education*, Lismore, NSW: Northern Rivers Mathematical Association.

Chinn, S. and Ashcroft, J. (1993) *Mathematics for Dyslexics*, London: Whurr.

Choate, J. (1997) *Successful Inclusive Teaching* (2nd edn), Needham Heights, MA: Allyn and Bacon.

Clay, M.M. (1985) *The Early Detection of Reading Difficulties* (3rd edn), Auckland: Heinemann.

Clay, M.M. (1990) 'The Reading Recovery program: 1984–1989', *New Zealand Journal of Educational Studies* 25, 1: 61–70.

Clay, M.M. (1993) *Reading Recovery: A Guidebook for Teachers in Training*, Auckland: Heinemann.

Colbert, P. and van Kraayenoord, C. (2000) 'Mapping of provisions: states, systems and sectors'. In C. van Kraayenoord, J. Elkins, C. Palmer, F. Rickards and P. Colbert (eds) *Literacy, Numeracy and Students with Disabilities*, v. 2, Canberra: Commonwealth of Australia.

Cole, C.L. (2000) 'Self-management'. In C.R. Reynolds and E. Fletcher-Janzen (eds) *Encyclopedia of Special Education* (2nd edn), New York: Wiley.

Cole, P. and Chan, L. (1990) *Methods and Strategies for Special Education*, New York: Prentice Hall.

Compton, D.L. (2002) 'The relationship among phonological processing, orthographic processing, and lexical development in children with reading disabilities', *Journal of Special Education* 35, 4: 201–10.

Conners, F.A. (1992) 'Reading instruction for students with moderate mental retardation: review and analysis of research', *American Journal on Mental Retardation* 96, 6: 577–97.

Connor, M. (1999) 'Children on the autistic spectrum: guidelines for mainstream practice', *Support for Learning* 14, 2: 80–86.

Cook, B.G. (2001) 'A comparison of teachers' attitudes toward their included students with mild and severe disabilities', *Journal of Special Education* 34, 4: 203–13.

Covington, M.V. and Teel, K.M. (1996) *Overcoming Student Failure: Changing Motives and Incentives for Learning*, Washington, DC: American Psychological Association.

Cowley, S. (2001) *Getting the Buggers to Behave*, London: Continuum.

Cox, C. (1999) *Teaching Language Arts* (3rd edn), Boston, MA: Allyn and Bacon.

Coyne, M.D., Kameenui, E.J. and Simmons, D.C. (2001) 'Prevention and intervention in beginning reading', *Learning Disabilities Research and Practice* 16, 2: 62–73.

Cramer, R.L. (1998) *The Spelling Connection: Integrating Reading, Writing and Spelling Instruction*, New York: Guilford Press.

Crawley, S.J. and Merritt, K. (2000) *Remediating Reading Difficulties* (3rd edn), New York: McGraw Hill.

Cripps, C. (1990) 'Teaching joined writing to children on school entry as an agent for catching spelling', *Australian Journal of Remedial Education* 22, 3: 11–15.

Croll, P. and Moses, D. (2000) *Special Needs in the Primary School: One in Five?* London: Cassell.

Cross, M. and Vidyarthi, A. (2000) 'Permission to fail', *Special Children* 126: 13–15.

Csoti, M. (2001) *Social Awareness Skills for Children*, London: Jessica Kingsley.

Cunningham, P., Moore, S., Cunningham, J. and Moore, D. (2000) *Reading and Writing in Elementary Classrooms* (4th edn), New York: Longman.

Cuvo, A.J., May, M.E. and Post, T.M. (2001) 'Effects of living room, Snoezelen room, and outside activities on stereotypic behaviors and engagement by adults with profound mental retardation', *Research in Developmental Disabilities* 22, 3: 183–204.

Dahl, K.L. and Farnan, N. (1998) *Children's Writing: Perspectives from Research*, Newark, DE: International Reading Association.

Dahl, K.L., Scharer, P.L., Lawson, L.L. and Grogan, P.R. (2001) *Rethinking Phonics*, Portsmouth, NH: Heinemann.

Davies, A. and Ritchie, D. (1996) *THRASS (Teaching Handwriting, Reading and Spelling Skills)*, London: Collins.

Davies, P. (2000) 'Differentiation: processing and understanding in teachers' thinking and practice', *Educational Studies* 26, 2: 191–203.

Dempsey, I. and Foreman, P. (2001) 'A review of educational approaches for individuals with autism', *International Journal of Disability, Development and Education* 48: 103–16.

Dempster, F.N. (1991) 'Synthesis of research on reviews and tests', *Educational Leadership* 48, 7: 71–6.

Department for Education and Employment (1997) *Excellence for All Children*, London: HMSO.

Department for Education and Employment (1998) *The National Literacy Strategy: Framework for Teaching*, London: HMSO.

Department for Education and Employment (1999) *The National Numeracy Strategy*, London: DfEE.

Deschenes, C., Ebeling, D. and Sprague, J. (1999) *Adapting the Curriculum in Inclusive Classrooms*, New York: National Professional Resources.

Dettmer, P., Thurston, L. and Dyck, N. (2002) *Consultation, Collaboration and Teamwork for Students with Special Needs* (4th edn), Boston, MA: Allyn and Bacon.

DETYA (Department of Education, Training and Youth Affairs) (1998) *Literacy for All: The Challenge for Australian Schools*, Canberra: Commonwealth Government Publishing Service.

Dixon, R. and Englemann, S. (1996) *Morphographic Spelling*, Sydney: McGraw Hill.

Drew, C.J. and Hardman, M.L. (2000) *Mental Retardation: A Life Cycle Approach* (7th edn), Upper Saddle River, NJ: Merrill.

Driscoll, M.P. (2000) *Psychology of Learning for Instruction* (2nd edn), Boston, MA: Allyn and Bacon.

Dufflemeyer, F.A. (2002) 'Alphabet on the internet', *The Reading Teacher* 55, 7: 631–5.

Duncan, H. and Parkhouse, S. (2001) *Improving Literacy Skills for Children with Special Educational Need*, London: RoutledgeFalmer.

Dymock, S. and Nicholson, T. (1999) *Reading Comprehension: What is it?* Wellington: New Zealand Council for Educational Research.

Dymond, S.K. and Orelove, P. (2001) 'What constitutes effective curriculum for students with severe disabilities?' *Exceptionality* 9, 3: 109–22.

Eaves, R.C. (1992) 'Autism'. In P.J. McLaughlin and P. Wehman (eds) *Developmental Disabilities*, Boston, MA: Andover Medical.

Eells, J.M. (2000) 'Cloze technique'. In C.R. Reynolds and E. Fletcher-Janzen (eds) *Encyclopedia of Special Education* (2nd edn), New York: Wiley.

Eggen, P. and Kauchak, D. (2001) *Educational Psychology: Windows on Classrooms* (5th edn), Upper Saddle River, NJ: Merrill.

Elbaum, B., Vaughn, S., Hughes, M. and Moody, S. (2000) 'How effective are one-to-one tutoring programs in reading for elementary students at risk for reading failure? A meta-analysis of intervention research', *Journal of Educational Psychology* 92: 605–19.

Elksnin, L.K. and Elksnin, N. (1995) *Assessment and Instruction of Social Skills* (2nd edn), San Diego, CA: Singular Publishing.

Elksnin, L.K. and Elksnin, N. (2001) 'Messages from guest editors', *Exceptionality* 9,1: 1–2.

Elliott, C., Pring, T. and Bunning, K. (2002) 'Social skills training for adolescents with intellectual disabilities: a cautionary note', *Journal of Applied Research in Intellectual Disabilities* 15, 1: 91–6.

Elliott, P. and Garnett, C. (1994) 'Mathematics power for all'. In C. Thorton and N.S. Bley (eds) *Windows of Opportunity: Mathematics for Students with Special Needs*, Reston, VA: National Council for Teachers of Mathematics.

Enright, B.E. and Choate, J.S. (1997) 'Arithmetic computation: from concrete to abstract'. In J.S. Choate (ed.) *Successful Inclusive Teaching*, Boston, MA: Allyn and Bacon.

Evans, D. (1995) 'Human diversity and schools'. In F. Maltby, N. Gage and D. Berliner (eds) *Educational Psychology: An Australian and New Zealand Perspective*, Brisbane: Wiley.

Falvey, M.A., Givner, C.C. and Kimm, C. (1996) 'What do I do Monday morning?' In

S. Stainback and W. Stainback (eds) *Inclusion: A Guide for Educators*, Baltimore, MD: Brookes.

Farrell, P. (2001) 'Special education in the last twenty years: have things really got better?' *British Journal of Special Education* 28, 1: 3–9.

Fawcett, A.J., Nicolson, R.I., Moss, H., Nicholson, M. and Reason, R. (2001) 'Effectiveness of reading intervention in junior school', *Educational Psychology* 21, 3: 299–312.

Fenwick, G. (1988) *USSR: Uninterrupted Sustained Silent Reading*, Reading: University of Reading.

Fisher, B. and Medvic, E.F. (2000) *Perspectives on Shared Reading: Planning and Practice*, Portsmouth, NH: Heinemann.

Fisher, D. and Frey, N. (2001) 'Access to the core curriculum', *Remedial and Special Education* 22, 3: 148–57.

Fisher, R. and Williams, M. (2000) *Unlocking Literacy: A Guide for Teachers*, London: Fulton.

Fitzgerald, J. and Shanahan, T. (2000) 'Reading and writing relations and their development', *Educational Psychologist* 35, 1: 39–50.

Fleischner, J.E. and Manheimer, M.A. (1997) 'Math intervention for students with learning disabilities: myths and realities', *School Psychology Review* 26, 3: 397–413.

Flores, A. (2002) 'Learning and teaching mathematics with technology', *Teaching Children Mathematics* 8, 6: 308–10.

Foreman, P. (ed.) (2001) *Integration and Inclusion in Action* (2nd edn), Melbourne: Nelson-Thomson.

Fountas, I.C. and Pinnell, G.S. (1996) *Guided Reading*, Portsmouth, NH: Heinemann.

Fountas, I.C. and Pinnell, G.S. (2001) *Guiding Readers and Writers in Grades 3–6*, Portsmouth, NH: Heinemann.

Franco, D., Christoff, K., Crimmins, D. and Kelly, J. (1983) 'Social skills training for an extremely shy adolescent', *Behaviour Therapy* 14: 568–75.

Frederickson, N. and Cline, T. (2002) *Special Educational Needs, Inclusion and Diversity*, Buckingham: Open University Press.

Frieman, J. (2002) *Learning and Adaptive Behavior*, Belmont, CA: Wadsworth.

Friend, M. and Bursuck, W.D. (2002) *Including Students with Special Needs: A Practical Guide for Classroom Teachers* (3rd edn), Boston, MA: Allyn and Bacon.

Galloway, D., Rogers, C., Armstrong, D. and Leo, E. (1998) *Motivating the Difficult to Teach*, London: Longman.

Galton, M., Hargreaves, L., Comber, W., Wall, D. and Pell, A. (1999) *Inside the Primary Classroom, 20 years on*, London: Routledge.

Gang, M. and Siegel, L.S. (2002) 'Sound-symbol learning in children with dyslexia', *Journal of Learning Disabilities* 35, 2: 137–57.

Gettinger, M. and Stoiber, K.C. (1999) 'Excellence in teaching: review of instructional and environmental variables'. In C.R. Reynolds and T.B. Gutkin (eds) *The Handbook of School Psychology* (3rd edn), New York: Wiley.

Gillingham, A. and Stillman, B. (1960) *Remedial Teaching for Children with Specific Disability in Reading, Spelling and Penmanship*, Cambridge, MA: Educators Publishing Service.

Glang, A., Singer, G.H. and Todis, B. (eds) (1997) *Students with Acquired Brain Injury: The School's Response*, Baltimore, MD: Brookes.

Glass, L., Peist, L. and Pike, B. (2000) *Read! Read! Read! Training Effective Reading Partners*, Thousand Oaks, CA: Corwin Press.

Goddard, A. (1995) 'From product to process in curriculum planning: a view from Britain', *Journal of Learning Disabilities* 28, 5: 258–63.

Goldsworthy, C.L. (2001) *Sourcebook of Phonological Awareness Activities*, San Diego, CA: Singular Publishing.

Good, T. and Brophy, J. (2000) *Looking in Classrooms* (8th edn), New York: Longman.

Goodman, K.S. (1967) 'Reading: a psycholinguistic guessing game', *Journal of the Reading Specialist* 6: 126–35.

Graham, J. and Kelly, A. (2000) *Reading Under Control* (2nd edn), London: Fulton.

Graham, S. (2000) 'Should the natural learning approach replace spelling instruction?' *Journal of Educational Psychology* 92, 2: 235–47.

Graham, S., Harris, K. and Loynachan, C. (1996) 'The Directed Spelling Thinking Activity: application with high frequency words', *Learning Disabilities: Research and Practice* 11, 1: 34–40.

Grainger, J. and Frazer, T. (1999) 'Using private speech to overcome learned helplessness'. In A.J. Watson and L.R. Giorcelli (eds) *Accepting the Literacy Challenge*, Sydney: Scholastic.

Graves, D.H. (1983) *Writing: Teachers and Children at Work*, Exeter, NH: Heinemann.

Greene, G. (1999) 'Mnemonic multiplication fact instruction for students with disabilities', *Learning Disabilities Research and Practice* 14, 3: 141–8.

Gregg, N. and Mather, N. (2002) 'School is fun at recess: informal analyses of written language for students with learning disabilities', *Journal of Learning Disabilities* 35, 1: 7–22.

Gregory, G.H. and Chapman, C. (2002) *Differentiated Instructional Strategies: One Size Doesn't Fit All*, Thousand Oaks, CA: Corwin Press.

Grenot-Scheyer, M., Fisher, M. and Staub, D. (2001) *At the End of the Day: Lessons Learned in Inclusive Education*, Baltimore, MD: Brookes.

Gresham, F.M. (2002) 'Social skills assessment and instruction for students with emotional and behavioral disorders'. In K.L. Lane, F.M. Gresham and T.E. O'Shaughnessy (eds) *Interventions for Children with or at risk for Emotional and Behavioral Disorders*, Boston, MA: Allyn and Bacon.

Gresham, F.M., Sugai, G. and Horner, R.H. (2001) 'Interpreting outcomes of social skills training for students with high-incidence disabilities', *Exceptional Children* 67 (3): 331–44.

Griffin, P., Smith, P.G. and Ridge, N. (2001) *The Literacy Profiles in Practice*, Portsmouth, NH: Heinemann.

Gross, J., Berger, A. and Garnett, J. (1999) 'Special needs and the Literacy Hour'. In A. Berger, and J. Gross (eds) *Teaching the Literacy Hour in an Inclusive Classroom*, London: Fulton.

Gucker, G. (1999) 'Teaching mathematics to students with different learning styles', *Mathematics Teachers' Journal* 49, 1: 39–41.

Gunning, T.G. (1995) 'Word building: a strategic approach to the teaching of phonics', *The Reading Teacher* 48, 6: 484–8.

Gunning, T.G. (2001) *Building Words: A Resource Manual for Teaching Word Analysis and Spelling Strategies*, Boston, MA: Allyn and Bacon.

Hall, S. (1997) 'The problem with differentiation', *School Science Review* 78, 284: 95–8.

Hallahan, D.P. and Kauffman, J. (2000) *Exceptional Learners* (8th edn), Boston, MA: Allyn and Bacon.

Hammill, L. and Everington, C. (2002) *Teaching Students with Moderate to Severe Disabilities: An Applied Approach for Inclusive Environments*, Upper Saddle River, NJ: Merrill.

Harlen, W. and Malcolm, H. (1997) *Setting and Streaming: A Research Review*, Edinburgh: Scottish Council for Research in Education.

Harniss, M.K., Carnine, D.W., Silbert, J. and Dixon, R.C. (2002) 'Effective strategies for teaching mathematics'. In E.J. Kameenui and D.C. Simmons (eds) *Effective Teaching Strategies that Accommodate Diverse Learners* (2nd edn), Upper Saddle River, NJ: Merrill-Prentice Hall.

Harris, K.R. and Graham, S. (1996) 'Memo to constructivists: skills count too', *Educational Leadership* 53, 5: 26–9.

Harrison, C. (2001) 'The reading process and learning to read'. In C. Harrison and M. Coles (eds) *The Reading for Real Handbook* (2nd edn), London: RoutledgeFalmer.

Hart, B. (2002) 'Anger management', *Special Children* 143: 17–19.

Harwayne, S. (2001) *Writing Through Childhood*, Portsmouth, NH: Heinemann.

Hastings, N. and Schwieso, J. (1995) 'Tasks and tables: the effects of seating arrangements in primary classrooms', *Educational Research* 37, 3: 279–91.

Hazler, R (1996) *Breaking the Cycle of Violence: Interventions for Bullying and Victimization*, Washington, DC: Accelerated Development.

Heilman, A.W. (2002) *Phonics in Proper Perspective* (9th edn), Upper Saddle River, NJ: Merrill-Prentice Hall.

Heller, K.W., Alberto, P.A., Forney, P.E. and Schwartzman, M.N. (1996) *Understanding Physical, Sensory and Health Impairments*, Pacific Grove, CA: Brooks-Cole.

Heller, K.W., Forney, P.E, Alberto, P.A., Schwartzman, M.N. and Goeckel, T.M. (2000) *Meeting Physical and Health Needs of Children with Disabilities*, Belmont, CA: Wadsworth.

Hess, M. and Wheldall, K. (1999) 'Strategies for improving the written expression of primary children with poor writing skills', *Australian Journal of Learning Disabilities* 4, 4: 14–20.

Hill, F. and Parsons, L. (2000) *Teamwork in the Management of Emotional and Behavioural Difficulties*, London: Fulton.

Hilty, E.B. (1998) 'The professionally challenged teacher: Teachers talk about school failure'. In B.M. Franklin (ed.) *When Children Don't Learn*, New York: Teachers College Press.

Ho, I.T., Salili, F., Biggs, J. and Hau, K.T. (1999) 'The relationship among causal attributions, learning strategies and the level of achievement: a Hong Kong Chinese study', *Asia Pacific Journal of Education* 19, 1: 44–58.

Hockenbury, J.C., Kauffman, J.M. and Hallahan, D.P. (2000) 'What is right about special education?' *Exceptionality* 8: 3–11.

Hoffman, J.V. and Duffy, G.G. (2001) 'Beginning reading instruction: moving beyond the debate over methods into the study of principled teaching practices'. In J. Brophy (ed.) *Subject-specific Instructional Methods and Activities*, Amsterdam: JAI Elsevier Science.

Hoffman, J.V. and McCarthey, S.J. (2000) 'Our principles and our practices'. In J.V. Hoffman. J. Baumann and P. Afflerbach (eds) *Balancing Principles for Teaching Elementary Reading*, Mahwah, NJ: Erlbaum.

Holdaway, D. (1990) *Independence in Reading* (3rd edn), Sydney: Ashton Scholastic.

Honig, B. (2001) *Teaching Our Children to Read* (2nd edn), Thousand Oaks, CA: Corwin Press.

Hoon, A.H. (1996) 'Visual impairments in children'. In A.J. Capute and P.J. Accardo (eds) *Developmental Disabilities in Infancy and Childhood*, v. 2, Baltimore, MD: Brookes.

Hoover, J. and Patton, J. (1997) *Curriculum Adaptations for Students with Learning and Behaviour Problems* (2nd edn), Austin, TX: ProEd.

Huinker, D.A. (2002) 'Calculators as learning tools for young children's explorations of number', *Teaching Children Mathematics* 8, 6: 316–21.

Hunt, P. and Goetz, L. (1997) 'Research on inclusive educational programs, practices, and outcomes for students with severe disabilities', *Journal of Special Education* 31, 1: 3–29.

Hunting, R.P. (1996) 'Does it matter if Mary can read but can't add up?' *Education Australia* 33: 16–19.

Hutchinson, R. and Kewin, J. (1994) *Sensations and Disability: Sensory Environments for Leisure, Snoezelen, Education and Therapy*, Exeter: ROMPA.

IRA (International Reading Association) (1997) *Position Statement: The Role of Phonics in Reading Instruction*, Newark, DE: IRA.

Isaacs, A. and Carroll, W. (1999) 'Strategies for basic-facts instruction', *Teaching Children Mathematics* 5, 9: 508–15.

Isaacson, S.L. (1987) 'Effective instruction in written language', *Focus on Exceptional Children* 19, 6: 1–12.

Jacobsen, D.A., Eggen, P. and Kauchak, D. (2002) *Methods for Teaching: Promoting Student Learning* (6th edn), Upper Saddle River, NJ: Merrill.

James, F. and Brown, K. (1998) *Effective Differentiation*, London: Collins.

Janney, R. and Snell, M.E. (2000) *Modifying Schoolwork*, Baltimore, MD: Brookes.

Jenkinson, J., Sparrow, W.A. and Shinkfield, A.J. (1996) 'Cognitive and motor functions'. In J. Annison, J. Jenkinson, W. Sparrow and E. Bethune (eds) *Disability: A Guide for Health Professionals*, Melbourne: Nelson.

Johnson, D.W. and Johnson, R.T. (2000) *Joining Together: Group Theory and Group Skills* (7th edn), Boston, MA: Allyn and Bacon.

Kaiser, A.P. (2000) 'Teaching functional communication skills'. In M.E. Snell and F. Brown (eds) *Instruction of Students with Severe Disabilities* (5th edn), Upper Saddle River, NJ: Merrill.

Kameenui, E. and Simmons, D. (1999) *Towards Successful Inclusion of Students with Disabilities: The Architecture of Instruction*, Reston, VA: Council for Exceptional Children.

Kavale, K.A. and Forness, S.R. (1999) 'Effectiveness of special education'. In C.R. Reynolds and T.B. Gutkin (eds) *The Handbook of School Psychology* (3rd edn), New York: Wiley.

Kavale, K.A. and Forness, S.R. (2000) 'History, rhetoric and reality: analysis of the inclusion debate', *Remedial and Special Education* 21, 5: 279–96.

Kavale, K., Mathur, S., Forness, S., Rutherford, R. and Quinn, M. (1997) 'Effectiveness of social skills training for students with behavior disorders'. In T.E. Scruggs and M. Mastropieri (eds) *Advances in Learning and Behavioral Disabilities*, v. 2, Greenwich: JAI Press.

Kenward, H. (1997) *Integrating Pupils with Disabilities in Mainstream Schools*, London: Fulton.

Kerry, T. and Kerry, C.A. (1997) 'Differentiation: teachers' views of the usefulness of recommended strategies in helping the more able pupils in primary and secondary classrooms', *Educational Studies* 23, 3: 439–57.

Kewley, G.D. (2001) *Attention Deficit Hyperactivity Disorder*, London: Fulton.

Killen, R. (1998) *Effective Teaching Strategies: Lessons from Research and Practice* (2nd edn), Katoomba, NSW: Social Science Press.

Kilpatrick, J., Swafford, J. and Findell, B. (eds) (2001) *Adding It Up: Helping Children Learn Mathematics*, Washington, DC: National Academy Press.

Kirk, S., Gallagher, J.J. and Anastasiow, N.J. (2000) *Educating Exceptional Children* (9th edn), Boston, MA: Houghton Mifflin.

Klinger, J. and Vaughn, S. (1999) 'Students' perceptions of instruction in inclusive classrooms: implications for students with learning disabilities', *Exceptional Children* 66, 1: 23–37.

Klinger, J., Vaughn, S., Hughes, M.T., Schumm, J. and Elbaum, B. (1998) 'Outcomes for students with and without learning disabilities in inclusive classrooms', *Learning Disabilities Research and Practice* 13, 3: 153–161.

Knight, A., Arnold, G., Carter, M., Kelly, P. and Thornley, G. (1995) 'The mathematical needs of school leavers', *The Best of SET Research Information for Teachers: Mathematics*, Melbourne: Australian Council for Educational Research.

Lampert, M. (2001) *Teaching Problems and the Problems of Teaching*, New Haven, CT: Yale University Press.

Lane, K.L., Gresham, F.M. and O'Shaughnessy, T.E. (eds) (2002) *Interventions for Children with or at risk for Emotional and Behavioral Disorders*, Boston, MA: Allyn and Bacon.

Lang, G. and Berberich, C. (1995) *All Children are Special*, Armadale, Vic: Eleanor Curtain Publishing.

Leech, G., Rayson, P. and Wilson, A. (2001) *Word Frequencies in Written and Spoken English: Based on the British National Corpus*, Harlow: Longman.

Leigh, H.J. (1996) 'Physical impairment and multiple disabilities'. In J. Annison, J. Jenkinson, W. Sparrow and E. Bethune (eds) *Disability: A Guide for Health Professionals*, Melbourne: Nelson.

Lever, M. (1999) 'An introduction: teaching mathematics to children with specific learning difficulties', *Equals: Mathematics and Special Educational Needs* 5, 2: 10–11.

Levin, J. and Nolan, J.F. (2000) *Principles of Classroom Management* (3rd edn), Boston, MA: Allyn and Bacon.

Leyser, Y. and Ben-Yehuda, S. (1999) 'Teacher use of instructional practices to accommodate student diversity: views of Israeli general and special educators', *International Journal of Special Education* 14, 1: 81 – 95.

Lindberg, J.A. and Swick, A.M. (2002) *Common-sense Classroom Management*, Thousand Oaks, CA: Corwin Press.

Llewellyn, A. (2001) 'What does inclusion mean for children with physical disabilities?' *Special Children* 135: 36–7.

Lloyd, S. (1992) *Jolly Phonics*, Chigwell, Essex: Jolly Learning.

Louden, W. (2000) 'Mapping the territory: overview', in W. Louden, L. Chan, J. Elkins, D. Greaves, H. House, M. Milton, S. Nichols, M. Rohl, J. Rivalland and

C. van Kraayenoord (eds) *Mapping the Territory: Primary Students with Learning Difficulties in Literacy and Numeracy*, Canberra: Department of Education, Training and Youth Affairs.

Lovaas, O.I. (1993) 'The development of a treatment research project for developmentally disabled and autistic children', *Journal of Applied Behavior Analysis* 26 (4): 617–30.

Lovitt, T.C. (2000) *Preventing School Failure: Tactics for Teaching Adolescents* (2nd edn), Austin, TX: ProEd.

Lowe, P. and Reynolds, C.R. (2000) 'Attention-deficit hyperactivity disorder'. In C.R. Reynolds and E. Fletcher-Janzen (eds) *Encyclopedia of Special Education* (2nd edn), New York: Wiley.

Lyle, S. (1996) 'An analysis of collaborative group work in the primary school and factors relevant to its success', *Language and Education* 10, 1: 13–31.

Lyndon, H. (1989) 'I did it my way: an introduction to Old Way–New Way', *Australasian Journal of Special Education* 13: 32–7.

MacArthur, C., Feretti, R., Okolo, C. and Cavalier, A. (2001) 'Technology applications for students with literacy problems: a review', *Elementary School Journal* 101: 273–301.

McCarrier, A., Pinnell, G.S. and Fountas, I.C. (2000) *Interactive Writing*, Portsmouth, NH: Heinemann.

McCarty, H. and Siccone, F. (2001) *Motivating Your Students*, Boston, MA: Allyn and Bacon.

McEwan, E.K. (1998) *The Principal's Guide to Raising Reading Achievement*, Thousand Oaks, CA: Corwin Press.

McGrath, M. (1998) *The Art of Teaching Peacefully*, London: Fulton.

McGrath, M. (2000) *The Art of Peaceful Teaching in the Primary School*, London: Fulton.

McInerney, D.M. and McInerney, V. (1998) *Educational Psychology: Constructing Learning* (2nd edn), Sydney: Prentice Hall.

MacInnis, C. and Hemming, H. (1995) 'Linking the needs of students with learning disabilities to a whole language curriculum', *Journal of Learning Disabilities* 28, 9: 535–44.

McKinnon, D.H. and Gordon, C. (1999) 'An investigation of teachers' support needs for the inclusion of students with disabilities in regular classrooms', *Special Education Perspectives* 8, 2: 3–14.

McNamara, S. and Moreton, G. (1997) *Understanding Differentiation: A Teacher's Guide*, London: Fulton.

McNamara, S. and Moreton, G. (2001) *Changing Behaviour* (2nd edn), London: Fulton.

Manset-Williams, G., St John, E., Hu, S. and Gordon, D. (2002) 'Early literacy practices as predictors of reading related outcomes: test scores, test passing rates, retention, and special education referral', *Exceptionality* 10, 1: 11–28.

Margalit, M. (1995) 'Effects of social skills training for students with intellectual disability', *International Journal of Disability, Development and Education* 42, 1: 75–85.

Mariotti, A.S. and Homan, S.P. (2001) *Linking Reading Assessment to Instruction* (3rd edn), Mahwah, NJ: Erlbaum.

Marrone, A.S. and Schutz, P.A. (2000) 'Promoting achievement motivation'. In K.M.

Minke and G.C. Bear (eds) *Preventing School Problems, Promoting School Success*, Bethesda, MD: National Association of School Psychologists.

Marston, D. (1996) 'A comparison of inclusion only, pull-out only, and combined service models for students with mild disabilities', *Journal of Special Education* 30, 2: 121–32.

Martin, K.F. and Manno, C. (1995) 'Use of check-off system to improve middle school students' story compositions', *Journal of Learning Disabilities* 28, 3: 139–49.

Martinez, J.G.R. and Martinez, N.C. (2001) *Reading and Writing to Learn Mathematics*, Boston, MA: Allyn and Bacon.

Mastropieri, M.A., Scruggs, T.E. and Butcher, K. (1997) 'How effective is inquiry learning for students with mild disabilities?' *Journal of Special Education* 31, 2: 199–211.

Mazur, J.E. (1998) *Learning and Behavior* (4th edn), Upper Saddle River, NJ: Prentice Hall.

Meese, R.L. (2001) *Teaching Learners with Mild Disabilities: Integrating Research and Practice* (2nd edn), Belmont, CA: Wadsworth-Thomson.

Meier, D.R. (2000) *Scribble Scrabble: Learning to Read and Write*, New York: Teachers College Press.

Merrell, K.W. (2001) 'Assessment of children's social skills: recent developments, best practices, and new directions', *Exceptionality* 9 (1–2): 3–18.

Meyer, R.J. (2002) *Phonics Exposed*, Mahwah, NJ: Erlbaum.

Meyerson, M.J. and Kulesza, D.L. (2002) *Strategies for Struggling Readers: Step by Step*, Upper Saddle River, NJ: Merrill-Prentice Hall.

Miller, L.L. and Felton, R.H. (2001) 'It's one of them . . . I don't know: case study of a student with phonological, rapid naming, and word-finding deficits', *Journal of Special Education* 35, 3: 125–33.

Minton, P. (2001) 'Effectively integrating the computer to teach children with literacy difficulties', *Australian Journal of Learning Disabilities* 6, 1: 35–7.

Moats, L.C. (1995) *Spelling: Development, Disability and Instruction*, Baltimore, MD: Brookes.

Moody, S.W., Vaughn, S., Hughes, M.T. and Fischer, M. (2000) 'Reading instruction in the resource room: set up for failure', *Exceptional Children* 66, 3: 305–16.

Moore, D.W., Prebble, S., Robertson, J., Waetford, R. and Anderson, A. (2001) 'Self-recording with goal setting: a self-management programme for the classroom', *Educational Psychology* 21: 255–65.

Morrow, L.M. (2001) *Literacy Development in the Early Years: Helping Children Read and Write* (4th edn), Boston, MA: Allyn and Bacon.

Morrow, L.M. and Woo, D.G. (2001) *Tutoring Programs for Struggling Readers*, New York: Guilford Press.

Neale, M.D. (1999) *Neale Analysis of Reading Ability* (3rd edn), Melbourne: Australian Council for Educational Research.

Nelson, J.R., Crabtree, M., Marchand-Martella, N. and Martella, R. (1998) 'Teaching good behavior in the whole school', *Teaching Exceptional Children* 30, 4: 4–9.

Nelson, J.R., Ferrante, C. and Martella, R.C. (1999) 'Children's evaluation of the effectiveness of in-class and pull-out service delivery models', *International Journal of Special Education* 14, 2: 77–91.

Nelson, N. and Calfee, R.C. (1998) *The Reading–Writing Connection*, Chicago, IL: National Society for the Study of Education.

Nichols, R. (1985) *Helping Your Child Spell*, Earley: University of Reading.

Nind, M. (1999) 'Intensive interaction and autism: a useful approach?' *British Journal of Special Education* 26, 2: 96–102.

Nind, M. (2000) 'Teachers' understanding of interactive approaches in special education', *International Journal of Disability, Development and Education* 47, 2: 183–99.

OECD (Organisation for Economic Cooperation and Development) (1999) *Inclusive Education at Work: Students with Disabilities in Mainstream Schools*, Paris: OECD Centre for Educational Research and Innovation.

OECD (Organisation for Economic Cooperation and Development) (2000) *Special Needs Education: Statistics and Indicators*, Paris: OECD Centre for Educational Research and Innovation.

OFSTED (Office for Standards in Education) (1993) *The Teaching and Learning of Number in Primary Schools*, London: HMSO.

Olweus, D. (1993) *Bullying at School*, Oxford: Blackwell.

Orange, C. (2002) *The Quick Reference Guide to Educational Innovations*, Thousand Oaks, CA: Corwin Press.

Orelove, F. and Sobsey, D. (1996) *Educating Children with Multiple Disabilities* (3rd edn), Baltimore, MD: Brookes.

Ormrod, J.E. (2000) *Educational Psychology: Developing Learners* (3rd edn), Upper Saddle River, NJ: Merrill.

Osborn, J. and Lehr, F. (eds) (1998) *Literacy for All: Issues in Teaching and Learning*, New York: Guilford Press.

Ostad, S.A. (1999) 'Developmental progression of subtraction strategies: a comparison of mathematically normal and mathematically disabled children', *European Journal of Special Needs Education* 14, 1: 21–36.

Ott, P. (1997) *How to Detect and Manage Dyslexia*, Oxford: Heinemann.

Owens, J. (1995) 'Hearing impairment'. In J. Annison, J. Jenkinson, W. Sparrow and E. Bethune (eds) *Disability: A Guide for Health Professionals*, Melbourne: Nelson.

Pagliano, P. (2002) 'Using all the senses'. In A. Ashman and J. Elkins (eds) *Educating Children with Diverse Abilities*, Sydney: Prentice Hall-Pearson Educational.

Paris, S.G. and Paris, A.H. (2001) 'Classroom applications of research on self-regulated learning', *Educational Psychologist* 36, 2: 89–101.

Paris, S.G., Byrnes, J.P. and Paris, A.H. (2001) 'Constructing theories, identities and actions of self-regulated learners'. In B.J. Zimmerman and D.H. Schunk (eds) *Self-regulated Learning and Academic Achievement* (2nd edn), Mahwah, NJ: Erlbaum.

Parmar, R.S., Cawley, J.F. and Frazita, R.R. (1996) 'Word-problem solving by students with and without mild disabilities', *Exceptional Children* 62, 5: 415–29.

Pavri, S. and Monda-Amaya, L. (2001) 'Social support in inclusive schools: student and teacher perspectives', *Exceptional Children* 67, 3: 391–411.

Peetsma, T., Vergeer, M., Roeleveld, J. and Karsten, S. (2001) 'Inclusion in education: comparing pupils' development in special and regular education', *Educational Review* 53: 125–35.

Pettig, K.L. (2000) 'On the road to differentiated practice', *Educational Leadership* 58, 1: 14–18.

Pierangelo, R. and Giuliani, G.A. (2001) *What Every Teacher Should Know About Students with Special Needs*, Champaign, IL: Research Press.

Plant, G. (1990) 'Profound deafness'. In S. Butler (ed.) *The Exceptional Child*, Sydney: Harcourt Brace Jovanovich.

Pollington, M.F., Wilcox, B. and Morrison, T.G. (2001) 'Self-perception in writing: the effects of writing workshop and traditional instruction on intermediate grade students', *Reading Psychology* 22: 249–65.

Porter, L. (2000) *Behaviour in Schools: Theory and Practice for Teachers*, Buckingham: Open University Press.

Powell, R.R., McLaughlin, H.J., Savage, T.V. and Zehm, S. (2001) *Classroom Management*, Upper Saddle River, NJ: Merrill-Prentice Hall.

Power, D. (1998) 'Deaf and hard of hearing students'. In A. Ashman and J. Elkins (eds) *Educating Children with Special Needs* (3rd edn), Sydney: Prentice Hall.

Pressley, M. (1994) 'State-of-the-science primary grade reading instruction or whole language?' *Educational Psychologist* 29, 4: 211–15.

Pressley, M. (1998) *Reading Instruction That Works: The Case for Balanced Teaching*, New York: Guilford Press.

Pressley, M. (1999) 'Self-regulated comprehension processing and its development through instruction'. In L.B. Gambrell, L.M. Morrow, S.B. Neuman and M. Pressley (eds) *Best Practices in Literacy Instruction*, New York: Guilford Press.

Pressley, M. and McCormick, C.B. (1995) *Advanced Educational Psychology for Educators, Researchers and Policymakers*, New York: HarperCollins.

Quinn, M., Kavale, K., Mathur, S., Rutherford, R. and Forness, S. (1999) 'A meta-analysis of social skills interventions for students with emotional or behavioural disorders', *Journal of Emotional and Behavioural Disorders* 7 (1): 54.

Rasinski, T. and Padak, N. (2000) *Effective Reading Strategies: Teaching Children who Find Reading Difficult* (2nd edn), Upper Saddle River, NJ: Merrill.

Rea, P.J., McLaughlin, V.L. and Walther-Thomas, C. (2002) 'Outcomes for students with learning disabilities in inclusive and pullout programs', *Exceptional Children* 68, 2: 203–22.

Reddy, G.L., Ramar, R. and Kusuma, A. (2000) *Education of Children with Special Needs*, New Delhi: Discovery Publishing House.

Reynolds, D. and Farrell, S. (1996) *Worlds Apart? A Review of International Surveys of Educational Achievement Involving England*, London: HMSO.

Reynolds, D. and Muijs, D. (1999) 'Contemporary policy issues in the teaching of mathematics'. In I. Thompson (ed.) *Issues in Teaching Numeracy in Primary Schools*, Buckingham: Open University Press.

Reys, R., Suydam, M., Lindquist, M. and Smith, N. (1998) *Helping Children Learn Mathematics* (5th edn), Boston, MA: Allyn and Bacon.

Rholes, W.S., Palmer, D.J. and Thompson, S.K. (2000) 'Learned helplessness'. In C.R. Reynolds and E. Fletcher-Janzen (eds) *Encyclopedia of Special Education* (2nd edn), New York: Wiley.

Riley, J. and Reedy, D. (2000) *Developing Writing for Different Purposes*, London: Paul Chapman.

Robbins, B. (1996) 'Mathematics', in B. Carpenter, R. Ashdown and K. Bovair (eds) *Enabling Access: Effective Teaching and Learning for Pupils with Learning Difficulties*, London: Fulton.

Robbins, P.R. (1998) *Adolescent Suicide*, London: MacFarland.

Robert, M.F. (2002) 'Problem solving and at-risk students', *Teaching Children Mathematics* 8, 5: 290–5.

Robertson, P., Hamill, P. and Hewitt, C. (1994) 'Effective support for learning: Themes from the RAISE Project', *Interchange* 27, Edinburgh: Research and Intelligence Unit, Department of Education.

Rogers, B. (1995) *Behaviour Management: A Whole-school Approach*, Sydney: Ashton Scholastic.

Rose, R. (2001) 'Primary school teacher perceptions of the conditions required for including pupils with special educational needs', *Educational Review* 53, 2: 147–56.

Rosencrans, G. (1998) *The Spelling Book: Teaching Children How to Spell, not What to Spell*, Newark, DE: International Reading Association.

Rosenshine, B. (1995) 'Advances in research on instruction', *Journal of Educational Research* 88, 5: 262–268.

Rosenshine, B. and Meister, C. (1994) 'Reciprocal teaching: a review of research', *Review of Educational Research* 64, 4: 479–530.

Ross, S.R. (2002) 'Place value, problem solving and written assessment', *Teaching Children Mathematics* 8, 7: 419–23.

Rubin, D. (2000) *Teaching Elementary Language Arts: A Balanced Approach*, Boston, MA: Allyn and Bacon.

Rubin, D. (2002) *Diagnosis and Correction in Reading Instruction* (4th edn), Boston, MA: Allyn and Bacon.

Ruddell, R.B. (2002) *Teaching Children to Read and Write* (3rd edn), Boston, MA: Allyn and Bacon.

Rutter, M. (1985) 'The treatment of autistic children', *Journal of Child Psychology and Psychiatry and Allied Disciplines* 26: 193–214.

Ryba, K., Curzon, J. and Selby, L. (2002) 'Learning partnerships through information and communication technology'. In A. Ashman and J. Elkins (eds) *Educating Children with Diverse Abilities*, Sydney: Pearson Educational.

Sabornie, E.J. and deBettencourt, L.U. (1997) *Teaching Students with Mild Disabilities at the Secondary Level*, Upper Saddle River, NJ: Merrill.

Salend, S.J. (1998) *Effective Mainstreaming: Creating Inclusive Classrooms* (3rd edn), Upper Saddle River, NJ: Merrill.

Samuels, S.J. (1997) 'The method of repeated readings', *The Reading Teacher* 50, 5: 376–81.

Savage, J.F. (2001) S*ound It Out: Phonics in a Balanced Reading Program*, New York: McGraw Hill.

Sawada, D. (1999) 'Mathematics as problem solving: a Japanese way', *Teaching Children Mathematics* 6, 1: 54–8.

Schumm, J.S. and Vaughn, S. (1995) 'Getting ready for inclusion: Is the stage set?' *Learning Disabilities Research and Practice* 10, 3: 169–79.

Scott, B.J., Vitale, M.R. and Masten, W.G. (1998) 'Implementing instructional adaptations for students with disabilities in inclusive classrooms', *Remedial and Special Education* 19, 2: 106–19.

Sewell, K. (2000) *Breakthroughs: How to Reach Students with Autism*, Verona, WI: Attainment Company.

Shapiro, M., Parush, S., Green, M. and Roth, D. (1997) 'The efficacy of the "Snoezelen" in the management of children with mental retardation who exhibit maladaptive behaviours', *The British Journal of Developmental Disabilities* 43 (2): 140–55.

Sheridan, S.M. and Walker, D. (1999) 'Social skills in context: considerations for assessment, intervention and generalization'. In C.R. Reynolds and T.B. Gutkin (eds) *The Handbook of School Psychology* (3rd edn), New York: Wiley.

Sideridis, G. and Greenwood, C. (1998) 'Identification and validation of effective instructional practices for children from impoverished backgrounds and those with learning and developmental disabilities using ecobehavioural analysis', *European Journal of Special Needs Education* 13 (2): 145 – 54.

Silver, A.A. and Hagin, R.A. (2002) *Disorders of Learning in Childhood* (2nd edn), New York: Wiley.

Silverstone, B., Lang, M.A., Rosenthal, B.P. and Faye, E.E. (2000) *The Lighthouse Handbook on Vision Impairment and Vision Rehabilitation*, Oxford: Oxford University Press.

Slavin, R.E. and Madden, N.A. (2001) *One Million Children: Success for All*, Thousand Oaks, CA: Corwin Press.

Smith, C. (1998) *Learning Disabilities: The Interaction of Learner, Task and Setting* (4th edn), Boston, MA: Allyn and Bacon.

Smith, D.D. (2001) *Introduction to Special Education* (4th edn), Boston, MA: Allyn and Bacon.

Smith, M.G. (2000) 'Secondary teachers' perceptions toward inclusion of students with severe disabilities', *NASSP Bulletin* 84, 613: 54–60.

Smith, N.B. (1969) 'The many faces of reading comprehension', *The Reading Teacher* 23: 249–59 and 291.

Smith-Burke, M.T. (2001) 'Reading Recovery: a systematic approach to early intervention'. In L.M. Morrow and D.G. Woo (eds) *Tutoring Programs for Struggling Readers*, New York: Guilford Press.

Snell, M.E. and Brown, F. (2000) *Instruction of Students with Severe Disabilities* (5th edn), Upper Saddle River, NJ: Merrill.

Soodak, L.C. and Podell, D.M (1998) 'Teacher efficacy and the vulnerability of the difficult-to-teach student'. In J. Brophy (ed.) *Advances in Research on Teaching*, v. 7, Greenwich, CT: JAI Press.

Sparzo, F.J. and Poteet, J.A. (1997) 'Managing classroom behavior to enhance teaching and learning'. In J.S. Choate (ed.) *Successful Inclusive Teaching* (2nd edn), Boston, MA: Allyn and Bacon.

Spiegel, D.L. (1999) 'Meeting each child's literacy needs'. In L. Gambrell, L. Morrow, S. Neuman and M. Pressley (eds) *Best Practices in Literacy Instruction*, New York: Guilford Press.

Squires, G. (2001) 'Dyslexia: strategies for support', *Special Children* 149: 23–6.

Stahl, S. (1992) 'Saying the "p" word: nine guidelines for exemplary phonics instruction', *The Reading Teacher* 45, 6: 618–25.

Stahl, S. and Kuhn, M.R. (2002) 'Making it sound like language: developing fluency', *The Reading Teacher* 55, 6: 582–4.

Stahl, S. and Miller, P.D. (1989) 'Whole language and language experience approaches for beginning reading: a quantitative research synthesis', *Review of Educational Research* 59: 87–116.

Stanovich, K.E. (1999) 'Foreword'. In R. Sternberg and L. Spear-Swerling (eds) *Perspectives on Learning Disabilities: Biological, Cognitive and Contextual*, Boulder, CO: Westview Press.

Stanovich, K.E. (2000) *Progress in Understanding Reading: Scientific Foundations and New Frontiers*, New York: Guilford Press.

Stauffer, R. (1980) *The Language-experience Approach to the Teaching of Reading* (2nd edn), Cambridge, MA: Harper and Row.

Staves, L. (1999) 'Making it count', *Special Children* 120: 23–6.

Steinberg, A.G. and Knightly, C.A. (1997) 'Hearing: sounds and silences'. In M.L. Batshaw (ed.) *Children with Disabilities* (4th edn), Sydney: Maclennan and Petty.

Sternberg, R. and Grigorenko, E.L. (2001) 'Learning disabilities, schooling, and society', *Phi Delta Kappan* 83, 4: 335–8.

Stevens, S. (2000) 'A teacher looks at the elementary child with ADHD'. In B.P. Guyer (ed.) *ADHD: Achieving Success in School and in Life*, Boston, MA: Allyn and Bacon.

Stewart, D.A. and Kluwin, T.N. (2001) *Teaching Deaf and Hard of Hearing Students: Content, Strategies and Curriculum*, Boston, MA: Allyn and Bacon.

Stewart, E. and Ritter, K. (2001) 'Ethics of assessment'. In R.G.Beattie (ed.) *Ethics of Deaf Education*, San Diego, CA: Academic Press.

Stieler, S. (1998) 'Students with physical disabilities'. In A. Ashman and J. Elkins (eds) *Educating Children with Special Needs* (3rd edn), Sydney: Prentice Hall.

Stigler, J.W., Fernandez, C. and Yoshida, M. (1996) 'Traditions of school mathematics in Japanese and American classrooms'. In L. Steffe and P. Nesher (eds) *Theories of Mathematical Learning*, Mahwah, NJ: Erlbaum.

Strickland, D.S. (2000) 'Classroom intervention strategies: supporting the literacy development of young learners at risk'. In D.S. Strickland and L.M. Morrow (eds) *Beginning Reading and Writing*, New York: Teachers College Press.

Strickland, D.S., Ganske, K. and Monroe, J.K. (2002) *Supporting Struggling Readers and Writers*, Portland, ME: Stenhouse.

Sue, D., Sue, D.W. and Sue, S. (2000) *Understanding Abnormal Behaviour* (6th edn), Boston, MA: Houghton Mifflin.

Sukumaran, P.S. (2000) *Parental Involvement in the Education of Mentally Handicapped Children*, New Delhi: Discovery Publishing House.

Sullivan, G.S., Mastropieri, M.A. and Scruggs, T.E. (1995) 'Reasoning and remembering: coaching students with learning disabilities to think', *Journal of Special Education* 29, 3: 310–22.

Swanson, H.L. (1999) *Interventions for Students with Learning Disabilities: Meta-analysis of Treatment Outcomes*, New York: Guilford Press.

Swanson, H.L. (2000a) 'What instruction works for students with learning disabilities?' In R. Gersten, E. Schiller and S. Vaughn (eds) *Contemporary Special Education Research*, Mahwah, NJ: Erlbaum.

Swanson, H.L. (2000b) 'Searching for the best cognitive model for instructing students with learning disabilities: a component and composite analysis', *Educational and Child Psychology* 17, 3: 101–21.

Taylor, J. and Baker, R.A. (2002) 'Discipline and the special education student', *Educational Leadership* 59, 4: 28–30.

Taylor, R.L., Sternberg, L. and Richards, S.B. (1995) *Exceptional Children: Integrating Research and Teaching* (2nd edn), San Diego, CA: Singular Publishing.

Templeton, S. (1992) 'New trends in an historical perspective: old story, new resolution – sound and meaning in spelling', *Language Arts* 69: 454–63.

Thomas, G. (1999) 'Foreword'. In R. Babbage, R. Byers and H. Redding, *Approaches to Teaching and Learning: Including Pupils with Learning Difficulties*, London: Fulton.

Thompson, M.E. and Watkins, E.J. (1990) *Dyslexia: A Teaching Handbook*, London: Whurr.

Threlfall, J. (1996) 'The role of practical apparatus in the teaching and learning of arithmetic', *Educational Review* 48, 1: 3–12.

Tiedt, P.L., Tiedt, I.M. and Tiedt, S.W. (2001) *Language Arts Activities for the Classroom* (3rd edn), Boston, MA: Allyn and Bacon.

Tomlinson, C.A. (1996) *Differentiating Instruction for Mixed-ability Classrooms*, Alexandria, VA: Association for Supervision and Curriculum Development.

Tomlinson, C.A. (1999) *The Differentiated Classroom: Responding to the Needs of All Learners*, Alexandria, VA: Association for Supervision and Curriculum Development.

Tomlinson, C.A. (2001) 'Grading for success', *Educational Leadership* 58, 6: 12–15.

Tompkins, G.E. (2002) *Language Arts: Content and Teaching Strategies* (5th edn), Upper Saddle River, NJ: Merrill-Prentice Hall.

Topping, K., Nixon, J., Sutherland, J. and Yarrow, F. (2000) 'Paired writing: a framework for effective collaboration', *Reading* 34, 2: 79–89.

Torgesen, J.K. (1999) 'Phonologically based reading disabilities'. In R. Sternberg and L. Spear-Swerling (eds) *Perspectives on Learning Disabilities: Biological, Cognitive and Contextual*, Boulder, CO: Westview.

Torgesen, J.K. and Mathes, P.G. (2000) *A Basic Guide to Understanding, Assessing and Teaching Phonological Awareness*, Austin, TX: ProEd.

Treiman, R. (1993) *Beginning to Spell*, New York: Oxford University Press.

Tucker, B., Singleton, A.H. and Weaver, T.L. (2002) *Teaching Mathematics to All Children*, Upper Saddle River, NJ: Merrill-Prentice Hall.

Tunmer, W.E., Chapman, J.W., Greaney, K.T and Prochnow, J.E. (2002) 'The contribution of educational psychology to intervention research and practice', *International Journal of Disability, Development and Education* 49, 1: 11–29.

Turnbull, R., Turnbull, A., Shank, M., Smith, S. and Leal, D. (2002) *Exceptional Lives: Special Education in Today's Schools* (3rd edn), Upper Saddle River, NJ: Merrill-Prentice Hall.

Tustin, F. (1992) *Autistic States in Children* (2nd edn), London: Routledge.

Udvari-Solner, A. (1998) 'Adapting the curriculum'. In M.F. Giangreco (ed.) *Quick Guides to Inclusion: Ideas for Educating Students with Disabilities*, Baltimore, MD: Brookes.

UNESCO (1994) *The Salamanca Statement and Framework for Action on Special Needs Education*, Salamanca: UNESCO.

Vacca, J.A., Vacca, R.T. and Gove, M.K. (2000) *Reading and Learning to Read* (4th edn), New York: Longman.

Valas, H. (2001) 'Learned helplessness and psychological adjustment: effects of learning disabilities and low achievement', *Scandinavian Journal of Educational Research* 45, 2: 101–14.

Van den Berg, R., Sleegers, P. and Geijsel, F. (2001) 'Teachers' concerns about adaptive teaching: evaluation of a support program', *Journal of Curriculum and Supervision* 16, 3: 245–58.

Van der Kaay, M., Wilton, K. and Townsend, M. (2000) 'Word processing and written composition: an intervention for children with mild intellectual disability', *Australasian Journal of Special Education* 24, 2: 53–9.

Van Kraayenoord, C. (2002) 'Focus on literacy'. In A.Ashman and J. Elkins (eds) *Educating Children with Diverse Abilities*, Sydney: Pearson Education.

Vaughn, S., Elbaum, B. and Boardman, A.G. (2001) 'The social functioning of students with learning disabilities: implications for inclusion', *Exceptionality 9* (1–2): 47–65.

Vaughn, S., Gersten, R. and Chard, D.J. (2000) 'The underlying message in LD intervention research: findings from research synthesis', *Exceptional Children 67*, 1: 99–114.

Visser, J. (2000) *Managing Behaviour in Classrooms*, London: Fulton.

Waksman, S. (1998) *The Waksman Social Skills Curriculum for Adolescents* (4th edn), Austin, TX: ProEd.

Walker, H.M. (1983) *The Walker Social Skills Curriculum*, Austin, TX: ProEd.

Ward, J. and Center, Y. (1999) 'Success and failure in inclusion: some representative case histories', *Special Education Perspectives 8*, 1: 16–31.

Warger, C.L. and Rutherford, R. (1996) *A Collaborative Approach to Social Skills Instruction*, Reston, VA: Foundation for Exceptional Innovations.

Waterhouse, S. (2000) *A Positive Approach to Autism*, London: Jessica Kingsley.

Watson, L., Gregory, S. and Powers, S. (1999) *Deaf and Hearing-impaired Pupils in Mainstream Schools*, London: Fulton.

Wearmouth, J. (ed.) (2001) *Special Educational Provision in the Context of Inclusion: Policy and Practice in Schools*, London: Fulton and Open University.

Webb, T. (1999) 'Look who's talking', *Special Children* 119: 31–3.

Webster, A. (1995) 'Differentiation'. In G. Moss (ed.) *The Basics of Special Needs*, London: Routledge

Weinstein, R.S. (1998) 'Promoting positive expectations in schooling'. In N.M. Lambert and B.L. McCombs (eds) *How Students Learn*, Washington, DC: American Psychological Association.

Weisel, A. and Tur-Kaspa, H. (2002) 'Effects of labels and personal contact on teachers' attitudes toward students with special needs', *Exceptionality* 10, 1: 1–10.

Wender, P.H. (2000) *ADHD: Attention-deficit Hyperactivity Disorder in Children and Adults*, New York: Oxford University Press.

Wendon, L. (2001) *Letterland*, Barton, Cambridge: Letterland International.

Weston, P., Taylor, M., Lewis, G. and MacDonald, A. (1998) *Learning from Differentiation*, Slough: NFER.

Westwood, P.S. (1998) 'Reducing educational failure', *Australian Journal of Learning Disabilities* 3, 3: 4–12.

Westwood, P.S. (2000) 'Learning difficulties: in search of effective methods', *Hong Kong Special Education Forum* 3, 1: 117–29.

Westwood, P.S. (2001) 'Differentiation as a strategy for inclusive classroom practice: some difficulties identified', *Australian Journal of Learning Disabilities* 6, 1: 5–11.

Westwood, P.S. and Graham, L. (2000) 'How many children with special needs in regular classes?' *Australian Journal of Learning Disabilities* 5, 3: 24–35.

Wheldall, K. (1995) 'Helping readers who are behind' *Education Monitor* 6, 1: 23–5.

Wheldall, K., Center, Y. and Freeman, L. (1993) 'Reading Recovery in Sydney primary schools', *Australasian Journal of Special Education* 17, 2: 51–63.

Wiest, L. (2001) 'Promoting reasoning through more effective work with word problems', *Focus on Learning Problems in Mathematics* 23, 2–3: 70–84.

Wilen, W., Ishler, M., Hutchison, J. and Kindsvatter, R. (2000) *Dynamics of Effective Teaching* (4th edn), New York: Longman.

Wilkins, J. (2001) *Group Activities to Include Students with Special Needs*, Thousand Oaks, CA: Corwin Press.

Winebrenner, S. (1996) *Teaching Kids with Learning Difficulties in the Regular Classroom*, Minneapolis, MN: Free Spirit Publishing.

Wing, L. (1996) *The Autistic Spectrum*, London: Constable.

Wolf, M. and Bowers, P.G. (1999) 'The double deficit hypothesis for the developmental dyslexias', *Journal of Educational Psychology* 91, 3: 415–83.

Wong, B., Butler, D.L., Ficzere, S. and Kuperis, S. (1996) 'Teaching low achievers and students with learning disabilities to plan, write and revise opinion essays', *Journal of Learning Disabilities* 29, 2: 197–212.

Wood, J.W. (1998) *Adapting Instruction to Accommodate Students in Inclusive Settings* (3rd edn), Upper Saddle River, NJ: Merrill.

Woodward, B. and Hogenboom, M. (2000) *Autism: A Holistic Approach*, Edinburgh: Floris.

Worthy, J., Broaddus, K. and Ivey, G. (2001) *Pathways to Independence: Reading, Writing and Learning in Grades 3–8*, New York: Guilford Press.

Wragg, J. (1989) *Talk Sense to Yourself*, Melbourne: Australian Council for Educational Research.

Xin, Y.P. and Jitendra, A.K. (1999) 'The effects of instruction in solving mathematical word problems for students with learning problems: a meta analysis', *Journal of Special Education* 32, 4: 207–25.

Yopp, R.H. and Yopp, H.K. (2001) *Literature-based Reading Activities* (3rd edn), Boston, MA: Allyn and Bacon.

Zimmerman, B.J., Bonner, S. and Kovach, R. (1996) *Developing Self-regulated Learners: Beyond Achievement to Self-efficacy*, Washington, DC: American Psychological Association.

Zirpoli, T.J. (2001) *Behavior Management Applications for Teachers* (3rd edn), Upper Saddle River, NJ: Merrill.

Zutell, J. (1998) 'Word sorting: a developmental approach to word study for delayed readers', *Reading and Writing Quarterly* 14: 219–38.

Index